GREEN PARTIES: AN INTERNATIONAL GUIDE

to
Colin and Douglas

Go and see the ecologists: if Humankind has
any future, then it lies with them

Denis de Rougement

GREEN
PARTIES

AN INTERNATIONAL GUIDE

SARA PARKIN

First published February 1989 by Heretic Books Ltd,
P O Box 247, London N17 9QR
World copyright © 1989 Sara Parkin.

British Library Cataloguing in Publication Data
Parkin, Sara
Green parties.
I. Title
324.2

ISBN 0-946097-27-5

Printed and bound in the European Community by
Nørhaven A/S, Viborg, Denmark

Contents

Acknowledgements

If I were to list all the people who have helped, either practically or by inspiration or both, to make this book possible, it would read like a telephone directory. A great number of colleagues and friends around the world have provided me with information, commented on drafts, and patiently answered my questions, and I thank them all most warmly. With the same breath I also absolve them of all responsibility for any errors that may occur in this book; for those the blame lies entirely with me.

Special thanks go to David Turbayne and Bob Brown in Australia, and Gene Frankland in the United States, who over the years have provided a stream of books, papers, cuttings and letters about developments in their countries that goes far beyond the call of duty or friendship. The work of several UK Green Party language monitors must be gratefully acknowledged too, notably that of Susan Miles and Elizabeth Adams. Measured by metre or by usefulness their work has illuminated the development of Green politics in Sweden and the Spanish-speaking countries respectively.

Particular thanks are also due to my family. With good-humoured kindness they have put up with the emotional gusts occasioned by the rotation of elation and despair that I am assured is an occupational disease among book writers, and when I used household chores variously as an excuse to put off tackling a particularly difficult bit or as an intolerable burden on my muse, no one has held this inconsistency against me.

Last but not least my thanks go to my editor, David Fernbach, who has sustained me with his calm confidence and who has shown great diligence in the face of my reluctance to be constrained by the rules of spelling and grammar in several languages.

Thanks everybody.

Foreword

The early days of the international Green movement have had a very considerable impact on the political scene in many different countries, not just in terms of the actual votes cast for the Green parties involved, but by way of a far-reaching influence on public opinion, on mainstream parties and on the media. Sara Parkin's lucid and interesting survey of Green political parties makes a timely and welcome contribution to the efforts of both activists and observers to assess this impact and look forward into the next decade.

Several common factors are revealed which may determine the apparent level of success of the different parties, including which electoral system they are operating in, the degree of general concern about the state of the environment, and the prominence and historical development of other radical social and political movements. But it is also very apparent that each country provides a very different model for the development of Green politics.

For aspiring Greens in the UK, endlessly on the receiving end of questions about their 'lack of success' in comparison with the Greens in Germany or other European countries, it is important (and reassuring!) to be able to assess the relative importance of these different factors. The extent and sustainability of any Green party's impact may well have to be measured in ways more complex than the simple number of Green bottoms on parliamentary seats!

It is of course a very short history with which we are dealing. As regards the long-term development of Green politics there is now much to be enthusiastic about. A gradual, if not dramatic, build-up of electoral support; a deepening awareness among ordinary people and in the media that Green politics really is different; increased confidence, expertise and political acumen among the Greens themselves that comes quite simply from more people gaining more experience; an impressive track record, particularly at the local level, which demonstrates beyond all doubt the practicality and the viability of Green politics; a growing international consensus on the need for new levels of cooperation to combat the multifarious symptoms of ecological breakdown. Amid all the doom and gloom of accelerating ecological mayhem, there is good cause to be thankful for such rays of hope.

But one can hardly claim that the international political scene is lit up by such Green enlightenment, however rapidly it may be growing. As this book makes abundantly clear, there is also much to be cautious about. All Green parties, whatever their level of electoral success, are still very young and very 'green' in the other sense of the word. Even in aspiring to build a wholly new political alternative it would seem that many of the old practices still recur. For some, it may be something of an eye-opener to see the way in which Greens have no built-in immunity to incompetence, insensitivity or chronic infighting. As Sara points out in her Introduction, there is a disturbing lack of sophistication in the Green analysis of the political climate in Europe today, leaving Green parties extremely vulnerable either to cooption by the major parties or to bouts of 'greener-than-thou' impossibilism, by which the advocacy of wholly unrealistic policies becomes a substitute for genuinely radical yet still effective politics.

What is more, certain profound and potentially irreconcilable differences in long-term strategy emerge very clearly from this book, not just by way of the inevitable factional disputes, but in terms of two particularly critical issues: to what extent should today's Green parties identify themselves specifically as parties of the left, and to what extent should they cooperate and work with mainstream parties, in temporary coalitions, in order to achieve even minimal reforms within the system? Much depends on how the Green movement resolves these differences both theoretically and practically.

It has not been an easy adolescence for the international Green movement. Some might claim that electoral success came too early and too easily to some of the European Green parties; having to learn on the job, breathlessly and painfully, is not always the best way of producing wise and mature practitioners in the art of Green politics. Many mistakes have already been made, and given an excessively healthy capacity on the part of some Green politicians for shooting themselves in the foot many more undoubtedly still will be. However, reading of the experiences (happy and unhappy) of colleagues in other countries may be as good a way as any to at least identify the worst of the pitfalls, if not actually avoid them. I therefore warmly recommend this refreshingly frank book to Greens everywhere, whether they are active in established or in embryonic movements. The breath of life and the sense of vision and purpose which the Greens have brought to their respective political systems more than compensates for any short-term failings of people inching their way up the learning curve.

Green politics can only get stronger as we all learn to articulate more clearly both our analysis and our prescriptions. It is no exaggeration to say that the world is now in a state of crisis as never before, even if so many still remain cut off from that perception by virtue of a temporary oil glut, the continuing availability of easy credit and a sickening readiness to isolate themselves from the desperate suffering of the Third World. Greater awareness of what is really happening, in terms of the inherent unsustainability of the whole precarious system, will inevitably lead to greater concern. It is the profound and wholly justifiable hope of the Greens that such concern will translate – soon rather than later – into a thoroughgoing revolution in attitudes and political support.

Green parties make up the vanguard of all those social and political movements which are, at last, coming to terms with the need for such a profound transformation. It is never easy being in the vanguard, but as Green politics has demonstrated beyond reasonable doubt, to all those who truly care about the Earth and all its inhabitants, there is really nowhere else to be.

Jonathon Porritt
September 1988

Abbreviations and Keys

International Organisations

EFTA	European Free Trade Association
NATO	North Atlantic Treaty Organisation
OECD	Organisation for Economic Cooperation and Development
UN	United Nations
WEU	Western European Union

Party Codes (used in tables of election results)

1 Communist
2 Independent Socialist
3 Social-Democrat
4 Liberal Radical
5 Centre/Christian-Democrat/Christian
6 Liberal Conservative
7 Conservative/Nationalist
8 Extreme Right
9 Regional and Ethnic
10 Green/Ecologist
11 Miscellaneous/Independents

INTRODUCTION

Going Green

By any standards the speed with which Green parties have established themselves on the political scene has been phenomenal; even the text on the cover of this book, subject to the necessary time-lags of the publishing process, has been surpassed by events. We can now say that in less than nine years Greens have been elected to eleven national parliaments around the world (see Table 1).

At first very few people noticed when Daniel Brélaz took his seat in the Swiss parliament in October 1979, and not many more were paying attention in 1981 when nine members of Agalev and Ecolo entered the Belgian parliament. But by 1983, when 28 members of Die Grünen were elected to the German Bundestag and two Finnish Greens to the Eduskunta quite a lot of people began to wonder about the Green wave that seemed to be breaking over European politics. 'Green revolution marches on Bonn,' declared *The Times* on 8 March 1983.

Since then those pioneering Green parties have seen colleagues elected to national parliaments in Austria, Italy, Luxembourg, Portugal and Sweden. Further afield, two Green/Anti-Nuclear senators now sit in the Australian parliament and, although they are not formally associated with the Greens, I like to add Iceland's Kvennalistinn to my tally of Green parties. In 1983 they became the first women's party to enter a national parliament, and although their programme does not mention the word Green once, it is as Green as Green can be.

Apart from the attention-grabbing breakers of Greens entering national parliaments, there has also been a ground-swell of Greens moving into local politics.Greens now sit at some level of local government in almost every west European country (see Table 1), and around the world, local Green groups are not only multiplying in number but their activities are also becoming more influential. Even in countries where access to democratic electoral processes is limited or proscribed, brave people are practising in their

everyday lives some of the Green ideas which have not yet
escaped from the cage of theory in the so-called advanced
democracies.

The breadth and the accelerating growth of the global
Green movement makes it difficult to pack everything I would
like to include into one book, so for this one I have
concentrated on the Green parties of western Europe and on
the development of Green politics in four other
countries – Australia, where Tasmanians became the first in
the world to take the issue of environmental protection to the
polls in March 1972; New Zealand, where the world's first
nationwide Green party was founded two months later; the
United States of America whose personalities and writers
had a major influence on the European movement; and
Canada, where in British Columbia an interesting combination of radical non-violent action, electoral campaigning,
feminism and high-quality journalism is at work.

In the final chapter, however, I point to Green ideas at
work in other countries – with detailed examples from
Poland, Hungary, Kenya and India – to illustrate how they
are able to inspire and influence even under the most difficult
of circumstances. My considerable desk-bound frustration at
not being able to properly research more of the many
interesting examples of local Green politics in action around
the world is tempered by plans to devote a whole book to them
in the not-too-distant future.

The main impetus to write *Green Parties* came in fact from
my letterbox. Since taking on the job of International Liaison
Secretary for the UK Green Party in 1983, the trickle of news
and requests for information about Green parties and Green
politics has swelled to a torrent. Moreover, from about the
time I became one of the co-secretaries of the Coordination of
European Green Parties in 1985, a growing number of these
requests required complicated answers. It was no longer
enough to pop a list of addresses, a manifesto and a friendly
note into an envelope. I found myself spending more and more
time assembling the ingredients for replies to sixth-formers
who were doing a project on the French Greens; or to the
postgraduate students who were 'elaborating a conceptual
model for analysing the dynamics between new social
movements and the Green parties'; not to mention the casual
enquirer wanting 'all the information you have on the Green
parties'! The contents of this book, therefore, have been
influenced by my desire to provide, not a complete answer to

all those questions, but at least a starting point for the growing number of people who are interested in the Green parties and their politics. A brief bibliography and the references throughout the book should help any reader who wishes to pursue their research further for pleasurable or scholarly reasons.

It is not every day that a new political force is born, so it might be helpful to review here the ideas which have inspired many Greens over the past few years and consider the prospects for Green politics as we move into the last decade of the century. Since people come to Green politics from many different directions, perhaps the simplest way to do this is to relate my own experience.

Salad Days

My background could with accuracy be described as non-political. As I grew up I added my name to the electoral register in much the same spirit as I put on high heels for the first time: both were signals that I wanted to be considered an adult, neither was evidence that I intended to take on adult responsibilities. My parents' generation had sacrificed their youth and in some case their lives so that we could be free and happy, they said, and I felt obliged not to waste that sacrifice. Being told by Harold Macmillan that I had 'never had it so good' further justified the considerable amount of effort I devoted to enjoying myself.

The first serious seeds of doubt that all was not perfect in the world were sown in my mind by a public lecture series organised by C. H. Waddington, the retired professor of animal genetics at Edinburgh university. 'Wad,' as he was widely and affectionately known, spent the all too brief period before his death establishing the School of the Man-Made Future in Edinburgh (now incorporated into the university's Centre for Human Ecology). His objective was to alert the public to the inevitable catastrophe that must occur if a rapidly growing population kept up its rate of plundering and polluting our planet's finite resources. However, Wad was not only concerned with the 'limits to growth' debate that was going on as the 1960s gave way to the 1970s, but also with the deeper philosophical questions that were implicit in any reassessment of the relationship between the human

species and its total environment. In another lecture series,
'The Nature of Mind', he observed: 'If one believes that a goal
is inherent in a set of circumstances – or to put it theologi-
cally, that God's will is immanent in his creations – then the
ultimate task for the rational mind is to discover what that
goal is. This, the discovery of natural ethics, or natural
religion is, surely, the greatest endeavour which mankind is
still engaged in.'[1]

Wad liked to frame the future scenarios he painted with his
conviction that it would be the poor who inherited the Earth
in the end; a conviction he backed with arguments that were
logical rather than biblical. He felt sure that any survivors of
the climax of human folly, whatever form it took, would be
among the most distant of Amazonian tribes or Asian
mountain dwellers. However ruthless the behaviour of the
rich towards the poor countries might become as the global
crisis developed, in the end it was the poor and not the rich
who had the sort of natural and human resources that were
the keys to survival.

I listened to Wad, read the books that appeared around
about this time and was deeply moved and influenced by them
all. Here are the last paragraphs of two of the best known of
these books – *The Limits to Growth* and *Only One Earth*. I
quote them because they still hold the challenges that I and
many others took up all those years ago:

> The last thought we wish to offer is that man must
> explore himself – his goals and values – as much as
> the world he seeks to change. The dedication to
> both tasks must be undending. The crux of the
> matter is not only whether the human species will
> survive, but even more whether it can survive
> without falling into a state of worthless
> existence.[2]

> Alone in space, alone in its life-supporting
> systems, powered by inconceivable energies,
> mediating them to us through the most delicate
> adjustments, wayward, unlikely, unpredictable,
> but nourishing, enlivening and enriching in the
> largest degree – is this not a precious home for all
> of us earthlings? Is it not worth our love? Does it
> not deserve all the inventiveness and courage and
> generosity of which we are capable to preserve it

from degradation and destruction and, by doing
so, to secure our own survival?[3]

The apocalyptic and passionate style of the early 1970s has
given way to the more tempered and 'respectable' evidence of
recent studies such as the *Global 2000* report[4] and *Our
Common Future,*[5] but sadly the same challenges remain. All
that seems to have happened is that ever more detailed
studies of our predicament have been called for. This raises
the dark suspicion that the human species seems more intent
on monitoring its own extinction than it is on avoiding it. Not
all the prophecies of the 1970s have come to pass of course,
but the continued destruction and degradation of our environment has been so little interrupted that, fifteen years after
the UN Conference on the Human Environment in
Stockholm, Lester Brown can write ominously:

> As we near the end of the twentieth century, we
> are entering uncharted territory. Localised
> changes in natural systems are now being overlaid
> with continental and global shifts, some of which
> may be irreversible. Everyday human activi-
> ties – driving automobiles, generating electricity,
> and producing food – may collectively cause
> changes of geological proportions within a matter
> of decades... With so many natural systems becom-
> ing unstable within such a short period of time,
> discontinuous, surprising and rapid changes may
> become commonplace.[6]

Picking Up Politics

It was not until I drew a little bit nearer to the centre of
Europe by moving from Edinburgh in Scotland to Leeds in
the north of England that I stumbled across members of the
British Green party. I was well aware that our predicament
required, among other things, a change of political direction,
but up till then had felt that, given the UK electoral system,
the big political parties would best be influenced through the
growing number of pressure groups. It was the 1979 general
election that removed any residual doubts I had about

becoming involved in party politics.

Some time before the election, on behalf of the Conservation Society, one of the pressure groups to which I belonged, I had written a letter to my Leeds MP, Sir Keith Joseph, posing a few questions about his confidently entitled booklet *The Right Approach to the Economy*. He replied very politely, suggesting I should read one or two more things before making an appointment so that he could answer my questions face to face. I did my homework, made an appointment for his constituency surgery a few weeks later and turned up stiff with facts ready to debate the ecological implications of Conservative economic strategy.

Sir Keith invited me to follow him into his room, passed before me and let the door swing back in my face. Sitting a good two feet higher than me on the far side of a large table, he had absolutely no recollection or record of my letter, nor of his reply to it, but what could he do for me? When he understood that I wished to discuss economic strategy and not holes in the pavement he became cross. When I rose to my feet and announced I had decided that the best way to get my views over would be to stand against him at the next general election, he sprang to his feet and became extremely charming. We parted on a warm handshake and he very carefully held the door open for me.

I give the details of this encounter by way of a parable to illustrate how the pressure point most respected by elected politicians lies inside the ballot box. Despite his safe majority, Sir Keith instinctively felt more threatened by my modest attack on his votes than he was by any logic contained in my arguments. My final faint hope that ginger groups working on the Labour and Liberal parties might fare better also evaporated during this election when another MP, Labour's Denis Healey, cheerfully remarked: 'You're quite right of course, but it's political suicide to say so.' Although he doesn't know it, his casual comment strengthened rather than weakened my conviction that for the forseeable future, at least in western Europe, independent Green parties have a crucial role to play in the defence and promotion of Green ideas.

Green Revolution

To begin with at least, many observers imagined that the
Green parties were simply a variation on the usual theme of
the liberal or socialist traditions which have dominated
world politics for centuries. But a closer look at the Green
parties' insistence that they are 'neither left nor right, but
out in front', reveals that it is indeed difficult to classify this
new political force, either by its policies or by its style. There
are not many political manifestos where a strong emphasis
on conservation and spiritual values may be found nestling
up to a commitment to redistribute wealth not merely
between classes but between continents and between
generations. And few parliamentarians have done so much to
take pomposity out of politics. Along with their flowers and
jeans Greens have brought a wide experience of real life into
parliaments which makes them as much at ease in the
chamber as on the street. This can only be good for politics, as
I have always thought it strange that we should have
abdicated so much power over our lives and the lives of our
children to a closed shop of grey-suited, narrowly educated
men. There are of course no tablets of stone engraved with
the commandment that there shall only be a left and a right in
politics, nor is there one which states that responsibility
shall only lie with he who possesses a pin-striped suit, but the
habits of such political myths unfortunately die hard.

Of course most ordinary people do want to live in secure,
convivial, non-polluted communities, and they don't con-
sciously choose to be menaced by dangerous technologies or
weapons of mass destruction. The real argument centres on
how to obtain such a lifestyle. Somehow the world has
become a place where a huge majority of people are more or
less dependent on a small minority; the atmosphere is so
polluted that we are faced with grave climatic disturbances;
and renewable resources like air, water, trees and soil are
fast being turned into non-renewable ones. Although we
thought increased travel and the concept of the global village
would smooth away conflicts through knowledge and
understanding, the divisions between men and women, black
and white, religions and cultures seem to have multiplied and
deepened.

It has always been impossible for me to subscribe to the
belief that our present predicament is the result of a plot

sustained over several centuries, although I readily agree
that it is the logical consequence of the consumer-driven
industrial regime which all of the rich and most of the
not-so-rich countries of the world endorse. My own diagnosis
is that this regime has been constructed out of a series of
wrong decisions – large and small, individual and collective – made over a considerable period of time. Building
bombs instead of convivial life-sustaining communities, and
failing to make our spirituality and our personal potential
the real challenges of our life on Earth, are examples of how
the human species has tended to gravitate towards the easier
option at moments of choice and decision, whether it be
practical or intellectual. We have managed to simplify the
immeasurable muddle of human relationships, customs and
beliefs into crisp, countable (and therefore totally unreal)
columns in the accounts of social analysis, and the environment in which all human activity *must* take place has been
reduced to the white page on which these calculations are
done. In short, we are living the consequences of a compound
error.

Now admitting to mistakes among our intimates is difficult
enough. Admitting to a collective error committed over
centuries will be even more difficult. It seems only sensible
therefore to seek the help of a strong guide and counsellor to
help us restore our relationship with ourselves, each other
and the planet to one of mutual respect and equal give and
take. I know of only one such arbiter that cannot be accused
of manipulative self-interest – and that is the Earth itself.
Greens are suggesting that by abandoning our obsession
with ourselves, and putting the Earth into the centre of all
the models and plans we make for our personal and collective
activities, we can discover that, in the words of Theodore
Roszak: 'The needs of the planet are the needs of the
person...the rights of the person are the rights of the planet'.[7]

The centrality of the Earth to Green thinking should not,
however, be confused with the sort of theological straitjacket
that ideologies such as monetarism or Marxism clamp onto
people. Putting the Earth first in our personal life and our
politics does suggest a new set of values and practices that is
considerably different from today's dominant ethos, but the
way in which Green thinking may be taken up and adapted to
suit local needs and customs is extremely varied, something I
hope *Green Parties* reveals. Celebrating the diversity of
human culture is, after all, much more in tune with the

immense variety to be found in nature than is trying to homogenise and then fossilise it into any ideology. Greens prefer to use nature as a living reference book, not as a bible.

Perhaps inevitably though, political scientists are keen to squeeze the Green parties into an ideological straitjacket, whether it be a stiff new one or a tattered old one. Already Greens have been called both a new 'class' of post-materialists, and the 'acid test' for left-wing politics.[8] However, the growth of groups practising a very Green sort of politics in Eastern Europe, Latin America and Africa rather knocks the post-materialist thesis on the head, and although some Green parties do owe their origins and development to a significant input from left-wing activists (in Luxembourg, Austria and West Germany for example), many were started by people who felt the need for politics to be based on an entirely new set of values that could not be found in any existing political tradition – socialist or liberal. This was the case with Agalev in Belgium, the UK Green Party and the Swedish Miljöpartiet, among others, and it is worth noting that the world's first national Green party, in New Zealand, was called the Values party.

Perhaps the most relevant test of the Green-ness of a political party (or indeed any person or organisation) should be its *approach* to a decision, a choice, a problem or an issue. How well has it understood the central role of the Earth in resolving the predicament of humankind? By the same token I feel that the maturity of a Green party is better assessed by how well it has managed to reflect that understanding in its policies, its style and its strategies than by how closely it has come to resemble any other political party.

The Green parties in this book are at very different stages of evolution. As Table 1 reveals, only two are more than ten years old, and most are experiencing the usual difficulties that go with youth and inexperience, whether they have had significant success at the polls or not. Being anxious to appear the antithesis to traditional political parties while operating in the same arena as them can promote arguments over strategy, organisation, power and leadership. In wishing to be what Petra Kelly calls an 'anti-party party', the tiny Green party in Eire, Comhaontas Glas, is no different to the biggest and best known Green party, Die Grünen. When I was speaking to a friend about writing this book he asked me: 'Which party do you think is the Greenest then?' But I could not give a straight reply. Each party has something good to offer and each has its black marks. In France, for example, Les Verts have one of the more interesting and efficient ways of organising, but so little theoretical substance that their programmes are weak and their presidential candidate could do no better than describe Green politics as a 'sort of humanism'. The British Greens, by contrast, have plenty of theory but can't organise a debate. It remains to be seen if the style of the Swedish Greens will survive their recent entry into parliamentary politics and if the Italian Federazione delle Liste Verdi can keep the Green light shining through their organisational anarchy.

Future Prospects

I suspect that Greens in Europe may look back on 1989 as a watershed in their development. The Swiss and the Belgian Greens have increased their number of parliamentary seats over three elections now, the Finnish and German Greens over two, but what next? As Table 2 shows, the total number of voters for Green parties in the 1984 European elections still fell considerably short of 5%. The urgency of the human predicament demands a strategy more profound than an increased couple of percent at the polls every four or five years, and the spectre of remaining a ghetto for the 10% protest vote looms large. Although quite correctly congratulating themselves for the role they have played in bringing environmental concerns to the top of the agenda in many countries, the Green parties must be aware that 10% of the popular vote is not enough to keep them a relevant political force into the next century, never mind fulfil the objective of the Green revolution which, given the global dimension of the problems we face, can be no less than the greening of the whole planet.

How the Greens might survive the power play of the other political formations and assemble popular majorities around Green ideas and policies is, unsurprisingly, something I have pondered a great deal, and researching and writing this book has suggested some critical features of the next ten years that will, I believe, be decisive in whether the Green parties flourish or falter. Recognising where their strongest opposition lies and having the courage to stick to their strongest points in the face of that opposition come first in my list, but

no less important is the need for Greens to come to terms with
the dynamics of power and to transmit Green ideas more
clearly and more widely than ever before.

1: Facing the Opposition

The rise of support for right-wing authoritarian politics and
the declining influence of libertarian and communitarian
ideals is given as evidence of a general disintegration of
political and cultural norms throughout Europe. Certainly
the message from election after election has been a rightward
drift of conservative and social-democratic parties and a
rapid fall-off of support for the more left-wing parties. Not
surprisingly there have been several calls for a renewal of the
pure socialist message, and for another go at the 'red'
revolution. Yet socialism in all its shapes and forms has
failed to face up to what George Lichtheim calls the 'inherent
conflict between two quite different and possibly irreconcilable goals: economic growth and social equality'.[9] Although
socialism has tried to topple the consumer-driven industrial
regime by rationing its supply of compliant people, it has
repeatedly failed to recognise the *pivotal* role of the environment in any successful revolution, and has never
understood how important it is for any vision of the future to
contain food for the spirit as well as for the body.

In fact, over the last few years all political parties have
assumed environmental policies to be an optional extra and
imagined that in order to wipe the Green parties off the
political map all they had to do was tack a few greenish
policies onto their own programmes. This has not worked. In
Italy for example, nearly all the parties added ecologists to
their lists for the 1987 parliamentary elections, but the brand
new Liste Verdi still won 15 seats. In the 'perfect' social
democracy of Sweden, the September 1988 elections saw the
environment as the number one issue and Miljöpartiet
become the first new party to enter the Swedish parliament
for 70 years. Furthermore, traditional parties, large and
small, are discovering that Green policies act like moles on
the rest of their programmes; policies for living a peaceful,
sustainable and convivial lifestyle in a green and pleasant
land seriously undermine the logic of the traditional economic, social and defence policies of any consumer-driven
industrial regime, regardless of whether those policies have

been crafted according to the dogma of left, right or centre.

So the sort of industries which grow fat in a climate of unrestrained consumption have been obliged to mount their own spirited offensive. They have given birth to the environment industry. John Elkington describes the efforts of some industries to incorporate environmental considerations into their product development as they compete with each other for the rewards of 'environmental excellence'. ICI, for example, waxes lyrical about the potential international market for its enzyme product Cyclear (which breaks down cyanide, a by-product of some industrial processes), running to 'tens of millions of dollars in North America, Europe and Japan'. The Green horror-scenario of sluicing one bucket of (bio)chemicals after another is being redrawn as sound industrial practice.[10] This sort of Green awareness has, of course, nothing to do with consuming *less* of the planet's resources, only about consuming them differently. Underneath, business goes on as usual.

Over the next few years the Greens will have to deal with a lot more kitsch greenery acting as camouflage for a major political offensive against them. Surviving the combined attacks of socialism wanting to have just one more go, and the consumer-driven industrial regime deploying 'pro-active strategies' in order to capture the 'frontiers of environmental science' for itself, means that Greens will have to mount a vigorous defence of their ideas. Unsurprisingly the best means of defence turns out to be attack.

2: Deploying Three Strategic Strengths

When considering Green party strategy, the current much publicised dilemma of the German Greens is instructive. Die Grünen have been persistently classified by political commentators and the other parties as a force to the left of the Social-Democrat party and have themselves done little to dispel this image. But if the tendency of a general rightward shift in politics goes on, how do Die Grünen plan to continue? If they intend to keep up the pressure for change according to their present strategy, then they too will have to play the left/right political game and chase the SPD to the right. The prominent 'Realos' who advocate compromise of their party's commitment to leave NATO and courting the 'yuppie' vote by investigating Green capitalism are doing just that – in order, they claim, to keep the SPD looking to the Greens as a coalition partner instead of to the liberal Free Democrats. Similarly the devotion with which some of the 'Fundi' faction are trying to breathe life back into the corpse of the extreme left suggests that they cannot read the political reality around them. Their equivocal position towards violence is also hard to square with a genuine Green philosophy, as violence has never proved a *sustainable* method of effecting change. However, I am not suggesting that Greens should stake out the centre of traditional politics for themselves. Being isolated on the flank of the political spectrum may be undesirable but being caught by a pincer movement at the centre is no better.

The lesson from Die Grünen is an important one for Greens everywhere. Pitch your policies and your strategies according to the other political parties and it is *they* who will decide how much political space you may have.

Clues for how the Green parties can not only survive but also flourish, however tough the opposition may get, are to be found in the very things that have made them the fastest growing political movement ever. The first is the close link in the minds of ordinary people between the Greens and environmental protection at a time when opinion polls reveal the environment to be one of their top concerns. The second is the fact that women and young people make up the majority of Green voters, and the third is the inspirational contrast that the Green vision offers to an otherwise bleak and frightening future.

Instead of back-pedalling on the environment in their desire to be perceived as a 'compleat' political party, Greens should be putting down roots on the political high ground of environmental concern, and *from there* put out multiple examples of how the environment touches every aspect of the lives of ordinary people, and is not something merely to be appreciated at weekends.

For example, if conservation and protection of the Earth were made the motor of our economic and social regime rather than its fuel, it would affect the health and well-being of not only the biosphere but people too. Social justice would be possible through conservation as it never was through consumption. We would be able to measure satisfaction with our lives, our well-being – our success – with real-life indicators such as health, cultural variety, clean air, safe water, unpoisoned food, secure and convivial neighbourhoods, even the number of species living there with us, rather than by what we consume expressed in very non-real indicators such as Gross National Product. Moreover, the currently fashionable but usually misused notions of 'Green growth' and 'sustainable development' take on their proper meaning and logic when considered in the context of an economic system based on protection of the environment. As there is a natural limit to what we may consume, but no natural limit to what we may conserve and protect, models for human activity based on nature would remain valid for the indefinite future.

Shifting the political debate from a left/right one to a Green/non-Green one is not something that can be done from a chronic minority position. So instead of rummaging around the fringes of other political parties for our coalitions and support we should be looking to the only *sustainable* majority that exists in society, a group whose interests and whose values already receive top billing in Green thinking – women. And how logical and sensible to go on and increase that majority by adding to it the section of society in which women have a massive vested interest and over which they have considerable influence – their children. The surveys that have been done on Green parties reveal that women and young people already make up an important part of their electorates and activists.

But apart from the mathematical sense of taking women as a starting point for building majorities around Green issues, there are other strategic reasons why the Green movement should focus on women. Per Gahrton, in a paper prepared for the 1987 European Green Congress, notes: 'There can be no doubt that men, middle-aged career men, are tremendously over-represented among those who have brought humankind to the brink of nuclear war and ecological disaster.' More directly some women writers wonder if the exploitation and manipulation of nature and women by men could be, as Ariel Sallah has suggested, 'one vast compensatory rage' for their 'rather small role in human reproduction'.[11] Whether men are motivated by revenge or a confused notion that they must appear strong in order to be considered worthy of protecting their mothers, it seems likely that only women have the power to absolve men and make it clear that women don't need their sort of defence. Per Gahrton 'seriously doubts whether man will ever recover without a period of matriarchy'.

Green parties should provide women with the skills and

resources they need to regain confidence in their considerable power to liberate, not simply women from men, but men from themselves, and to re-establish the confidence of *all* of us in the wisdom of natural instincts and patterns of life. Marita Haibach, who was Die Grünen's secretary of state for women's affairs in the Hesse state parliament for two years up to 1987, established an experimental cross-party women's affairs committee shortly after she was first elected in 1982. After a year, women from all four parties in the parliament agreed that the committee should continue. This example from Hesse is echoed by the experience of many Green women elected to various levels of local government. Heidi Hautala of the Finnish Greens believes this represents a kind of 'post-feminist consciousness'. Increasingly women are preferring to work together, even in mixed-sex environments, less because they want to create an identity against men and the male-oriented institutions than because they want to create positive alternatives.

Finally, Greens would be foolish to neglect the high ground of the amazing inspiration and hope contained in the Green vision of the future. Whether we like it or not, we all possess a spiritual dimension, and the Green celebration of diversity and interconnectednes of all life has strong echoes of ancient wisdoms and cultures where sprirituality played a positive and essential part in both society and politics. Today the search for spiritual satisfaction is taking people to extremist religions, or to substitute in despair the ephemeral holy grail of consumerism. Ever more live with a spiritual void and the destructive apathy that is bred of hopelessness. If Greens wish to rekindle people's desire to take responsibility over their own lives, then they must relight the fires of spiritual hope too.

Only if Greens pitch their policies and their strategies according to their strengths will the other parties have to follow or give way.

3: Participating in Power

Almost without exception, the Green parties are squeamish about power – in their own organisations and in the world around them. This is odd for a political movement which proposes the most radical redistribution of power and wealth ever contemplated – sharing it not merely between classes but between continents and with future generations. How these fine words can ever become reality without manipulating power, I do not know. Only by becoming experts in the nature and dynamics of power will Greens be able to applaud when it is used in ways of which they approve and shout 'foul' when it is being abused. Only by becoming experts in the nature and dynamics of power can Greens hope to redistribute it in ways that do not have undesirable side-effects.

As the organograms in this book show, most of the Green parties have a rather naive approach to organisation, which in the case of Die Grünen, Ecolo and the Greens in Finland for example has already posed considerable difficulties. Yet there are ways of organising, as suggested by systems theory, which could fulfil the Green parties' apparently incompatible demands for strength and flexibility, power and accountability, style and efficiency. The theory boils down to the (ecological) notion that description, maintenance and development of the relationships between discrete units are more important than the nature of the units themselves, and that the 'activity of systems involves a process known as transaction – the simultaneous and mutually interdependent interaction between multiple components'.[12] With a bit of development this theory could provide not only the sort of internal organisation the Green parties need but also a notion of what a Europe of regions might look like, what it might be like to live in it, and how it might relate to the rest of the world.

4: Developing True Internationalism

Perhaps the thing that has struck me most about the Green parties, especially those in Europe, is their parochialism. Not only is there a lack of knowledge about what goes on in other countries but a disturbing lack of interest too. Even the ambassadors of the richest and most travelled party, Die Grünen (though there are individual exceptions like Petra Kelly) are more concerned with a narrow sort of internationalism where foreign visits take place in a political and strategic vacuum and are often used merely as personal campaign medals back home.

At a time when environmental problems increasingly need solutions of a global nature, and shifts in economic and political power now take place between continents rather than countries, there is no way Green parties can justify isolationism in their activities. At the Fourth Congress of the European Greens in Antwerp in 1988, Agalev senator Ludo Dierickx pointed out: 'Before men were asked to lay down their lives for the sake of their country, today they are being asked to suffer for the sake of their national economy... It is against this ideology, powerful but without future, that the ideas of the Greens should be directed.' As there is no encyclopaedia of Good Green Housekeeping on the shelf, the only way Greens can enhance their effectiveness back home and project their ideas more widely is by learning from each other and working more efficiently together.

Internationalising their vision of what the future *can* be like, so that people all over the world, rich and poor, know that a Green choice does exist, is probably the biggest challenge facing the Green parties over the next decade. However, the European Green parties would be mistaken if they thought that they have more to teach than they have to learn. The Green revolution was triggered because the whole biosphere is in danger, and, unlike any previous revolution in the history of humankind, if we get it wrong the first time, there will be no second chance.

Sara Parkin
Lyon, October 1988

Notes

1 Christopher Longuet-Higgins et al, *The Gifford Lectures 1971/2: The Nature of Mind*, Edinburgh University Press, 1972, p. 132.
2 Club of Rome report, *The Limits to Growth*, Earth Island, 1972, p. 197.
3 Barbara Ward and René Dubos, *Only One Earth*, Penguin, 1972, p. 298.
4 *The Global 2000 Report to the President*, Penguin, 1982.
5 World Commission on Environment and Development, *Our Common Future*, Oxford University Press, 1987.
6 Lester Brown et al, *State of the World, 1987*, W. W. Norton, New York, 1987, p. 17.
7 Theodore Roszak, *Person/Planet*, Granada, 1981, p. 23.
8 Ronald Inglehart, 'Post-Materialism in an Environment of Insecurity', *American Political Science Review* 75/4, 1981. Werner Hülsberg, *The West German Greens*, Verso, 1987.
9 George Lichtheim, *A Short History of Socialism*, Fontana, 1975, p. 351.
10 John Elkington, *The Green Capitalists*, Gollancz, 1987, p. 126.
11 Ariel Sallah, in Drew Hutton (ed.), Green Politics in Australia, Angus & Roberston, Australia, 1987, p. 81.
12 Fritjof Capra, *The Turning Point*, Wildwood House, 1982, p. 287.

PART ONE:
WEST EUROPEAN GREENS

1: AUSTRIA *Die Grüne Alternative*

Area: 83,855 sq. km.   *founded: September 1986*
Population: 7.55 million (1985)   *members: not known*
Density: 90 per sq. km.

Member: UN, OECD, EFTA
Language: German
GNP per capita: US $8,739 (1985)

Background and Electoral System

Historians sometimes refer to the complexity of events in
Europe during the period 1914 to 1945 as the 'European civil
war'. Although the central issue in both World Wars was the
control of German power, and Europeans did see themselves
as some sort of unit, the often long-standing and multiple
strains and conflicts within and between the different
countries prevented any broader concept of European unity
from developing. Austria was at the heart of both wars. The
assassination of archduke Franz-Ferdinand at Sarajevo in
June 1914 acted as a starting pistol for what has been
described as the beginning of the end of European civilisation.

After the first Austrian republic was formed in 1918, the
contrast between the clerically dominated rural areas and
the huge urban 'red Vienna' was reflected in the delicate
balance between the two main political parties, the
Christian-Social (now People's) party and the Social-
Democrats. In 1933 the Christian-Social chancellor Dollfuss
suppressed the constitution and was assassinated in July
1934 during a Nazi uprising. So began the sticky course to
1938 when Hitler annexed Austria as part of his project to
create a Greater Germany with all people of German blood
reunited. After the defeat of Hitler, Austria was occupied by

the allies.The second republic was established in1945 but full
sovereignty not restored until 1955, when the 'Austrian state
treaty' was signed by the four Allied powers. When the last
foreign soldier left Austrian soil the national parliament
decided on 26 October 1955 that Austria would maintain
permanent neutrality.

When Austria regained its status as a constitutional republic,
the second post-World War I constitution of 1929 was
restored. A president is directly elected by the people every
six years. The two-chamber parliament has a 183-seat Nationalrat directly elected for a four-year term and a Senat whose
members are elected by the provincial councils in proportion
to the population of the province. At present the Senat has 63
members.

The nine Austrian provinces each directly elect a provincial parliament every five years (in Upper Austria every six
years), the size of the parliament depending on the size of the
province. Each parliament in turn elects members of an
executive. Communities also elect municipal councils who
appoint a Bürgermeister (mayor) and a committee to deal
with administrative and executive duties. The Austrian
capital of Vienna is run by a city council, with minor duties
devolved to 23 districts which directly elect their own
councils.

National elections in Austria are conducted under the
d'Hondt system of proportional representation with constituency lists. Some of the local elections require a certain
percentage to be polled before seats may be won. For example
at least 5% must be polled to gain seats on Vienna city
council. To form a political party in Austria requires simply
that the party's statutes be lodged with the ministry of the
interior, then published, and that the party indulge in no
'neo-Nazi agitation'. Signatures of support from the electorate are required to register a list at any election if the
party is not already represented in parliament or on the
council. At present the number of signatures required is
modest but the government is examining proposals to
increase it for national elections. Parties with at least five
members in the national parliament receive state funding for
political and educational work. Any other party which polls
over 1% of the vote receives a small sum of money per vote.

Factors Influencing the Development
of Green Politics

Although very influenced by the success of the West German
Green party, there is not the same tradition of local citizens'
initiatives behind the development of Die Grüne Alternative.
The issues and events that stimulated people to take up
Green politics in Austria were more of a national nature.

The Austrian peace movement, for example, is primarily
engaged in trying to safeguard Austria's increasingly fragile
status as a neutral country. Their battle, however, seems to
be a losing one. Austria is the sixth largest exporter of arms
(mostly to Third World countries) of all the OECD countries.
In 1985 the Socialist-led coalition government bought 24
Saab-Draken fighter planes from that other neutral country,
Sweden, for the Austrian army. The army had been created in
1955 to defend Austria's frontiers, but as Freda Meissner-
Blau, a long-time peace activist and now a Green MP, points
out: 'If they {Russia or America} want to march through
Austria, all we can do is open our frontiers and say "go
through as quickly as you can"... any army we have will
perhaps stop them for a day or two, with terrible losses, but it
won't prevent them.' The generals' demand for the Swedish
fighters she sees as simply 'toys for the boys', but fears that
the next demand will be for rockets and other accessories to
go with them. Although the Greens are fairly certain that
Austria is already secretly involved in defence plans for
Western Europe, they are strongly against Austria joining
the European Community. They believe this would give
Austria an unacceptably close relationship to NATO, thus
ending even the present pretence over the country's neutral
status.[1]

The Greens point to two other major events that have
contributed to their development. The first, the campaign
against the commissioning of Austria's first nuclear power
station at Zwentendorf, not very far from Vienna, was
completely successful. On 5 November 1978 – three months
before the accident at Harrisburg, USA – over half the
people of Austria voted against the use of nuclear power in
their country in the only referendum to be held since 1945.[2]
Subsequent tentative suggestions that a new referendum
should take place on nuclear power have been firmly scotch-
ed by the accident at Chernobyl, from which Austria experi-

enced considerable radioactive fall-out.

The second campaign, against the proposal to build a hydroelectric dam on the Danube at Hainburg, was also a victory but rather a Pyrrhic one. This time, the last river forest in Europe was at stake. Thousands of demonstrators followed the example of the Indian Chipko movement (see Chapter 20) by hugging the trees as the contractors moved into the forest. Thus the demonstrators prevented the clearance of the trees for four freezing cold December weeks in 1984. By the time the government sent in 2,000 police who acted with considerable brutality, a large number of Austrian people had been alerted to the problem. Horrified by the violence of the police 40,000 people took to the streets of Vienna on 19 December 1984. This caused the government to pause for thought, and to think even deeper when the high court decided a few days later that the clearing of the forests was illegal. The project was halted. For many people this was a turning point in Austria's history. Not only was it the first real case of mass civil disobedience, but it had been successful, proving that people could do something against those in power.

Unfortunately, the Austrian government not only had big contracting firms all dressed up and ready to build a dam, it also had investors. The whole project was shifted downstream into Czechoslovakia and Hungary where protest would be more easily supressed. The Austrian government in effect 'lent' the expertise and money, and arranged for it to be repaid in electricity. Although the Danube goes through a wide flat plain at the proposed site and is therefore entirely unsuitable for damming, the Austrian offer was taken up. In the event, this stimulated one of the most sustained attempts at non-violent mass civilian defiance in an Eastern bloc country (see Chapter 20). The Hungarian Duna Kör (Danube Circle) were unsuccessful in their own protest, but maintain close contacts with the Austrian Greens who appreciate that their democratic freedom to protest merely transferred the same ecologically unsound project into a country where protest was that much harder.

Die Grüne Alternative

Although many small parties and organisations sprang up in
Austria at the beginning of the 1980s, only two put up
candidates for the elections to the Nationalrat in April 1983.
One, Vereinte Grüne Österreichs (VGÖ – United Greens of
Austria), was founded on 2 December 1982, mainly from
moderate groups who had taken part in the campaign against
nuclear power. The other, Alternative Liste Österreich
(ALÖ – Austrian Alternative List), was founded one month
earlier on 5 November in Graz, by activists from ecological,
feminist, peace, Third World and student movements etc.[3]
Neither party won any seats – VGÖ polling 1.9% of the votes
and ALÖ 1.4% – but they did contribute to the Socialist party
losing its overall majority, which obliged it to form a
coalition with the right-wing Freedom party (FPÖ). Dr Bruno
Kreisky, the long-reigning Socialist chancellor, resigned.

In some provinces VGÖ and ALÖ formed joint lists for
provincial elections (Salzburg, Tyrol, Vorarlberg and Styria)
but frequently there were several Green lists standing
against each other. The first major success in a provincial
election took place inOctober 1984,when anALÖ-VGÖ list in
Vorarlberg polled 13% and won 4 seats on the 36-seat
council.[4] Greens have subsequently been elected to one other
provincial council – Styria – where an ALÖ-VGÖ list obtained 3.7% and 2 seats.[5]

When Freda Meissner-Blau polled 5.5% in the first round
of the presidential elections in May 1986, forcing Kurt
Waldheim into a second-round run-off, the disparate and
frequently feuding Green groups looked up. Freda had a long
and honourable reputation as an activist. She had taken part
in the protest against the nuclear plant at Zwentendorf and
had been one of the ten people who had negotiated with the
government after 'Black Wednesday' – the day the police
descended on the demonstrators in the Hainburg forests.
Within a few months many members of VGÖ and ALÖ had
joined with the Bürgerinitiative Parlament (BIP — Citizens'
Parliamentary Initiative) founded by Hainburg activist,
journalist and ex-Socialist party member Günther Nenning,
as well as other small provincial groups including the
Slovene Koroška Enotna Lista (KEL — Carinthian United
List), and Die Grüne Alternative was founded in September
1986. In the November 1986 elections to the Nationalrat, Die

Grüne Alternative, with Freda Meissner-Blau at the head of
the list, polled 4.8% of the vote and won 8 seats.

Since 1986, Die Grüne Alternative has done less well than
it hoped in provincial and municipal elections. This is due
not only to internal arguments but also to the fact that some
members of VGÖ have split away from the new party and put
up competing candidates, while the FPÖ has started to
revamp its image under a new leader. In October 1987 the
Greens polled only 2.2% in the Burgenland provincial
elections, but the Die Grüne Alternative-affiliated Bürgerlis-
te (citizens' list) managed to poll 10.1% and win 4 seats on the
Salzburg city council. In November 1987, Die Grüne Alternative polled 4.4% and won no seats in elections to the Vienna
city council, but it did gain 55 out of a total of 1,082 seats in
the Vienna district council elections which were held simultaneously. At least one seat was won in each of the 23
districts. Another setback occurred in the 24 January 1988
elections to the Graz city council, where the Die Grüne
Alternative-affiliated Alternative Liste Graz lost 2 of its 4
seats on the city council with a poll of 4.9%.[6]

Future Prospects

According to the party itself Die Grüne Alternative is a
coalition of 'moderate ecologists, former leftist Socialist
party members who were discontented with the new Austrian
federal chancellor, Franz Vranitzky {a technocratic right-
wing social democrat}, peace activists, Eurocommunists and
other former radical leftists as well as anti-nuclear power
activists, Hainburg activists and critical Christians.'[7]
However the strains of so many people with differing
interests – objectives even – trying to work as one are
beginning to show, and arguments are particularly intense
about the way the money allocated to political parties with
parliamentarians should be spent. The Austrian citizen's
inevitable confusion over the lack of coherence within Die
Grüne Alternative must be compounded by the presence of
many other small local parties in Austria that lay claim to the
title Green.

This disarray of the party outside parliament is unfortunate, to say the least, since inside parliament the Socialist
party and the People's party formed a 'grand coalition' in

January 1987. Left in opposition are only the right-wing Freedom party and the Greens. While this certainly imposes an enormous workload on the 8 Green MPs, who are faced with 23 parliamentary commissions for example, it also offers an almost ideal backdrop against which to contrast Green policies. Within 18 months, the Green MPs made over 60 proposals for legislation and asked over 400 written questions – more than any other party. By putting questions that the other parties had never thought of before (and by throwing back any answers with which they were not satisfied) the Greens say they have been able to keep up such pressure on the parliamentary agenda that the other parties have been forced to face the issues. This tactic paid off in March 1988 when the Greens' proposal to oblige the National Statistical Bureau to correct calculations of gross national product for environmental losses was accepted unanimously by the environmental committee.[8]

Obviously the Greens in opposition will be unable to affect as many practical changes by this government as they would like, but if they can resolve their internal problems, they have a real chance of increasing their vote significantly in the next elections to the Austrian parliament. By that time, if they can keep up the pressure, the *next* government might be ready to wax a bit greener. As Freda Meissner-Blau puts it:

> The only way you can instigate change is to threaten them in their power. This language they understand. They are very quick to know when they start to get insecure in their position. That means that the only way we can force them to change or stop what they're doing or do what needs to be done is by the force of people...That's our only chance because that threatens their power. If they have to worry that they're not elected, they will do what's expected of them.[9]

Notes

1 'Austria: Race Against Time', interview with Freda Meissner-Blau, *Sanity*, July 1987.
2 Gerhard Jordan, 'The Peace Movement and the Greens in Austria – A Short History', 1986, unpublished.
3 ibid.

4 Die Grüne Alternative report to the European Greens, November 1986.
5 'Resultat Grüner Parteien bei Landtagswahlen in Österreich, 1987,'
Die Grüne Alternative document.
6. ibid.
7 Die Grüne Alternative report to the European Greens.
8 The Austrian Greens' proposal was based on work done by Roefie
Hueting and Christian Leipert. See their discussion paper 'Economic
Growth, National Income and the Blocked Choices for the Environment', International Institute for Environment and Society, West
Berlin, 1987, for an introduction to how these calculations may be made.
It also has a good bibliography.
9 As note 1.

Main Party Publications

Offenes Kurzprogramm, 1986 (election programme).
Nagymaros, Grüne Bildungswerkstatt, Vienna, 1988 (bilingual booklet
on Danube dam project published on behalf of Hungarian protest
groups).
Un-mut, Der Beginn einer Protestbewegung, Grüne Bildungswerkstatt,
Vienna, 1988.
Die Republik im Fieber. Ein Jahr Grüne-Alternative im Parlament, Grüne
Bildungswerkstatt, Graz, 1988.

Grüner Rundbrief, party magazine.

Studies of Green Politics

'Die Grünen – Momentaufnahme einer Bewegung in Österreich', KOHL
A. & STIRNEMANN A., *Österreichisches Jahrbuch für Politik '82*,
Verlag für Geschichte und Politik, Vienna, 1983.
'Grün-Alternative Bewegungen in Österreich', *Zeitschrift für Erwach-
senenbildung und Politische Bildung* 2, 1983.
Umdenken. Analysen Grüner Politik in Österreich, Junius-Verlag,
Vienna, 1984.

Addresses

Die Grüne Alternative   Parlamentsklub der Grünen
Millergasse 40/9   Dr Karl Rennerring 3
1060 Vienna   1017 Vienna

tel: (43) 222 5979182   tel: (43) 222 4804691

Election Results

NATIONAL
(Nationalrat)

	1986 Nov	1983 Apr	1979 May
7 Freedom Party (FPÖ)	**18** *9.7*	**12** *5.0*	**11** *6.1*
6 People's Party (ÖVP)	**77** *41.3*	**81** *43.2*	**77** *42.0*
3 Socialist Party (SPÖ)	**80** *43.1*	**90** *47.7*	**95** *51.0*
1 Communist Party (KPÖ)	*0.7*	*0.7*	*1.0*
10 Greens			
- Die Grüne Alternative	**8** *4.8*		
- ALÖ		*1.4*	
- VGÖ		*1.9*	

PRESIDENTIAL (May 1986)

	first round	second round
Waldheim (People's)	*49.6*	*53.9*
Steyrer (Socialist)	*43.7*	*46.1*
Meissner-Blau (Green)	*5.5*	
Scrinzi (extreme-right)	*1.2*	

REFERENDUM ON NUCLEAR POWER (November 1978)

For	*49.5*
Against	*50.5*

Key: **Seats** in bold, *Percentages* in italics.

References
The Statesman's Year Book (ed. John Paxton), Macmillan.
SMITH Gordon, *Politics in Western Europe*, Heinemann, 1984.
Austrian Embassy, London.
Green Party documents.

2: BELGIUM

Agalev

Ecolo

Area: 30,519 sq. km.   *founded: Agalev, March 1982*
Population 9.86 million (1986)   *Ecolo, March 1980*
Density: 323 per sq. km.   *members: about 1,000 each*

Member: UN, OECD, NATO, WEA,
      European Communities
Languages: Dutch (57%), French (42%), German (1%)
GNP per capita: US $7,870 (1984)

Background and Electoral System

A revolt against the Dutch in 1830 led to the establishment of an independent and predominantly Catholic kingdom of Belgium under Leopold I. Since then linguistic disputes between the Dutch-speaking Flemings in the north (Flanders) and the French-speaking Walloons in the south (Wallonia) have progressively intensified, to the point where a mayor in the tiny rural district of Fourons (Voeren in Dutch – population 4,500), was able to bring down the national government in 1987 by refusing to take a test in Dutch.[1]

Dutch-speaking Belgians had a long struggle to gain equality for their language in higher education, the courts of law and administrative bodies, and as late as 1968 clashes over language took place at Leuven university. In the 1970s the main political parties split along linguistic lines. Finally, in 1981, Belgium devolved considerable powers to regional assemblies in Flanders and Wallonia, with Brussels becoming an official bilingual region whose executive remained part of central government.

Far from resolving the linguistic tensions, devolution simply institutionalised them. It also highlighted the shift of economic power that was taking place from the once rich Wallonia to the formerly poor and predominantly agricultural Flanders. While Walloons were reeling from the depression of their steel and other heavy industries, the Flemish (who already had the largest concentration of people anywhere in the world speaking four languages) were using their surplus labour and relatively low wages to make full use of their major port, Antwerp, and to attract investment in new high-technology industries.

Belgium is a constitutional and hereditary (male) monarchy. The 212-seat Chamber of Representatives sits for a maximum of four years. Senators are elected both directly and indirectly. Those directly elected must number exactly half the members of the Chamber, i.e. 106. The remaining senators are indirectly elected, either by the provincial councils in proportion to their population or by cooption. The coopted senators must number half the provincial senators. At present there are 183 senators in the national parliament.[2]

As well as being divided into linguistic regions – Flanders, Wallonia, bilingual Brussels and a small German-speaking region – Belgium is also divided into nine provinces. These are further subdivided into electoral *arrondissements* (constituencies) for the purpose of national elections and into 589 communes for the purpose of local and provincial elections. Deputies and the directly elected senators also serve in the regional assemblies.

Elections to national and European Parliaments and to the regional assemblies are conducted under the d'Hondt system of proportional representation, with lists based on the *arrondissements* for elections to the national parliament and linguistically divided lists for the other two. This system gives reasonable proportionality but means that the smaller the *arrondissement* the higher the percentage vote required to gain a seat. This favours larger political parties. For local elections a variation on the d'Hondt system – the Imperiali system – is used which is even more biased towards larger parties. To allocate the final seats, the Belgian electoral system aggregates 'surplus' votes from the several districts within each province. Voting in Belgium is obligatory.

There are no financial requirements for candidates, who must simply be resident Belgian nationals, not less than 25 years old to enter the Chamber, regional assemblies and European Parliament, and not less than 40 to enter the Senate. Lists in each constituency require the signatures of a few outgoing members of parliament or a larger number of registered electors – 5,000 for the European elections, 200 for both the House of Representatives and the Senate, 50 for the provincial councils. There is no public financing for political parties in Belgium, and media time during national election campaigns is linked to the number of seats held by the party in the outgoing parliament. A small amount of time is allocated to smaller parties who have lists in every constituency.

Factors Influencing the Development of Green Politics

The Belgian Green parties first entered their national parliament in 1981, some time before their better known German counterparts. But it is hard to find in the context of Belgium the same constellation of factors that were in place in neighbouring Germany at the end of the 1970s.

Social scientists apply the *verzuiling* (pillar-isation) theory in their analysis of Belgian and Dutch society.[3] However the *zuilen* they identify are more accurately a complex cross-meshing of social groups which make the traditional 'class' analysis inappropriate. The original *zuilen* were Catholic and lay pillars which were both crossed by linguistic divisions. Each *zuil* had separate organisations – trade unions, youth organisations, schools, cultural organisations and so on – most divided linguistically. Eventually the lay *zuil* subdivided into liberal and socialist pillars while the Christian pillar became more secularised and united. Now there are conservative, liberal and socialist *zuilen* each topped by their political parties, but still cross-meshed by the religious, linguistic and socio-economic groupings. Each small 'compartment' tends to be fiercely protective, parochial and competitive, but broadly speaking Flanders is politically more conservative, while Wallonia is more socialist. Not only does the *verzuiling* theory help to explain the deadlocks that can occur in Belgium when it tries to form a government and the fragility of the eventual coalitions; it also explains why no broad social movements have developed, as they did in nearby Germany.

Certainly the Belgian environmental movement has proved unable to stop Belgium being surpassed only by France in its reliance on nuclear power (over 60% of Belgium's electricity is generated by nuclear plants) or prevent some of the worst examples of postwar inner-city development. With justification, present-day Belgium is called the crossroads of Europe. For a small, densely populated country it is extravagantly criss-crossed with railways and motorways, and of course Brussels acts as Europe's unofficial capital by providing the headquarters for NATO and the European Communities.

Because of the linguistic divide there are two Green parties in Belgium – Agalev in Flanders and Ecolo in Wallonia. Although their origins are very different they both owe their beginnings and style to their founders and each is influenced by the political and cultural history of its linguistic region. Agalev started from a Catholic-inspired lifestyle movement and Ecolo from a group within one of the Walloon parties that was particularly concerned with democratic structures.

The basic programmes of both parties are similar in content although differently accented and expressed, and each party maintains a relatively informal organisation, holding regular joint meetings to deal with matters of common interest, especially in connection with parliament.

Both Green parties have made a point of objecting strongly to the use of language or religion as a political weapon (as in the case of the mayor of Fourons/Voeren). Agalev senator Ludo Dierickx points out how fortunate it is for Belgium that while politicians and the papers shout and hassle ordinary people remain calm. 'Such issues have already resulted in bloodbaths in other places – like the Basque country or Northern Ireland.'[4]

The Green MPs have enshrined their collaboration in both Chamber and Senate in a formal agreement. Agalev and Ecolo are the only 'opposite language' parties to form a single parliamentary group both in the Chamber and in the Senate, although rules governing the Senate do not even cater for 'interlinguistic groups'. All proposals for legislation are signed by both parties. They have also achieved the unique distinction of being the only 'opposite language' parties to put forward a joint proposal to solve the dilemma of Fourons/Voeren. Their proposition for 'linguistic courtesy' in political and administrative affairs was given a practical demon-

stration in the way Ecolo and Agalev MPs took the oath
when the new parliament convened in January 1988. Each of
their Brussels MPs responded in both languages. Apart from
the minister of the interior, who is responsible for 'linguistic
peace', they were the only ones to do so.

Agalev

In the early 1970s, Luc Versteylen, a Jesuit and teacher,
brought together a group of thinkers in De Brouwerij, an old
brewery at Viersel, near Antwerp. Described as a charismatic man, Versteylen ran a group in the brewery where
youngsters came to play and talk about their problems. He
became aware of the stress they were experiencing in the
increasingly competitive school system and, with other
adults in De Brouwerij, started to develop a critique of
education. Very quickly this expanded to a general critique
of consumer-driven society and the group began to elaborate
some 'counter-values'. Disillusioned with present-day Catho-
licism they returned to the ideals and symbolism of early
Christianity. The three bad values of *competitie, consumptie*
and *concurrentie* (rivalry, consumption and competition)
should be replaced by three good values of *stilte, soberheid*
and *samenhorigheid* (peace, frugality and community). These
values became very important to the new movement, Anders
Gaan Leven, that grew up in and around Antwerp.

Anders Gaan Leven (meaning 'to go and live differently')
spread their ideas via pamphlets which they published and
distributed themselves and by their activities. They participated in colourful environmental campaigns, founded an
alternative village school and established the well-known
'green cyclists' movement De Groene Fietsers. Gradually the
movement spread to other parts of Flanders.

Discussion over how institutions and political leaders
could be won over to the new values began in the new, but
still very diverse and unstructured movement. Opinion was
divided over the desirability of taking part in elections. Some
felt the movement should not take part at all while others
preferred to run 'tactical voting' campaigns – offering advice
to voters on the most suitable candidates. Eventually a
working group called Agalev was formed for the sole purpose
of directly contesting elections.

The first engagement of Agalev in the electoral process took place in the local elections of October 1976, but only in the Antwerp region. Then in the December 1978 national elections Agalev stood some candidates in every region and polled 0.1% nationwide.[5]

For the first direct elections to the European Parliament in 1979, Agalev polled 2.3% in Flanders and the subsequent publicity attracted many people from other parties and from environmental and peace groups. Then in the national elections of 1981 Agalev obtained 3.9% in Flanders which gave them two seats in the Chamber and one seat in the Senate.[6] In the simultaneously held elections to the provincial councils Agalev won a total of 7 seats: 4 in Antwerp, 2 in East Flanders and 1 in West Flanders.[7]

With elected parliamentarians, the debate about whether Agalev should or should not become involved in elections became more than overtaken by events. Many people from diverse backgrounds were keen to create an ecological party and in March 1982 Agalev split from the movement Anders Gaan Leven and constituted itself as a political party. Despite a few early difficulties the relationship between the movement and the party remained fairly close, with several of the movement's originators to be found in the party. Anders Gaan Leven still exists and attracts young people and, on the whole, the party's style still reflects the three 'counter-values' that inspired the movement.

1982 also saw the newly founded party gain 44 seats in the 64 Flemish communes where it stood. The average vote in those communes was 5.6%; 28 of the seats were in Antwerp, 7 in Brabant, 7 in East Flanders and 2 in West Flanders. Agalev continued its occasional practice of supporting local 'green lists' for these elections, with the result that a further 12 'Agalev-approved' candidates were elected. But attempts to establish majority coalitions with different parties in the communes of Schoten and Meise didn't last.

The June 1984 elections to the European Parliament saw Paul Staes, a dynamic environmental journalist, elected with a vote of 7.08% in Flanders and an impressive 4.4% nationwide. Staes attracted a local vote of 9.25% from the Antwerp region, where he lives.

The following year, in the national elections of October 1985, Agalev won 6.3%[8] of the vote in Flanders and increased its representation to 4 seats in the Chamber and 3 in the Senate.

The story of Agalev's progress is remarkable for its
smoothness, in contrast to the usually turbulent development of the other Green parties. Most people give credit for
this to one man, Leo Cox, who has been its full-time paid
political secretary since it was founded. Cox's original remit
was to oversee the transformation of a tiny inexperienced
group of people into a democratic and efficient political
party. Strong internal organisation had to be matched by
external relationships (with the press, institutions, etc.)
which would command respect for the party. Many members
acknowledge that Agalev's success so far is largely due to
Cox's ability to balance the needs of different factions within
the party and to judge correctly how Agalev should prepare
for and react to external political events. Cox remains firmly
in the background, shunning the media spotlights and
playing a low-key role at party conferences. The modesty
with which he handles his position of considerable power
ensures that he is trusted and respected throughout the
party.

After the 1985 elections the local parties did express some
frustrations with the way the party was concentrating on the
national aspects of Green politics, and a decision was made
that one-tenth of the annual working budget would go to
local parties. It was thought that this *dotatiefond* could help
increase party membership, which, although restricted to
activists, remains low. The party also tried a *witte vlekken*
(white spots) campaign in which it attempted to stimulate
membership in areas where there was no local organisation.
However, despite improving local elections results neither
the *dotatiefond* nor the white spot campaign brought in many
new members. Also during this period the party bought and
restored a building in Brussels. Despite the reservations of
the local groups and the steering group over the cost of this,
the project was completed and the house now offers working
and meeting conditions entirely in tune with the values of
Anders Gaan Leven. It has also provided a strong signal to
the outside world – the electorate, the media and the other
political parties – that Agalev means serious business and
will not be easily marginalised.

Members of Agalev also point to several areas where they
have made a particular point of taking the lead in Belgian
politics. Firstly as a 'whip' on the peace movement, sections
of which were anxious to avoid compromising the Christian-
Democrat party. (This party has several wings and is

therefore prone to prevaricate over anti-nuclear policies.)
Belgium also has an old-fashioned abortion law. Although
many doctors interpret the law fairly leniently, abortion is in
fact illegal. The Christian-Democrats have also dragged their
feet over reform, and the Socialist and Liberal parties have
provoked rebellion rather than reform by proposing
extremely radical amendments. Agalev, coming from a
Christian background, and with the support of its founder,
was able to propose a sensible amendment to the law, in a
framework of understanding both the anti- and pro-abortion
moral positions but not accepting that one should dominate
the other. This caused considerable confusion in all the other
parties and much attention from the press.

Agalev's strategy has undoubtedly paid off in electoral
terms. In the December 1987 elections to the national
Parliament, the party obtained 6 seats for 4.5% of the vote in
the lower house and 5 seats in the Senate for 4.9%, exactly
what Leo Cox hoped would happen. The sort of steady
progress which doesn't destabilise a still inexperienced party
but does mean that 'no other party can ever leave the Green
bits of a political programme to one side. They all must follow
some form of Green politics, they can no longer say that the
environment or the missiles are not important. In this sense
we have managed to change the debate.'[9]

Ecolo: Early days

No one studying the history, the development and the style of
Ecolo can fail to be struck by the influence of one man – Paul
Lannoye. A physicist in his late forties, he was instrumental
in the formation of Ecolo during the 1970s and is now one of
the three Ecolo senators in the Belgian parliament.

At the time of the 1971 national elections, Lannoye was a
member of the French-language federalist party, Rassemblement Wallon (RW — Walloon Union). Although the RW
was then at the height of its fortunes, he left, and with some
friends founded Démocratie Nouvelle (DN), a movement of
'reflection' on the state of Belgian democracy. Its manifesto
published in February 1973 called for an integrated federa-
lism, implying autonomy and self-management for local
communities with most decisions being made by referendums
initiated by the people. It also outlined proposals for a new

economy differentiating between fundamental needs or needs associated with self-realisation (which should get priority) and superficial or polluting needs – economic intervention was to place people's living conditions and environment at the level of their own lives. Finally the DN committed its own organisation to assuring the autonomy and decision-making power of each member.

These same themes were given priority in the Ecolo manifestos for the 1981 and 1985 national elections. Only since then have policies for 'eco-development' and for dealing with unemployment received higher billing than policies dealing with the organisation either of Belgium or of Ecolo itself.

In March 1974, DN participated in the national elections in a cartel with the Union Démocratique et Progressiste (UDP), but only in the province of Namur. The top result was 2.4% in Namur city. Over the next two years members of DN made contact with several groups concerned with environmental protection in Wallonia and also with members of Friends of the Earth in France and America. In March 1976 Les Amis de la Terre Belgique (ATB) was founded. Among the founding members were Georges Trussart, who was eventually to become an Ecolo Senator, and Nicole Martin, wife of Paul Lannoye. The statutes of ATB were quite clear about the political role of the organisation and laid down a structure founded on the 'dual principle' of autonomy for local groups and coordination for joint activities. The contradiction enshrined in this principle was to plague ATB and then Ecolo for the next ten years.

Before the local elections of October 1976 DN appealed to a variety of local groups to form a joint list. Combat Pour l'Ecologie et l'Autogestion (CPEA — Struggle for Ecology and Self-Management) scored 1.9% in Namur, but after failing to come to an agreement on future cooperation with other lists standing on similar themes in the elections the CPEA dissolved. Meanwhile ATB were setting up local groups and adopting a manifesto not dissimilar to that of the CPEA.

In the national elections of April 1977 several lists evoking ecology appeared – Ecolo, Ecolog, Wallonie-Ecologie, Ecologie-Wallonie – none scoring more than 2.3% and all more or less dissolving after the elections. In January 1978, Wallonie-Ecologie was reborn in Namur, with local groups established in each electoral district. These sent delegates to a permanent central council who were in turn charged with elaborating a political programme. This programme was adopted at a meeting in Liège in August 1978 and bore a strong resemblance to the ATB manifesto. A few weeks later, at their general assembly at Tihange in October, ATB split. The majority, who wanted a federal structure for the movement, contained many people who were to go on and found Ecolo 18 months later. The minority, who insisted on the primacy of autonomy for local groups, went on to form the Réseau Libre des Amis de la Terre (RLAT — Free Network of Friends of the Earth).

Again, several lists vied for the ecology ticket in the national elections of December 1978 – Ecopol (with many members of RLAT), Ecolog and Wallonie-Ecologie. The first list, standing in Brussels, gained only 0.47% of the vote, Ecolog 1.01%, but Wallonie-Ecologie did far better, scoring up to 5.21% in its stronghold of Namur.

Although attempts at reconciliation were made, the bitterness of the split in ATB increased to the point of legal action being started by both sides. Only intervention by Friends of the Earth in other countries and the approach of the 1979 European elections defused the situation.

With some difficulty, a single list Europe-Ecologie was established for these elections. Of the 17 people on the list headed by Paul Lannoye, 13 were members of ATB, and their platform, agreed at a meeting in Huy in February 1979, consisted of proposals for a Europe of regions, referendums, an ecological economy, solidarity with the Third World, an end to reliance on nuclear weapons and withdrawal from NATO. The result was 5.1% in the French-speaking region of Belgium, with higher scores in Namur (7.7% for the *arrondissement* and 10.1% in the canton). 22% was obtained in the German-speaking canton of Saint-Vith.[10]

At two meetings on 8th and 23rd March 1980, held in Opheylissem and Huy respectively, the decision was made to found Ecolo as 'a permanent structure based on the self-managing and federalist model, with the objective of putting ecological demands into the political area in terms of social management'.[11] But old conflicts remained, and although Ecolo was the only one to have candidates in every constituency for the national elections of November 1981, other lists also sought the ecological vote – Ecolo-J, Ecolo-Bxl, Ecolos. Some were objecting to the way Ecolo was organised rather than to its programme, others were promoting quite a different sort of politics. Ecolos for example was considered to be extremely right-wing and Ecolo successfully obtained a legal ban on its name. In the end the smaller lists gained a total of 1.5% while Ecolo scored a result that surprised even itself. With an overall score of 5.9% in Wallonia and 3.1% in Brussels, it received 2 seats in the Chamber and 3 in the Senate. In the provincial elections held simultaneously, Ecolo gained 4 seats in Liège, 3 in Namur, 1 in Hainaut and 1 in Luxembourg.

For the local elections in October 1982, Ecolo prepared a manifesto headed 'Une autre manière de vivre sa commune' (a different kind of community living) and only considered cartels with local groups who agreed with this programme. In the area of Brussels some lists were shared with Agalev. The result was an overall 7.1% and 75 seats for Ecolo.[12] In several communes Ecolo held the balance of power but, with the exception of the city of Liège, no majority coalitions were formed. The 'Liège experiment' is examined in more detail below.

When Ecolo attracted François Roelants, ex-secretary general of Interenvironnement-Wallonie, to head its list in the June 1984 elections to the European Parliament it obtained 9.9% in Wallonia and one seat. In October the following year Ecolo polled 6.5% in Wallonia for 5 seats in the Chamber and 3 seats in the Senate of the national parliament. The party's place in Belgian politics seemed secure. But underneath the slowly improving election results, the tensions and the contradictions that had plagued the genesis of Ecolo began to reappear.

Ecolo: The Crisis

Ecolo had never resolved its own confusion about whether to be a political party, a movement or both. Despite their concern over democratic processes and organisation, the founders of Ecolo not only institutionalised this confusion but also found themselves trapped in contradictions essentially of their own making. When conflict and difficult decisions had to be dealt with, the framework and process for dealing with them proved to be inadequate; so decisions were put off and conflict bottled up. As the movement grew, the 'dual principle' of local autonomy and democratic cooperation had not been translated into practical structures; tasks remained associated with personalities rather than posts. New members attracted by the success of the party often held different conceptions about what the party stood for; the contrast between urban Brussels and provincial Wallonia sharpened.

Soon disillusion with the rapidly deteriorating atmosphere in a party that gave top priority to 'Une autre manière de faire de la politique' (a different style of politics) was added to deep confusion over the role and objectives of Ecolo.

At an assembly of the party in May 1986, Paul Lannoye and two of his supporters lost a motion to 'professionalise' the party's executive. They withdrew their nominations for the vacant posts on the executive and Lannoye, described variously as the 'father of the movement' or its 'historic leader', unambiguously gave his point of view in several interviews with the press at the beginning of March.

Shortly afterwards the widely popular chair of the Agalev/ Ecolo group in the Chamber of Representatives, Olivier Deleuze, resigned his seat and his Ecolo membership. The press secretary and the secretary to the party executive also resigned over the same issue. The executive of Ecolo had just approved a proposal to 'assure a quorum' for the Liberal (i.e. conservative) group who held just one seat more than the Socialists in the Wallonia regional assembly. The idea was that Ecolo would provide a 'constructive opposition' which would mean providing a majority for certain issues approved by Ecolo in return for support on specific projects.[13]

As the implication of the agreement seemed to be that, by not assuring a quorum, Ecolo would simply close its eyes to issues of which it did not approve, Deleuze was furious. He said it was impossible for him to belong to any party that contemplated a relationship with the right under such feeble conditions. While many were scandalised at the proposed agreement because they frankly viewed Ecolo as a party of the left, others were more disturbed at the way in which the matter had been dealt with by the party. The agreement had been established by Paul Lannoye and some colleagues, and then presented to the federal council of the party in what several people felt to be an unacceptable take-it-or-leave-it basis at their meeting of 21 March 1986.

On 11 May, at an assembly described afterwards by Paul Lannoye as a big 'clean-out', the delegates present voted their disapproval of the way the agreement in the Wallonia regional council had been handled; but they also declared that they did not consider the agreement a political error, nor did they disapprove of the contents of the agreement. The meeting also sanctioned an 'internal audit' of the party's organisation which would indicate suitable amendments to the statutes designed to 'ensure internal coherence'. The professionalisation of the secretariat was approved and Paul Lannoye voted back onto the executive committee.

Finally, after all the agony, the Liberals in the Wallonia regional assembly rejected the terms of the coalition agreement.

Deleuze was neither the first nor the last MP to resign. In 1982 Alphonse Royen had resigned as senator giving as his reason: 'The Senate can manage without me but my family cannot.' After Deleuze came François Roelants, Member of the European Parliament, maintaining: 'Ecolo is an empty vessel,' although his departure was influenced more by his financial differences with the party and frustration over trying to pursue his political career in the GRAEL group of the European Parliament (see Chapter 15). Georges Dutry then left for 'personal reasons' and Georges Flandres was forced by his region to resign over his refusal to accept the party's policy on abortion. Under the Belgian electoral system the vacated seats may be filled by the party from its list. However, Roelants refused to give up his seat, continuing as an independent, and the replacement for Deleuze, Jacques Preumont, promptly founded another party as soon as he took up his seat. Only when Verts pour une Gauche Alternative (VEGA — Greens for an Alternative Left) failed to attract more than a handful of supporters did Preumont leave parliament and return the seat to Ecolo.

All these resignations were of course widely reported in the press and did a lot of damage to Ecolo's political credibility. They also caused the party severe financial problems. 98% of the party's finance is obtained from the salaries of its parliamentarians, who are paid around 156,000 Belgian francs per month, or from the other financial assistance given to parliamentary groups. This they hand over to the party along with any other allowance. In turn Ecolo pays its parliamentarians a more modest salary and controls the appointment of parliamentary assistants. Although he gave political and organisational ineffectualness as his reasons, financial difficulties are considered to have played an important role in the resignation of Roelants, who kept his salary. By the time Preumont returned his mandate and therefore his salary to Ecolo in October 1987, the party had acute financial problems.

The Liège Experiment

In the local elections of October 1982, the left-wing coalition Rassemblement Progressiste et Socialiste Wallon (RPSW) won 23 seats on the Liège city council, the right-wing coalition Union Pour Liège (UPL) winning 21. Both instantly contacted Ecolo who held the balance of power with 6 seats. A meeting of the local party was overwhelmingly in favour of joining a ruling coalition on the city council but was clear that it preferred the RPSW to the UPL as partners.

After ten days of negotiations an agreement of 21 pages was signed, backed by a more detailed 150-page document. Ecolo's priorities were:

> * to increase the participation of the citizens of
> Liège in the running of their city,
> * to make town planning respect the quality of life
> in the city,
> * to end Liège's financial involvement in the
> production of nuclear power, and
> * to end all political patronage.

The party also negotiated 3 out of the 11 *échevinats* (alderman posts):

> * Town Planning and Public Transport (held by
> Raymond Yans, who also became a *premier éche-
> vin*,
> * Local Communities, Youth and Sport,
> * Housing and Public Building.

To exercise control over its councillors and act as liaison between them and other party members (who met at a general assembly each month) the local party formed a Structure Politique Intermédiaire (SPI) of 7 people elected from the local group.[14] Each Ecolo *échevin* was also put under the 'guardianship' of a working group. As all 11 *échevinats* were also allocated a 'commission d'accompagnement mixte' (a

working group made up of members of the RPSW and Ecolo),
the strain on the relatively small local party became quickly
obvious.

So too was Ecolo's inexperience revealed. Although the
agreement included many of the party's demands, it also
contained a key phrase in the section devoted to the city's
finances which said that the new Liège council would 'take
on board the constraints caused by the financial situation'.
Liège was in fact heavily in debt. This put an end to many of
Ecolo's more ambitious projects. Ecolo had also underesti-
mated the length and complexity of certain procedures – the
setting up of rules for conducting referenda, for
example – and the inertia of the whole machine of local
government. Jean Henrottay describes Ecolo's 'confrontation with the town planning department in Liège' in some
detail. He notes ruefully that major projects like roads are
decided at national level and big building schemes that give
shape to the city, like banks, are developed by private
agencies. The town planning department, he feels, is reduced
to rubber-stamping plans that are elaborated elsewhere.[15]

However some successes can be recorded. Neighbourhood
councils have been set up and some of their projects have
been financed by the city. An 'urban boutique' has been
established where citizens may ask to see official city
documents and where projects are displayed. By-laws have
been passed to protect trees and open spaces and to assure
access to public places for disabled people. In 1985 Liège sold
the city's shares in the nuclear power company Socolie.
Unfortunately these shares were quickly bought up by the
surrounding communities and the money gained by Liège,
instead of going to alternative energy projects, was swall-
owed up by the overall debt.

To many the 'Liège experiement' has shown the dangers
awaiting a Green party that embarks on power-sharing too
soon. The strain on a small, undeveloped party has been
considerable – active membership in Liège declined seriously after 1983, only picking up again in 1987. An opinion
poll commissioned by the party and published in September
1987 also revealed that support for Ecolo in Liège had
dropped by 2% since 1982, the most significant drop for all the
political parties. However, the national elections of 1987 did
not bear out these dismal forecasts and Ecolo did not expect
to lose seats in the next elections to Liège city council due
late 1988.

Nevertheless, perhaps understandably, when the sirens of power-sharing called again from the Wallonia regional council in December 1987, this time from the Socialist party, Ecolo did not heed them. The party has perhaps learnt the lesson of premature adventuring into power politics from a position of programmatic and strategic weakness. It must have also heeded the warning from the electorate. Although the elections to the national parliament in December 1987 gave the Greens the same percent of the vote they had in 1985 (6.5% in Wallonia), this was not enough to prevent them falling victim to the vagaries of the Belgian electoral system. The French-speaking party lost two of its five seats in the Chamber and only kept its three seats in the Senate by the skin of its teeth.

Future Prospects

Ecolo must be reassured by the fact that, despite the publicity given to its internal problems, its vote has largely held up. This confirms that it has a fairly secure base of support among French-speaking Belgian people. However, the party will have to keep up its effort to not only re-establish some internal cohesion and stability but also to promote an image to the outside world of political competence. When commitment to 'a different way of working' becomes associated with chaos, a party may remain attractive only to the more anarchic and marginal political activist. This in turn becomes reflected in the programmatic content and the strategy of the party and a downward spiral of political credibility sets in. To Ecolo's credit, it has understood this and has gone a fair way towards reversing this trend. An opinion poll published in *De Standaard* (24 August 1988) estimated Ecolo's support in Wallonia at 10.9%.

Agalev, on the other hand, has not been troubled by the scandals of dissident parliamentarians, though it acknowledges that, in the beginning at least, this was due more to luck than good management. The parliamentarians have been integrated into the meetings of the party steering group and the executive, with political priorities being worked out together. To Agalev the main task is the consolidation of Green ideas in the minds of the public as well as the politicians. Ludo Dierickx makes the broader point like this:

To succeed we must have theory. All the really big power-brokers like the financial institutions, industry and the trade unions adopt theoretical models for their long-term vision of progress. Once the model was based on the US experience but now it is based on Japan. To compete, the Green parties have to become an equivalent transnational force by developing a long-term theoretical model for the future that is intellectually irreproachable and only open to cooption as a whole. Governments speak the language of the banks, of the OECD or the EEC when they tell their citizens that they must suffer unemployment and pollution today in order to become competitive tomorrow... The Greens have to get themselves into a strong enough position to combat these myths, and give confidence and hope to people who are living the consequences of gross pollution and unemployment.[16]

The primary task, according to Dierickx, is to 'prevent the bourgeois forces doing to ecology what they have done to socialism; if they do then we are sunk.' Keeping the Green profile distinctive is also a preoccupation of arch-strategist Leo Cox. 'Our challenge is to insert ourselves into the classical social problems without falling into the positions and habits of an ordinary movement of the left. We have to maintain a position where *any* government feels threatened by the presence of Agalev.

Notes

1 *The Times*, 27 October 1987.
2 *Memento Politique* , Kluwer, Antwerp, 1987.
3 e.g. J. Fitzmaurice, *The Politics of Belgium*, Hurst, 1983, or L. Huyse, 'Pillarization Reconsidered' in *Acta Politica*, 19/1, 1984.
4 Interview with author, October 1987.
5 CRISP (Centre de Recherche et d'Information Socio-Politique) 1095-6, 8 November 1985; rue du Congrès 35, 1000 Bruxelles.
6 ibid.
7 ibid, 1061, 7 December 1984.
8 CRISP 1095-6, 8 November 1985, p. 55 (figure given as 6.1% on p. 5).
9 Leo Cox, interview with author, 27 October 1987.
10 CRISP, 1045-46. 22 June 1984.

11 *Statutes du Mouvement Ecolo*, 1981.
12 CRISP, 1045-46.
13 *Libé-Belgique*, 24 March 1986.
14 CRISP, 1045-46.
15 Jean Henrottay, 'Cinq ans de présence Ecolo a l'échevinat de l'urbanisme de la ville de Liège', paper given at Fourth Congress of the European Greens, Antwerp, April 1988.
16 Interview with author, 26 October 1987.

Main Party Publications

AGALEV

Declaration of Principles, 1982.
Op Mensenmaat, Werkgroep Ekonomie Agalev, 1985.
1987 Election Programme.

Bladgroen, three-weekly party newsletter.
Berichtenblad, information bulletin for local councillors.
De Groenen, monthly journal, Blekersdijk 14, 9000 Gent.

ECOLO

Déclaration des Principes, 1985.
Four Years of Political Action, 1985.
Election Programme 1987.

Studies of Agalev

DIERICKX Ludo, *Groen is de Helling*, Soethoude, Antwerp, 1983.
STOUTHUYSEN Patrick, 'De Politieke Identiteit van de Vlaamse Groene Partÿ Agalev', *Res Publica* 15/2-3, 1983.
BUYLE Daniel, 'Van Pechstrook Naar Paradigme De Groenen in Vlaanderen', *De Neiuwe Maand*, 28/1, 1985.
DESCHOUWER K. & STOUTHUYSEN P., 'L'Electorat d'Agalev', CRISP 1060 (1984) 35 rue du Congrès, 1000 Brussels.

Studies of Ecolo

DEFEYT P., 'Radioscopie d'Electorat Ecologiste', unpublished, 1985.
MAHAUX P. & MODEN J.,'Le Mouvement Ecolo',CRISP 1045-46 (1984).

Addresses

Agalev
Tweekerkenstr 78
1050 Brussels

tel: (32) 2 2306666

Ecolo
26 rue Basse Marcelle
5000 Namur

tel: (32) 81 227871

Agalev Parliamentary Group
Palais des Nations
Rue de la Loi
1000 Brussels

tel: Chamber (32) 2 5199418/19
    Senate (32) 2 5158679

Ecolo Parliamentary Group
Rue de la Sablonnière 9
1000 Brussels

tel: (32) 2 2183035

Organogram: Agalev

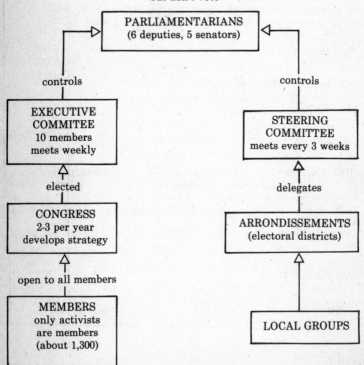

attend steering committee
but don't vote

PARLIAMENTARIANS
(6 deputies, 5 senators)

controls   controls

EXECUTIVE
COMMITEE
10 members
meets weekly

STEERING
COMMITTEE
meets every 3 weeks

elected   delegates

CONGRESS
2-3 per year
develops strategy

ARRONDISSEMENTS
(electoral districts)

open to all members

MEMBERS
only activists
are members
(about 1,300)

LOCAL GROUPS

Organogram: Ecolo

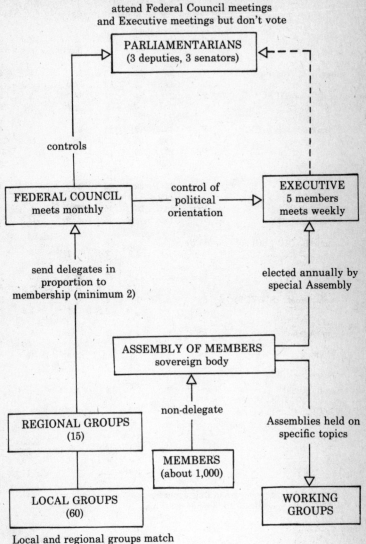

attend Federal Council meetings
and Executive meetings but don't vote

PARLIAMENTARIANS
(3 deputies, 3 senators)

controls

FEDERAL COUNCIL
meets monthly

control of
political
orientation

EXECUTIVE
5 members
meets weekly

send delegates in
proportion to
membership (minimum 2)

elected annually by
special Assembly

ASSEMBLY OF MEMBERS
sovereign body

REGIONAL GROUPS
(15)

non-delegate

MEMBERS
(about 1,000)

Assemblies held on
specific topics

LOCAL GROUPS
(60)

WORKING
GROUPS

Local and regional groups match
administrative (electoral) areas

Election Results

		NATIONAL Chambre des Représentatives)					EURO-PEAN	
		1987 Dec	1985 Oct	1981 Nov	1978 Dec	1984 Jun	1979 Jun	
6 Freedom & Progress (PVV)	Fl		**25**	**22**	**28**	**22**	**2**	**2**
			11.5	*10.7*	*12.9*	*10.4*	*8.6*	*9.4*
Liberal Reform (PRL)	Fr		**23**	**24**	**24**	**14**	**3**	**2**
			9.4	*10.2*	*8.6*	*6.4*	*9.4*	*6.9*
5 Christian People's (CVP)	Fl		**43**	**49**	**43**	**57**	**4**	**4**
			19.5	*21.3*	*19.3*	*26.1*	*19.8*	*29.5*
Social Christian (PSC)	Fr		**19**	**20**	**18**	**25**	**2**	**3**
			8.0	*8.0*	*7.2*	*10.1*	*7.6*	*8.2*
3 Socialist (SP)	Fl		**32**	**32**	**26**	**26**	**4**	**3**
			14.9	*14.6*	*12.6*	*12.4*	*17.1*	*12.8*
Socialist (PS)	Fr		**40**	**35**	**35**	**32**	**5**	**4**
			15.7	*13.8*	*12.7*	*13.0*	*13.3*	*10.6*
1 Communist (KPB/PCB)	Fl/Fr				**2**	**4**		
			0.8	*1.2*	*2.3*	*3.3*		
9 Volksunie (VU)	Fl		**16**	**16**	**20**	**14**	**2**	**1**
			8.0	*7.9*	*9.8*	*7.0*	*8.5*	*6.0*
Rassemblement (RW/FDF)	Fr		**3**	**3**	**8**	**15**		**2**
			1.4	*1.4*	*4.2*	*7.1*	*2.5*	*7.6*
10 Green (Agalev)	Fl		**6**	**4**	**2**		**1**	
			4.5	*3.7*	*2.3*	*0.1*	*4.4*	*1.4*
Green (Ecolo)	Fr		**3**	**5**	**2**		**1**	
			2.6	*2.5*	*2.2*		*3.9*	*2.0*
11 Miscellaneous			**2**	**2**	**4**	**3**		

SENATE

		1985 Oct	1981 Nov	1978 Dec
Agalev		**5**	**3**	**1**
		4.9	*3.8*	*2.4*
Ecolo		**3**	**3**	**4**
		2.8	*2.9*	*2.6*

Key: **Seats** in bold, *Percentages* in italics and for the whole of Belgium.
 Fl = Flemish-speaking, Fr = French-speaking.

References:
CRISP: CH 104 5-46, 22 June 1984; CH 1061, 7 December 1984; CH 1095-96, 8 November 1985; Brussels.
The Times Guide to the European Parliament, Times Books, 1984.
Ministère de l'Interieur, Brussels.

3: DENMARK
De Grønne

Area: 43,092 sq.km. | *founded: 16 October 1983*
Population: 5.12 million (1986) | *members: 800-1,000*
Density: 119 per sq. km.

Member: UN, NATO, OECD and
European Communities
Language: Danish
GNP per capita: US $10,250 (1984)

Background and Electoral System

Denmark is one of the oldest states in Europe and moved from the rule of kings to a democratic constitution in 1849, when the Folketing (lower house of parliament) was established.

In 1953 a new constitution abolished the Landstinget (upper house of parliament) and introduced referenda as a means of overseeing parliamentary decisions. All constitutional changes must be approved by at least 40% of the electorate and some parliamentary bills can be subjected to a referendum if one-third of the Folketing demand it. However, Denmark offers no exception to the general rule that, outside Switzerland, referenda are unpopular with most political parties because the results frequently cut across party lines. Successive Danish governments have become adept at bending sufficiently to pressure from the parties around them (especially over internal affairs) in order to avoid triggering the sort of parliamentary rebellion that might lead to a referendum.

The power of this very direct form of pressure on the decision-making process has resulted in the large number of political parties now represented in the Danish parliament – some of them splinters from traditional parties, some of them new.

Some political commentators view the proliferation of

parties as 'electoral chaos' because it has stopped the
government taking tough measures to deal with Denmark's
growing economic problems. But as the distribution of
support for the eight parties at present represented in
parliament is generally agreed to be an accurate reflection of
the views of the Danish people, an interesting dilemma for
democratic constitutionalists is posed.

The basis of the Danish constitution is the 1953 Grundlov
charter. Although legislative power lies jointly with the
queen and the Folketing, and executive power with the
queen, she delegates her powers to her government which is
in turn answerable to the 179-member Folketing. As men-
tioned above, a check on the Folketing is assured by the
provision of referenda. Both Greenland and the Faroe islands
have a separate legislature and executive to handle local
matters but send two representatives each to the Folketing.

Fourteen *amtskommuner* (counties) and two city municipalities for Copenhagen are administered by directly elected
councils, as are the 275 *kommuner* (municipalities).

For national elections, which are conducted under a
system of proportional representation, Denmark is divided
into 17 constituencies which send a total of 135 members to
the Folketing. To assure proportionality in the parliament,
the remaining 40 *tillaegsmandater* (additional seats) are
allocated to the parties failing to obtain seats in the constituencies but gaining more than 2% of the vote. There is no
threshold for elections to the local councils.

There are no financial restrictions on contesting elections,
and since 1987 parties are reimbursed with 3 kroner, 2 kroner
and 5 kroner per vote for the local, regional and national
elections respectively. In order to contest any election a
party must apply for registration to the minister of the
interior, furnishing in support of its application the signatures of 1/175 (about 20,000) of votes cast in the last election.
At election time Danish television broadcasts a 30-minute
programme on each party, 10 minutes being produced by the
party itself (60,000 kroner provided for this) plus a 20-minute
interview with three party representatives. There is also
special televised debate between representatives from each
of the parties standing.

Factors Influencing the Development
of Green Politics

Denmark is one country where the founding and development of a distinct Green party seems to have taken place
despite the prevailing situation in the country. Environmental protection has a high priority for most Danes[1] and their
frequently better environmental standards have led to a
sometimes uneasy relationship with the EEC and neighbouring countries. Denmark has no civil nuclear power and views
the Swedish Barseback nuclear plant, 20 kilometres across
the water from Copenhagen, with dismay. Most energy
production comes from imported coal but there is growing
investment in alternative energy sources. Although a
member of NATO and committed to providing 'facilities' in
case of war, no nuclear weapons or foreign bases are officially
stationed in Denmark.

In parliament many issues close to the heart of a Green
party are dealt with by other parties, the increasingly
popular Socialist People's party (SF) in particular. This split
from the Communist party in 1958, drawing most of its
members and support from the many public-sector employees
in Denmark. By adding anti-EC, anti-NATO, pacifist and
environmental policies to a fairly classic left-wing programme the party attracted a lot of young voters during the 1970s
and 1980s. But one of the reasons the SF has failed to
convince everyone that it has a fundamental commitment to
Green politics was underlined in the run-up to the 1987
election. The SF leader, Gert Petersen, announced that the
party would modify its positions towards NATO and the EEC
should it form a government with the Social Democrats,
demonstrating how easy it would be to muffle the so-called
'greenest' voice in the Danish parliament.

De Grønne, however, do not view either the greenish SF or
the already Green-inclined Danish public as the only obsta-
cle that has prevented them up to now from making a
significant impact on a reasonably accessible political
system. They lay most of the blame on the Revolt From The
Centre movement that grew out of the publication of a book
of the same title by Niels I. Meyer, a physicist, K. Helveg
Petersen, Liberal government minister between 1967 and
1970, and Villy Sørensen, a philosopher. Published in October 1978, this caused a long and heated debate throughout

Denmark, widely reported by newspapers, radio and tv and involving everyone from the ordinary citizen to the prime minister. The book, which sold over 120,000 copies in Denmark and has been translated into several languages,[2] was written at a time when the make-up of the Danish parliament reflected simultaneously the post-1968 fondness for Marxism and the growth of the extreme-right Progress party (in the 1977 elections this won 26 seats, coming second only to the Social Democrats). In the book the authors described their vision of a 'humane, ecologically sustainable society' and the political programme they believed necessary to attain it. They saw this programme not only as a rejection of both political extremes but also as a revolt from the democratic centre of politics.

But the promise and excitement inspired by the book and the subsequent intellectual movement that developed around it did not translate into political activity. Petersen and Sørensen withdrew due to age and ill-health and Meyer, from the earliest meetings of the movement, consistently argued against the development of a Green party.[3] Nor did the democratic centre parties take up the challenge – either individually or as a coalition. The Radical Liberal party, the traditional king-maker in Danish politics, supported right-wing coalitions while the Social Democrats had an uneasy relationship with the Socialist People's party.

Meyer went on, though his contacts with the Norwegian Erik Dammann, author of *The Future in Our Hands*, to become involved with the Alternative Nordic Futures project. This essentially amounted to scientists applying to Scandinavian governments for funding for research projects associated with the new 'holistic vision...such as alternative energy systems, organic farming, decentralised production, Nordic self-reliance in basic commodities, formal and informal economy, local autonomy, new working and production concepts etc.'[4] Many Greens feel frustrated by and disappointed in Meyer, who is a prominent public figure in Denmark. They feel he has quite rightly staked out the intellectual ground for Green ideas but regret that he has not only failed to follow through on the political consequences of those ideas but has also guarded them jealously for himself.

De Grønne

The founding of a distinct Green party was seriously mooted for the first time at a 1980 meeting of small grassroots environmental groups. These were involved in different local campaigns and were struggling with all the difficulties that such campaigns entail. At subsequent meetings opinions about whether to found a political party or not were divided along age lines – older people wanted to, younger people did not. Then in August 1982 an advertisement appeared in *Information*, a cooperatively owned Copenhagen Sunday newspaper, in the name of the Greens, calling all those interested in forming a new political party to a meeting. This attracted about 50 people who, stimulated by the success of the German Greens, eventually founded De Grønne on 16 October 1983.

Members were attracted from the environmental movement and from the Revolt From The Centre movement more than from other political parties. As Flemming Andersen, a past international secretary, put it: 'Many people felt that the left-wing parties, while having peace and environmental policies that were quite developed, were moving backward in time – taking up old positions.'[5]

At the same time another party was being conceived in the northern part of Jutland, and Danmarks Miljøpartiet (Environment Party of Denmark) was officially founded on 1 September 1984 in Arhus.[6] The two parties spent two years in protracted negotiations over a merger. Danmarks Miljøpartiet wanted a programme and an organisation to be elaborated by a few people and then agreed widely in the movements before a party was launched. De Grønne became increasingly impatient: 'We came to the conclusion after two years of hard, fruitless negotiation that we were going ahead, we were not going to wait for them.'[7]

De Grønne then set about collecting the 20,000 signatures that were needed in order to take part in national elections. They were finally approved by the minister of the interior in December 1984, too late for the party to participate in the national elections of that year. Danmarks Miljøpartiet remained a very local party with about 50 members.

In the November 1985 local elections De Grønne scored 2.8% nationwide and obtained 12 seats on municipal councils and 6 seats on provincial councils. This brought considerable attention from the media and assured the party a place in the opinion polls where it regularly scored between 2 and 3%. Danmarks Miljøpartiet failed to make any impact, only managing to score 32 votes to De Grønne's 277 on its home ground in Frederikshavn in North Jutland.

De Grønne were caught on the hop by the announcement of an early election in September 1987, and the amount of time spent in negotiations with Danmarks Miljøpartiet and collecting signatures to the exclusion of political debate and efficient organisation began to show. Lack of satisfying activity had resulted in a swift turnover of party officials and serious discontinuity. The disappointing result of 1.3% was therefore not a surprise to many people. However, under the Danish *tillaegsmandater* system De Grønne posed more of a threat to all small parties than to any particular position on the traditional left-right spectrum. Therefore the entry into the Folketing for the first time with 2.2% of the vote and 4 seats of Faelleskurs (Common Cause) – 'a party that combines an unorthodox Marxism with a strong distaste for Asian refugees' (*Economist*, 12 September 1987) – must have been a particularly bitter blow to De Grønne. Despite the key issue of the next general election held only 8 months later being the visit to Danish ports of ships carrying nuclear weapons, the Danish Greens were unable to improve on their score of 1.3%.

Future Prospects

The party has indeed turned in on itself. It has a very decentralised system of organisation with no central focal point either for members or for outsiders. Spokespeople have to stick by what has been agreed at infrequent meetings. Critics of the party say that its claims to be Green are false because it is not Green by action. Its present attitudes, that policy can be reduced to beautiful slogans and that such (dis)organisation is democratic, are naive and dangerous, they add, and leave the party open to manipulation by internal power politickers. Others feel that the extreme decentralisation of De Grønne is the essence of Green politics and that everyone should do what they feel to be right on their own patch. This, they say, is the road to collective salvation.

Notes

1 *Economist*, 31 Jan 1986.
2 English edition published by Marion Boyars, 1981.
3 Kaare Rasmussen, interview with author, 6 August 1987.
4 Niels Meyer, *Alternative Nordic Future*, paper circulated by Future In Our Hands, 25 September 1984.
5 interview with author, 6 August 1987.
6 Kai Mogens Lang, letter to author, 16 March 1985.
7 Lisbeth Heap, founder member, interview with author, 6 August 1987.

Main Party Publications

1987 election programme

Rodnettet, monthly newsletter.

Address

De Grønne
c/o Walter Turnowsky
Voonporten 14-108
1220 Albertslund

tel: (45) 2 642037

Organogram: De Grønne

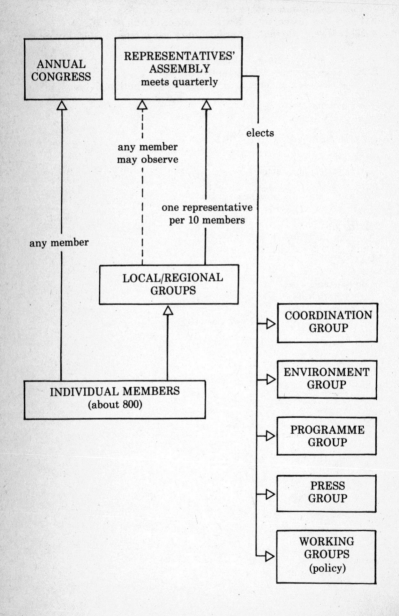

Election Results

	NATIONAL (Folketing)[1]					EURO-PEAN	
	1988 May	1987 Sep	1984 Jan	1981 Dec	1979 Oct	1984 Jun	1979 Jun
8 Progress Party	**16**	**9**	**6**	**16**	**20**		**1**
	9.0	*4.8*	*3.6*	*8.9*	*11.0*	*3.5*	*5.8*
7 Conservative People's Party	**35**	**38**	**42**	**26**	**22**	**4**	**2**
	19.3	*20.8*	*23.4*	*14.4*	*12.5*	*20.8*	*14.1*
6 Centre Democrats	**9**	**9**	**8**	**15**	**6**	**1**	**1**
	4.7	*4.8*	*4.6*	*8.3*	*3.2*	*6.6*	*6.2*
6 Christian People's Party	**4**	**4**	**5**	**4**	**5**		
	2.0	*2.4*	*2.7*	*2.3*	*2.6*		
5 Liberal Democrats (Venstre)	**22**	**19**	**22**	**20**	**22**	**2**	**3**
	11.8	*10.5*	*12.1*	*11.3*	*12.5*	*12.5*	*14.5*
4 Radical Liberals	**10**	**11**	**10**	**9**	**10**		
	5.6	*6.2*	*5.5*	*5.1*	*5.4*		
3 Social Democrat Party	**55**	**54**	**56**	**59**	**68**	**3**	**3**
	29.8	*29.3*	*31.6*	*32.9*	*38.3*	*19.4*	*21.9*
2 Socialist People's Party	**24**	**27**	**21**	**21**	**11**	**1**	**1**
	13.0	*14.6*	*11.5*	*11.3*	*5.9*	*9.2*	*4.2*
2 Left Socialists			**5**	**5**	**6**		
	0.6	*1.4*	*2.7*	*2.7*	*3.7*		
1 Communists	*0.8*	*0.9*	*0.7*	*1.1*	*1.9*		
2/8 Common Cause (Faelleskurs)		**4**					
	1.9	*2.2*					
10 Greens (De Grønne)	*1.3*	*1.3*					
11 People's Movement Against EEC						**4**	**4**
					20.8	*20.1*	

Key: **Seats** in bold, *Percentages* in italics.

References
The Times Guide to the European Parliament, Times Books, 1984.
The Danish Embassy, London and Paris.

Note
1 Greenland and the Faeroe Islands have two seats each in the Folketing.

4: EIRE   *Comhaontas Glas*

Area: 68,889 sq. km.   *founded: December 1981*
Population: 3.54 million (1986)   *members: about 300*
Density: 51 per sq. km.

Member: UN, OECD, European Communities
Languages: Irish and English
GNP per capita: US $4,440 (1984)

Background and Electoral System

Since the 14th century, rulers of England have claimed, with
varying degrees of success, overlordship of Ireland. During
the 17th century British (Protestant) landowners uprooted
native Irish (Catholic) farmers, particularly in the north-east
of the country.

It was fear of Irish sympathy for the French revolution that
prompted Great Britain to incorporate Ireland into the
United Kingdom in 1801. The Irish peasants had substantial
grievances against their mostly absentee, non-Irish landlords, and the predominantly Catholic population greatly
resented paying tithes (taxes) to the Protestant church, also a
substantial landowner in Ireland. Catholics could not hold
seats in parliament, nor could they hold public office.

A central figure in the Irish struggle for Home Rule
through their own parliament was Daniel O'Connell. He
secured Catholic emancipation (including the right to build
churches, hold office etc.) and in 1829 became a Member of
Parliament. In 1839 liability for tithes was passed to the
landlords but O'Connell – 'The Liberator' – died without
achieving his great purpose, repeal of the 1801 Act of Union.

After long agitation, Home Rule was accorded in 1914 but
suspended during the Great War. Anti-British feeling
however was exacerbated when they executed six organisers
of the 'Easter rising' in 1916. After considerable violence the

Irish Free State Act of 1922 formally divided Ireland into a predominantly Catholic South and a predominantly Protestant North, establishing parliaments in both Belfast and Dublin.

Twenty-six of the 32 Irish counties subsequently approved by referendum a new constitution and became Eire (the Irish Republic) in 1937. Article 2 of this constitution also affirmed that the remaining six northern counties were part of Irish 'national territory'. Although the majority of people in these remaining counties were Protestant and happy to owe continued allegiance to Great Britain, there was a significant minority of Catholics who bitterly resented this.

Two political parties dominate in Eire, the Fianna Fail (Soldiers of Ireland) and Fine Gael (United Ireland). They are more easily differentiated by the positions they supported at the time of partition than by any traditional left-right dichotomy. Fine Gael supported the treaty but Fianna Fail rejected its terms. Despite their constitutional commitment to a united Ireland, neither party has taken serious steps towards achieving it. Although a Fine Gael prime minister signed the Anglo-Irish agreement in 1985 (which included consultation with Eire over decisions made about Northern Ireland by a British government), it was Charles Haughey, the present Fianna Fail prime minister who set it in motion in 1979.

Since 1977 the two main parties have taken turns to form a government, Fine Gael usually forming a coalition with the Labour party. However a new party, the Progressive Democratic party, appeared on the electoral scene for the February 1987 elections. Although founded by Dessie O'Malley, a prominent member of Fianna Fail, and offering a programme of monetarist policies, it took votes principally from Fine Gael and the Labour party.

Eire is a sovereign independent republic. The 1949 Ireland Act, passed by the British parliament, provided for a special relationship between Eire and the United Kingdom whereby Eire would not be considered a foreign country and its citizens not treated as aliens.

The two-chamber Oireachtas (national parliament) consists of the 166-seat Dáil Eireann (lower house) and the 60-seat Seanad Eireann (senate). There is also a directly elected president who serves a 7-year term.

There are 27 county councils, 5 county borough corporations, 6 borough corporations, 49 urban district councils and 25 boards of town commissions. Most of the important tasks are carried out at county council level. Elected members of local government are provided with expenses and subsistence allowances only and have specific functions, such as setting the local tax rate and development plans. Each elected body works with a paid full-time manager who deals with the day-to-day administration and management of the local authority.

The constitution cannot be amended without consulting the people through a referendum.

Elections to the Dáil and to the local authorities are by the Single Transferable Vote (STV) system of proportional representation. Candidates must place a depost of IR £100 for national elections and IR £1,000 for European elections which are refundable if at least 5% of the vote is obtained.

Eleven members of the Seanad are nominated by the Taoiseach (prime minister), six are elected by the universities and 43 are elected from five panels of candidates representing different interests: 1) Language, culture and education; 2) Agriculture and fishing; 3) Labour, organised or unorganised; 4) Industry and commerce; 5) Public administration, social services and voluntary services. The electoral college of about 1,109 people is made up from members of the Dáil, Seanad, county boroughs and councils.

Any political party which contests at least 7 of the 41 constituencies in a national election is accorded 3 minutes of television and radio coverage. Further time is allocated according to the number of seats contested. There is no state financing for political parties.

Factors Affecting the Development of Green Politics

Eire is one of the countries where the presence of a Green party is more of a surprise than anything else. Apart from degradation of its more heavily populated areas, particularly in Dublin, Eire has been little affected by the industrialisation process which has scarred most European countries. (Such industrialisation as did take place in Ireland was mostly concentrated in the Belfast area.) By 1985, of those people in work, 16% were employed in the agricultural sector and 56% in the service sector. Unemployment runs at about 19%.[1]

As already noted the Irish political parties do not fit so easily into the usual left-right categories. They tend to be pragmatic over most issues and are often tied up with the personality of their leader. In a system which also disfavours small parties this makes it difficult for a Green party to obtain a high profile. Protest has, on the whole, been limited to the worst cases of urban pollution, like smog in Dublin (*Irish Times*, 2 February 1988) or directed against pollution of the Irish Sea by English nuclear plants.

Comhaontas Glas (Green Alliance)

It is unsurprising therefore to discover that the Green party in Eire was founded not as a natural development in public protest, but as a logical step in the thinking of a few people. A teacher in Dublin, Christopher Fettes, took the first step in December 1981 when he founded the Ecology Party of Ireland. He was influenced by the formation of similar parties in other European countries, particularly Great Britain, and was convinced that such a step would be necessary to influence opinion in Eire. Too new to mount a campaign, the party did not contest the February 1982 elections to the Dáil. It did however publish a leaflet promising voters that they would 'have the opportunity to vote for our radically sane policies on future occasions'.

Seven of the 41 constituencies did have a Green candidate when the minority government was forced to hold new elections in November of the same year. The Ecology Party of Ireland polled 0.2% nationwide, averaging 1.3% over the seven constituencies where it stood candidates. (Percentages given are for first preference votes.) The following year the party underwent considerable restructuring, and the Ecology Party of Ireland was replaced by Comhaontas Glas (Green Alliance), a coordination of independent local Green groups, each with its own constitution. Since then the party has concentrated mainly on policy development and information exchange, latterly facilitated by a smartly produced two-monthly newletter, *Nuacht Ghlas*, which is at present edited by Christopher Fettes. Uniquely, the Green parties of Eire and of the United Kingdom hold jointly agreed policies on Northern Ireland. These include a Bill of Rights to be guaranteed by some body outside of Northern Ireland, London or Dublin, either at European or at United Nations level; devolution of power in all Ireland and Great Britain to federated regions to be made a political option; 'preferenda' (a series of multiple-option referenda) to be used to facilitate step-by-step compromise.

Fettes stood in one of the four constituencies for the 1984 elections to the European Parliament and polled 1.9%, which gave a nationwide percentage of 0.5%. In the local elections of 1985 Comhaontas Glas stood 34 candidates, mostly in urban areas with 28 of them being in Dublin. Nationwide, the party polled 0.6% but averaged 2.3% over the constituencies it contested and obtained one seat on the urban district council of Killarney in County Kerry. In 1986 the still very tiny party experienced a split during which several members who were unhappy about even the minimal organisation of Comhaontas Glas left altogether.

In the February 1987 elections to the Dáil the party contested 9 of the 41 constituencies, only two more than in 1982. The poll was slightly more than 1982, 0.4% nationwide and an average of 1.8% over the 9 seats where it had candidates. Six of the seats were in Dublin.

Future Prospects

In the immediate future there seems little prospect of Comhaontas Glas making any significant electoral gains in Eire. An overriding commitment to consensus decision-making throughout the party and a distaste for 'leaders' makes attracting attention to themselves difficult in the personality-strewn environment of Irish politics. However the arrival on the political scene of the Progressive Democratic party in 1987 suggests that discontent with the two main parties is increasing and Eire, as one of the poorest 'peripheral' countries of Europe, will be particularly affected by the approach of the single European market, timetabled for 1992. The time for Comhaontas Glas, who vigorously opposed Eire's ratification of the Single European Act, may come then.

Notes

1 *Report on the Regional Problems of Ireland*, European Parliament Session Document A2-109/87.

Main Party Publications

A Green Manifesto: For a Simply Better Ireland, 1987 election manifesto.

Nuacht Ghlas, bimonthly newlsetter.

Address

Comhaontas Glas
5a Upper Fownes Street
Dublin 2

tel: (353) 1 771436

Organogram: Comhaontas Glas

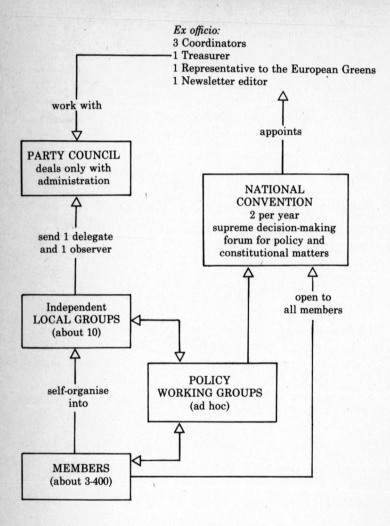

Ex officio:
3 Coordinators
1 Treasurer
1 Representative to the European Greens
1 Newsletter editor

work with

PARTY COUNCIL
deals only with
administration

appoints

NATIONAL
CONVENTION
2 per year
supreme decision-making
forum for policy and
constitutional matters

send 1 delegate
and 1 observer

Independent
LOCAL GROUPS
(about 10)

open to
all members

self-organise
into

POLICY
WORKING GROUPS
(ad hoc)

MEMBERS
(about 3-400)

Election Results

	NATIONAL (Dáil)				EURO-PEAN	
	1987 Feb	1982 Nov	1982 Feb	1981 Jun	1984 Jun	1979 Jun
7 Fianna Fáil	**81** 44.2	**75** 42.5	**81** 47.3	**78** 47.0	**8** 39.2	**5** 34.7
6 Progressive Democrats	**14** 8.4					
4 Fine Gael	**51** 27.1	**70** 39.2	**66** 37.3	**65** 39.1	**6** 32.1	**4** 33.1
3 Labour Party	**12** 6.4	**16** 9.4	**15** 9.1	**15** 9.0	**4** 8.4	14.5
2 Democratic Socialist Party	**1** 0.4				0.5	
2 Workers Party	**4** 3.8	**2** 3.3	**3** 2.3	4.3	4.3	3.3
10 Greens (Comhaontas Glas)	0.4[1]	0.2[2]			0.5[3]	
11 Miscellaneous	**3** 2.0	**3** 3.0	**4** 4.0	**8** 4.8	**1** 15.0	**2** 14.1

Key: **Seats** in bold, *Percentages* in italics.

References
The Times Guide to the European Parliament, Times Books, 1984.
Official Statistics, Department of the Environment, Dublin.

Notes
1 Nationwide percentage for 9 candidates who polled an average of 1.8% where they stood.
2 Nationwide percentage for 7 candidates who polled an average of 1.3% where they stood.
3 Nationwide percentage for 1 candidate who polled 1.9%.

5: FINLAND
Vihreä Liitto

Area: 319,230 sq. km.
(excluding inland water)   *founded: 28 February 1987*
Population: 5.09 million (1985)   *members: not known*
Density: 16.1 per sq. km.

Member: UN, OECD, EFTA
Languages: Finnish (93.5%) and Swedish (6.2%)
GNP per capita: US $11,007 (1985)

Background and Electoral System

Because distance and climate keep it off the main tourist trails, to most Europeans living south of the Baltic Finland remains more of a concept than a country. As the only non-communist European country to share a long border with Russia, Finland has become associated in the minds of many people with stories of spies and East-West intrigue, an impression seemingly confirmed by the pragmatic approach Finns have taken to living with their superpower neighbour.

But the way of life enjoyed by the majority of Finns bears more resemblance to that of their western neighbour, Sweden, than it does to Russia, while centuries of domination by one or another of them has left Finland with a well-honed sense of independence. The famous Finnish foreign policy that led to the term 'finlandisation' entering the political vocabulary is also generally misunderstood outside the country. The objective of the first two postwar presidents, Paasiikivi and Kekkonen, was to achieve reasonable relationships with their eastern neighbour within the framework of neutrality. While some measures taken to implement this ambitious foreign policy have grated on the Finns there is virtually no opposition to it in Finnish society.

There are no official restrictions to freedom of expression in Finland, but during the Kekkonen years (1956-1982) self-censorship became common practice. Articles which might 'damage Finland's relations with foreign countries' (i.e. which dealt with human rights abuses in the Soviet Union or other delicate matters) were often not printed in respectable newspapers and magazines. In the interests of foreign policy, many foreign books have not been translated into Finnish or published by Finnish publishers, although they are freely available in Finnish bookstores in the original language. Films such as *A Day in the Life of Ivan Denisovich* have not been shown in Finnish cinemas, though cold-war films such as *Ice Station Zebra* and all of the James Bond films have. It is doubtful if such measures actually had any positive effect on Finnish-Soviet relationships and they certainly aggravated the feelings of resentment and suspicion that the Finns have traditionally felt towards their eastern neighbour.[1]

Finland will be celebrating 70 years of independence in 1989 and obviously enjoys exhibiting the confidence that comes with maturity. The new factories and modern shipyards built after the 1939-44 war with Russia in order to produce goods necessary to meet substantial war reparations were released for Finland's own use in 1952 and gave the country's economy a considerable boost. Pragmatic as ever in their foreign policy, the Finns unload sugar cane from Cuba into their refineries while showing on their cinema and tv screens the new batch of Soviet films devoted to exposing the seamy side of socialism – from the horrors of Stalinism to today's drug-taking youth.

According to the constitution of July 1919 which remained intact after the war, Finland is a republic and has a one-chamber parliament of 200 members (Eduskunta) returned from 15 electoral constituencies. The president is elected for six years (limited to two terms) by a college of 301 electors who are in turn elected by the votes of citizens in the same way as members of parliament.

Local government consists of 12 *lääni* (provinces) that have a governor appointed by the president. The governor directs the provincial office and the local sheriffs (225 sheriff districts in 1986). 461 local communes (94 urban, 367 rural) raise local taxes and elect councils for four-year terms. Some communes come together to administer a common institution such as a hospital.

For elections to the Eduskunta Finland is divided into fifteen constituencies. Fourteen of them (excluding the autonomous county of Åland) send between 8 and 24 members elected by a system of proportional representation. The threshold for obtaining a seat varies between 4% and 12% depending on the size of the constituency and the number of seats. No financial deposit is required and any independent candidate is treated like a party. Once it has representatives in the Eduskunta a political party becomes eligible for public finance which amounts to approximately 250,000 Finnish marks per MP.

Factors Influencing the Development of Green Politics

Kalevala is the land in Finnish mythology where knowing the 'words' give not only magical power but also the practical power that comes with knowledge. All through the myths of Kalevala the power of the sword is looked down on; *real* heroes overcame their adversaries with words, often in the form of songs. The most famous folk hero, Väinämöinen, not only sang his opposition into a swamp, but was wise enough, when he felt his powers waning, to leave in a boat 'to make room for better singers'.

This diversion into the misty pasts of Finnish folklore is not entirely irrelevant because it makes it easier to understand the influence one man has had over the way Green thinking has developed in Finland. Love him or hate him, agree or disagree with him, Pentti Linkola is the yardstick against which Greens measure themselves. And his power is the way he uses words.

Recognised even by his detractors as one of the best writers in Finland, Linkola's style is provocative and compelling. An expert on wild birds, he left an academic career to live the simple life of a fisherman and from the 1950s onwards has been writing about the new set of values society would have

to adopt if the human species is to avoid destroying the
natural environment on which all life depends. His pamphlet
on pacifism, published in 1960, caused a sensation.[2] A
collection of articles published in 1971 had the title *Unelmat
Paremmasta Maailmasta (Dreams of a Better World)*.

But few listened to his warnings and before the turn of the
decade Linkola was so pessimistic about the possibility of
people changing their values voluntarily that he began to
write of violent action by the enlightened few as the only way
to secure the future of the species. Having abandoned hope of
a peaceful redressment of the balance between human beings
and the rest of nature he decided to take up the cudgel on
behalf of nature in order to defend it from the violent and
destructive actions of human beings. Another book of articles published at this time he entitled *Toisin – Ajattelijan
Päiväkirjasta (Diary of a Dissident)*, the literal translation of
the Finnish word for dissident being 'otherwise thinker'. It
caused an uproar not least because it was dedicated to
Andreas Baader and Ulrike Meinhof, whose example Linkola
felt offered the only road to saving the human species.

Linkola's friends, who often agree with his pessimistic
prophecies but rarely with his prescriptions, say he is
primarily committed to logic and truthfulness. They also say
that he is intentionally controversial, hoping by his extreme
words to stir up reasonable revolution. His personal manifesto contains extreme proposals for population reduction
and social organisation which he sometimes details with a
humour that is not always dark. But it also recommends
isolation, individualism and uncooperativeness as values to
be cherished above technology, socialism and solidarity.
Linkola does not see why killing other human beings should
be more punishable than destroying the environment which
he argues is also murdering people, indirectly perhaps, but
potentially on a massive scale.

In a leading article for a prominent Finnish weekly
magazine Linkola reveals the deep bitterness that has led his
passion for nature to overwhelm his compassion for the
human species. He is writing about the dilemma facing many
Finnish farmers who have no wives – the women having
moved from the country into the cities:

> We see efficiency as a busy life and change in the
> forest and the fields, as cutting down trees to build
> things – for extensions to our homes, for sheds to

store things, for saunas. All this 'progress' leaves
marks on nature because whenever human beings
fight, love, work or rejoice it is always nature that
suffers...

...loneliness is the best employer. What else can a
lonely and powerful man do to escape the lack of a
wife? Of course we extend the work day to make
lonely evenings in the house as short as possible.
We seek revenge for our loneliness and it is on
nature that we take it because we can't do it to any
other human being. With our tractors we run down
all the beautiful and tender gifts of nature.[3]

Other friends, and his enemies, say that Linkola is a
dangerous liability to the Green movement and he should
stay quiet – to leave room for other singers perhaps.

The 1960s and the 1970s also saw the growth of 'consensus'
politics in Finland. Although government coalitions were
left of centre – with the Centre party usually playing a
pivotal role – the balance of power between all parties in
parliament became institutionalised. High posts in the civil
service are divided among members of parties represented in
the national parliament, in proportion to their number of
seats. Differences over policy can thus be smoothed out at a
high level, cutting out consultation with the ordinary
citizen. The Finnish youth responded to the student radicalism which swept Europe at the end of the 1960s, but 'by the
1970s many of the young radicals were absorbed by the
various political parties, with the Soviet-oriented minority
faction of the Communist party having the most vocal youth
organisation and enjoying the largest number of recruits.'[4]

The stifling effect of 'consensus' politics and the ideological dead hand that the Communist point of view put on
intellectual debate made the 1970s a bleak time for quite a few
people. Even the peace movement was dominated by the
Finnish Peace Committee, an affiliate of the largly pro-Soviet
World Peace Council. In 1976, 15 people stood in the
municipal elections in Helsinki under the name Helsinki
Movement, polling 1,700 votes (0.7%) but gaining no seats.[5]
Osmo Soininvaara, now a Green MP, remembers that
although the platform was against growth policies it was
really a protest at dull political times – a gesture against the
ideological slump.

By 1979 several people who kept meeting each other in different places – trying to protect a small but unique bird lake in southern Finland from being drained, at anti-nuclear and peace demonstrations or Amnesty International meetings – had decided that they shared a similar view of the world. This relationship was cemented when the year-long but ultimately unsuccessful protest at the bird lake, Koijärvi, turned from trying to use legal channels to civil disobedience.

> The authorities were unprepared for such action from law-and-order conscious Finns. There were warnings of such actions leading to political terrorism and an insistence on the use of 'proper channels' to deal with grievances. The action at Lake Koijärvi led to a nationwide controversy on the relationship between justice and the letter of the law, and the moral right and duty to engage in civil disobedience, and on environmental protection in general.[6]

There is no doubt that for most Finns the Koijärvi protest was the starting point for Green politics in their country.

Electoral Success

In 1980, Ville Komski, a member of Amnesty International who played a prominent role in the Koijärvi protest, headed an Alternative Helsinki list in the elections to Helsinki city council. Emphasis was put on limiting the growth of the Helsinki area, on city planning and on traffic. The list obtained 1.7% and Ville was elected.

For the 1983 elections to the national parliament, Greens were on the ballot in the southern 7 of the 14 electoral districts, obtaining 40,000 votes or about 1.5% of the national total. The vote for the Greens was 3.3% and 4.5% in the province of Uusimaa and the city of Helsinki respectively. This result obtained two seats for the Greens, one for Ville Komski and one for Kalle Könkkölä, a wheelchair-bound activist from the disabled people's movement.

The following year, the Greens consolidated their success by getting 350 names onto the ballot in 69 of the 461

communes. They gained a nationwide average of 2.8% of the
vote (6% where they stood) and a total of 101 local council
seats for candidates claiming to be Green. Higher polls of up
to 11% in Espoo were recorded and 7 seats on the 85-member
Helsinki city council went to Greens.[7]

Although the 1987 national elections increased the Greens'
parliamentary representation by a further 2 seats they are
not viewed as the success they could have been. Opinion polls
were showing a potential support between 6% and 10% but in
the end only 4% of people actually voted Green. Opinion is
divided among the Greens as to why this happened. Some
believe the results could have been even more disastrous save
for a brilliant tv performance by Pekka Haavisto, one of the
new MPs, in a pre-election debate. Others believe the reason
lies in the fact that the Greens in Finland have never
formally become a party and remain a group of loosely
associated individuals. While voters seem to like the new
approach to politics, they are confused by people acting like a
political party while declaring that they are not.

In refusing to organise and become an officially registered
political party the Greens in Finland have ended up with the
worst of both worlds. From 1982 onwards they have held
annual national conferences open to members of various
ecological and alternative groups. Although individual
activists say that no meeting or body should have the moral
authority to decide on behalf of the whole movement, these
conferences have taken decisions of increasing importance.

In Jyväskylä in 1983, working groups developed policy and
examined the possibility of greater reliance on extra-
parliamentary action. In 1984 the meeting at Oulu produced a
resolution which was made public and is now known as the
Oulu theses:

1) The capacity of nature to endure the effects of
human action must not be exceeded;
2) The capacity of people to tolerate social and
economic pressures must not be exceeded;
3) The long-term effects of all policies must be a
primary aspect of decision-making;
4) The costs of public policy must not be left to
future generations to pay.[8]

By 1985 the disadvantages of a disorganised structure were
even more apparent. The 1984 local elections had seen people

elected on a Green ticket with a far from Green programme
and the 1985 Turku meeting simply increased the confusion
as to who the Greens really were. One Green described the
candidate selection process as the 'IEM-method' – I elect
myself.[9] A detailed policy programme prepared by the Turku
Greens was discussed and rejected by the meeting as being
too traditionally socialist in, for example, its dependence on
nationalisation and central state planning, and Linkola
made an impassioned speech which gained much publicity:

> He argued that the only real issue was survival of
> life on earth, which required an extensive
> abolition of modern social and economic struc-
> tures. He accused the Greens of indecisiveness and
> a 'summer soldier and sunshine patriot' mentality,
> and urged them to resort to open violence on
> behalf of nature conservation. The vast majority
> of Greens have explicitly rejected violence, but the
> issues raised by this address and a subsequent
> pamphlet developing its ideas (his personal mani-
> festo) have done much to alert the country to the
> seriousness of Green politics.[10]

Although still without any democratic organisational structure, some Greens decided to form a discussion group with a
view to establishing a clearer picture of what the Greens
were and what they weren't, although the group emphasised
that they would have no say over how Green politics is
executed in the parliament or in the local councils.

The accident at Chernobyl dominated the August 1986
meeting in Espoo where the Greens agreed a firm opposition
to the building of a fifth nuclear power station (which they
had not been able to do in Turku) and broached the question
of closing down existing plants. But the organisational chaos
remained, and a meeting was held in September in Tampere
to seek to resolve the problem before the 1987 elections to the
national parliament. Amid considerable confusion, a
resolution to form a party was defeated, but a group under
Jaakko Turkka, a political scientist, former Social-Democrat
and information secretary to the prime minister, was charged
with the task of establishing a Vihreä Liitto (Green Union).
Kalle Könkkölä was nominated chairman of the Union, with
two women, Manu Kaajakari and Voukko Laine-von Konow,
as second and third chairs.

The new Green Union was formally agreed at a congress on 28 February 1987 but it has in fact done little except enshrine the confusion of the Greens into 9 compartments.[11] No one is sure how many members there are – estimates vary between 700 and 1,000 – because people can belong to more than one section as well as to other political parties, and non-members' groups are allowed representatives on the council. Each section has an organiser and decides on its own rules and subscriptions, simply passing 20 Finnish marks per member on to the Vihreä Liitto. Few people take this organisation seriously. Ulla Antilla of the feminists describes it as 'a bit artificial' and no one even pretends that it is democratic. However, most people agree that it least provides a starting point from which to craft a democratic organisation which up to then had been impossible.

Future Prospects

The 1987 election to the national parliament brought an added dimension to the Finnish taste for consensus politics and to the relatively cosy style of politics made possible by a small one-chamber parliament. For the first time a coalition government has been established between the Conservatives and the Social-Democrats at national level, although cooperation between left and right occurs fairly frequently in local government.

Paradoxically the Greens feel that this situation is good for them. Many Social-Democrats and members of the Centre party (now in opposition) are not happy about the present government's plans for Finland. The Greens feel that both government and opposition listen to their ideas, especially since the traditional stronghold for Finnish intellectuals, the Communist party, is in decline and has now split. They are particularly proud that, in the tradition of offering public appointments to members from other parties represented in parliament, the Greens have obtained the newly created post of equality ombudsperson for one of their members – Paavo Nikula, a lawyer and former member of the Centre party.

Some Greens, however, sound warning bells about the dangers of continued ambivalence towards establishing a proper democratic organisation. They point to the craziness of taking part in the political game by seeking election yet voluntarily handicapping themselves by refusing the money that is available to legalised parties with elected MPs, and refusing to elaborate a coherent programme for the electorate. They are also concerned about the apparent domination of men amongst Green representatives at national level; the new equality ombudsperson is a man as well as all four of the Greens' MPs.

However, of the 81 Green municipal councillors recognised by the Vihräa Liitto, 46 are women (56.1%), markedly better than the 25.2% of all councillors who are women. In the city councils where the Greens are represented, concrete achievements in the form of legislation are few, although there is wide agreement that many issues, like waste recycling and pollution taxes, are being taken up by other parties in ways they would not have been without the influence of the Greens. At a meeting in Tampere in February 1988 it was at last agreed to begin the process of turning the Vihreä Liitto into a registered political party, the first step being the collection of 5,000 signatures. The more cynical among the Finnish Greens see dangerous echoes of the 1970s and fear that their radical ideas will become blunted if they are restricted to the 'proper channels' of Finnish consensus politics.

Notes

1 Kimmo Wilska, 'The Green Movement and the Political Mood in Finland', unpublished paper, 1985.
2 Jukka Paastela, 'Finland's New Social Movements', University of Tampere, 1987, p. 40.
3 *Suomen Kuvalehti*, 24 April 1987.
4 Kimmo Wilska, op. cit.
5 *The Greens in Finland*, booklet published by the Finnish Green Parliamentary Group, March 1988.
6 Wilska, op. cit.
7 *The Greens in Finland*, loc. cit.
8 Marketta Horn, 'The Greens in Finland: A General Survey', Green Parliamentary Group information sheet, autumn 1986.
9 Jukka Paastela, op. cit., p. 28.
10 Marketta Horn, op. cit.
11 See under 'Organisation', below.

Main Party Publications

HAAVISTO P. (ed.), *Tehtävä Napapiirillä – kadonnutta aatetta etsimässä* (Mission at the Arctic Circle – in search of the lost ideology), Perusta ry, 1983.
Waskipaino Karkkila, thoughts of the Greens in southern Finland before the parliamentary elections of 1987. In Finnish and Swedish.
SOININVAARA Osmo, *Vihreitä kysymuyksiä* (Green Questions), Helsinki Greens, 1987.
The Greens in Finland, Finnish Green Parliamentary Group (in English), 1988.

Vihreä Lanka (Green Thread), bimonthly newspaper with news and reports from the Green movement and the parliamentary group.
Suomi (Finland), monthly journal for the underground culture.

Studies of Green Politics

BORG O. & HARISALO R., *Vihreä Kirjo* (The Green Variety), University of Tampere, 1986.
SOININVAARA Osmo, *Correspondence with Pentti Linkola*, WSOY, 1986.
PAASTELA Jukka, *Finland's New Social Movements*, University of Tampere (in English), 1987.

Addresses

Vihreä Liitto (Green Union)
Lätinen Papinkatu 2-4
00530 Helsinki,

tel: (358) 0 7011613

Vihreä (Green parliamentary group)
Eduskunta
00102 Helsinki 10

tel: (358) 0 432 ext. 3273 or 3271

Organisation

Vihreä Liitto (Green Union)

'IDEALISTIC' GROUPS:

Vihreä Elämänsuojelun Liitto	ecologists
Vihreä Seura	social and ecology
Vihreä Feministit	feminists
Valomerkki	students
Vihreä Vaivaislhke	handicapped

DISTRICT GROUPS

Uudenmaan Vihreät	live near Helsinki (SE)
Etelä-Hämeen Vihreät	live near Hämeenlinna (SE)
Oolun Seudun Vihreät	live near Oulu (N)

DISTRICT & 'IDEALISTIC' GROUP

Vastedes	live near Tampere (SE)

Election Results

NATIONAL (Eduskunta)

	1987 Mar	1983 Mar	1979 Mar	1975 Sep
8 Rural Party	**9**	**17**	**7**	**2**
	6.3	*9.7*	*4.6*	*3.6*
8 Christian League	**5**	**3**	**9**	**9**
	2.6	*3.0*	*4.8*	*3.3*
8 Constitutional Party		**1**		**1**
	0.1	*0.4*	*1.2*	*1.6*
7 National Coalition Party	**53**	**44**	**47**	**35**
	23.1	*22.1*	*21.7*	*18.4*
6/5 Centre Party			**36**	**39**
			17.3	*17.6*
	40	**38**		
	17.6	*17.6*		
6 Liberal Party			**4**	**9**
	2.6	*3.0*	*4.8*	*3.3*
3 Social-Democratic Party	**56**	**57**	**52**	**54**
	24.1	*26.7*	*23.9*	*24.9*
1 Democratic League	**16**	**26**	**35**	**40**
	9.4	*13.5*	*17.9*	*18.9*
1 Democratic Alternative	**4**			
	4.2			
9 Swedish People's Party	**12**	**10**	**10**	**10**
	5.6	*4.9*	*4.3*	*5.0*
11 Finnish Pensioners' Party	*1.2*			
10 The Greens (Vihreä)	**4**	**2**		
	4.0	*1.5*[1]		

Key: **Seats** in bold, *Percentages* in italics.

References
The Statesman's Year Book (ed. John Paxton), Macmillan.
Economist, 21 March 1987.
Finnish Parliament Information Service.

Notes
1 Percentage nationwide, although only 7 of the 15 constituencies had a Green candidate.

6: FRANCE   *Les Verts*

Area: 543,965 sq. km.   *founded: 28/29 February 1984*
Population: 55.5 million (1987)   *members: 1,000*
Density: 102 per sq. km.

*Member: UN, OECD, NATO, WEA and European
          Communities*
Official language: French
GNP per capita: US $8,890 (1984)

Background and Electoral System

In its search for a politically stable system following the 1789
revolution France completed several full circles, rotating
monarchies, republics and empires twice before establishing
the Third Republic in 1870. Moreover, each change of power
was due either to a military coup, a military defeat or a
revolution, carried out more often than not in traumatic and
bloody fashion.

Although the Third Republic is the longest-lived of the
republics so far (it lasted from 1870 to 1940) it was less than a
year old when one of France's most divisive political experiences occured – the Paris Commune. Outraged by national
defeatism following occupation and defeat by the Prussians,
and inspired by the growing socialist movement, the people of
Paris rose in arms, barricaded the city and for 62 days
established a democratic, self-governing state. When military forces were ordered into Paris, the *communards* burnt
many buildings and executed hostages. The army is said to
have slaughtered about 25,000 people and arrested nearly
twice as many. This most bloody of all French civil wars
hardened the 'bunker mentality' of subsequent governments
and convinced many working people that their struggle for
Liberté, Egalité, Fraternité would always be hard and violent.

Weakened by the First World War, which killed 10% of the active male population, caused widespread damage to agriculture and industry and left many people shattered emotionally, France was ill-prepared to withstand the invasion of Hitler's army. People reacted to this occupation in different ways. Some actively welcomed and supported the Nazis' 'new order' for Europe; some – including the Pétain government and its supporters – preferred to consider themselves nationalists and endorsed the Vichy regime which was in fact a collaborationist police state; others participated actively in the Resistance movement. Most people, though, simply waited to see what would happen, concentrating on the day-to-day difficulties of meeting their basic needs in meagre and dangerous times.

After the Second World War political stability remained elusive and the Algerian war brought Charles de Gaulle out of retirement to 'save' France once again. Although in the end he agreed to total independence for Algeria – everything France had fought against – the French public accepted his decision. It is hard not to see in de Gaulle an echo of past French empires. The Fifth Republic was designed to legitimise his executive style of governing and he had an ill-concealed contempt for political parties, preferring to use referenda to test approval of his policies.

Paradoxically de Gaulle's regal example proved particularly useful when legislative elections in 1986 resulted in the constitutionally unexpected event of a parliamentary majority coming from a different political grouping than the sitting president. The Socialist president, François Mitterand, although no longer able to practise hands-on politics as he had done when his party held the parliamentary majority, did retain his political legitimacy and even gained increased public respect by playing the role of a wise, rather monarchical president.

France is a constitutional democracy and the Fifth Republic came into force in 1958. Although sovereignty resides with the people via their elected representatives (and through referenda), the president enjoys considerable powers. He is elected directly every seven years and is, amongst other things, responsible for respect of the constitution and the proper functioning of public authorities, being also the 'protector of national independence and territorial integrity'. It is the president who appoints the prime minister and who presides over the council of ministers that he, acting on the prime minister's advice, appoints and dismisses. Civil and military offices are filled by presidential appointees, and in times of crisis the president has substantial emergency powers.

The 577 members of the Assemblée Nationale (lower house) are elected for five years from single-member constituencies in France and its overseas territories. The 319 senators enjoy a nine-year term and are elected by an electoral college in each department or overseas territory. The government determines and conducts policy, is responsible for national defence and for the execution of laws. However, under article 23 of the constitution, ministers in the French government must not be members of parliament.

The constitution also allows for a constitutional council, which oversees the fairness of elections and referenda and acts as guardian of the constitution.

In 1982 the Socialist majority in parliament passed legislation that decentralised much more power to the 22 directly elected regional councils which replaced the state-appointed regional prefects. The Conseils-Générales of the 96 departments also saw their powers expanded, taking over local administration and expenditure from the departmental prefects. The other important level of local government is the 36,394 communes, which vary in size and population and directly elect a municipal council every six years. The mayor of the commune is both its representative and the agent of the central government. The 324 *arrondissements* and 3,509 cantons are of less administrative importance.

Since 1958, the main system for conducting elections has been the double ballot. This involves two rounds of voting, usually on consecutive Sundays. In each electoral constitutency voters may cast one vote for the candidate of their choice in the first round. Any candidate who obtains 50% plus one of the votes cast is automatically elected and the election stops there. Should no candidate obtain a majority in the first round, a play-off is staged between the two highest polling candidates.

To stand in the presidential elections a candidate needs signatures of support from at least 500 parliamentarians or *maires* of local councils (there is a pool of about 38,000 eligible signatures). All candidates have 90 minutes television time and a full reimbursement of the official election material, that is, voting slips, official poster and one leaflet delivered per household.

For legislative, regional and all other local elections no signatures are required and any candidate polling more than 5% is entitled to reimbursement of their official election expenses. During legislative elections access to two hours of television time is shared between the parties in proportion to their representation in the outgoing parliament, and a half hour is shared between the smaller parties. In the 1984 elections to the European Parliament the Entente Radicale Ecologiste list had enough good connections to profit from an electoral rule which gives any list with the support of at least 15 sitting senators access to the 'big' parties' air-time.

Factors Affecting the Development of Green Politics

Until the 1960s most French environmentalists were concerned with nature conservation. This mainly involved the establishment of reserves and the regulation of hunting and shooting, which were the main threats to wildlife. Until relatively recently a large proportion of the French people depended on the land in one way or another for their livelihood. So, as one of the larger countries of Europe with a relatively low population density, the impact of industrialism on France was not as immediately apparent as it was in Britain or Belgium for example.

Most environmental groups in France have been formed under the 1 July 1901 law of association. This law defines, categorises, and in some cases allocates government subsidies to groups of people who register under it.

But in order to understand modern French society a bit better it is useful to know that the 1901 law replaced one which was passed shortly after the 1789 revolution. This law enshrined the belief of philosopher Jean-Jacques Rousseau that each citizen should be free to have a direct relationship with the state, unhampered by any intervening body or institution. The electoral system established at the same time was in the same spirit. Under it, an elected deputy was considered to be responsible to the *nation* rather than to the constituency that elected him. All this helped establish the cult of individualism which has became a dominant feature of French society, with de Gaulle arguably its best-known practitioner. Indeed modern-day politics in France is far more concerned with competition between personalities than it is with prescribing a coherent set of policies for the country.

The legacy of France's history of bloody revolution has also proved hard to overcome. The state rarely consults any special interest group (apart from perhaps the massively powerful business and farming lobbies – viewed by some as the new aristocracy) and the groups themselves have difficulty in rising above internecine squabbles, and so rarely manage to mount a coherent lobby round a well-defined set of ideas. Several attempts to bring grievances to the attention of both the public and the state through demonstrations have ended in violence and little real change – like, some say, the earlier revolutions. Now, on the whole, both the special interest groups and the state are deeply entrenched in their dislike, distrust and, worse still, their fear of each other.

When the Torrey Canyon oil tanker sank and spilt its cargo in 1967, ecological disaster and environmental protection became linked in the minds of many conservation groups for the first time. The black oil covered the beaches of Brittany and coated thousands of sea-birds. Then in 1968 it was discovered that the government had approved a plan by private interests to commercially develop the Vanoise national park. This provoked a huge uproar and for the first time environmental groups got together to coordinate what turned out to be a successful campaign against the development. These two events did much to politicise the conservation movement in France.

Other changes were taking place too. In May 1968 student grievances culminated in university occupations. Their protest centred in part on their own concerns – overcrowding, elitist and authoritarian university administration and lack of jobs for leavers. But they were also influenced by the international student movement and the Vietnam war. As the police responded with their usual heavy-handedness, the protest expanded to cover hierarchical authority in general and the lack of democracy in all aspects of French life. Workers responded in sympathy with the students' aims, occupying factories and generally paralysing the whole system. The Gaullist government defused the 'revolution', first with some concessions and then with a June general election which they won convincingly, blaming the unrest on 'Communist agitation'.

At the beginning of the 1970s the environmental movement began to split. On the one side were the nature conservationists who wished to keep ecology a natural and not a political science and who preferred to take up particular conservation causes as and when they came along, mostly at a local level. On the other side were environmentalists who felt that they needed to directly intervene in order to alter government priorities and change the path of society if they were to achieve an ecologically balanced society. Many had been influenced by the 'limits to growth' literature and debate that was taking place in other countries.

The arguments raged in a growing number of 'ecojournals' and became more complicated when some left-oriented groups took over the political ecologists' side of the debate, assuming that they would provide the best vehicle for environmental demands. The intervention of traditional left-wing thinking at this stage of the movement's development was to prove a major handicap to the political ecologists as they fell victim to the same minute arguments over ideology and strategy that dominated the other political formations.

No scene-setting for the development of Green politics in France would be complete without reference to the French civil and military nuclear programme. In its own terms the nuclear power programme is a remarkable achievement. In the early seventies, only a tiny proportion of electricity was generated by nuclear power. This proportion rose to 59% by 1985 and is planned to reach about 80% by 1990.[1] There is little doubt that the nuclear programme was made possible by the very centralised and closed decision-making process in France. But that doesn't explain the general consensus that exists in support of it and the parallel and interlinked development of the French nuclear missile programme, the *force de frappe*. The phenomenon of such uncritical acceptance of unconstrained technological development is better explained through the tradition of French individualism. The desire of France to be totally independent of foreign imports for her energy supplies, to provide her own nuclear defence programme and to presumably become world leader in the associated technologies could be interpreted as French individualism expressing itself in the international community.

If anything, the anti-nuclear campaign divided the environmentalists even more. The conservation groups backed off from taking a stand on nuclear energy while the political ecologists joined with the other anti-nuclear movements in the 1970s to demonstrate against both the potential of the nuclear industry to commit the ultimate environmental disaster and the whole long-term threat that a 'plutonium economy' would present to France.

With no other channels open to them the anti-nuclear campaigners put much of their effort into direct action. History seemed to repeat itself again as protest disintegrated into violence, with one person killed and 200 injured at the massive demonstration on 31 July 1977 on the site of the Super-Phénix fast-breeder nuclear reactor at Creys-Malville. Afterwards the anti-nuclear movement succumbed to the same problems as the rest of the environmental movement and arguments developed over how to proceed; some wished to keep the movement outside party politics, others not. The threat of violence made public demonstration a closed option for all but the most hardened and courageous of activists. Ordinary people, however passionately they felt about the issue, began to stay at home.

Les Verts

The French ecologists first tested the electoral waters of France during the legislative elections of March 1973. Ecologie et Survie was a group founded in the Alsace home of Solange Fernex. A committed anti-nuclear activist, Fernex was also a member of the Association Féderative Régional pour la Protection de la Nature. Along with some colleagues she felt that the time had come to establish a political organisation parallel to the usual environmental groups. Present at this meeting was Antoine Waechter who eventually became the presidential candidate for Les Verts in 1988. The theme for Ecologie et Survie was *'halte à l'expansion'* and their candidate Henri Jenn obtained 3.7%, slightly more than the candidate for the Parti Socialiste Unifié (PSU — United Socialist Party).[2]

In April 1974 Georges Pompidou died, bringing forward the presidential elections which were not normally due until 1976. Journalist Jean Carlier rallied support, notably from Les Amis de la Terre (AdlT — Friends of the Earth) and other journalists concerned with environmental matters as well as some environmental groups, including Ecologie et Survie. The candidate was René Dumont, the internationally known agronomist and expert on the Third World. He polled a modest 1.3% with 336,114 votes but the campaign drew the public's attention to the political nature of ecological issues.

In 1976 a few candidates stood in the March cantonal elections, with some candidates in Alsace polling over 10%. That same year, a by-election in the 5th *arrondissement* of Paris for a seat in the National Assembly attracted the attention of the Amis de la Terre. A campaign called Paris-Ecologie was mounted with an AdlT spokesperson, Brice Lalonde, as candidate and René Dumont acting as *suppléant* (stand-in). The programme covered policies for ameliorating the quality of life in the neighbourhood, called for a halt to nuclear power stations (particularly those planned for rivers that supply Paris), and demanded a shorter working week, also proposing that more power should be transferred to the provinces and referenda by popular initiative become law. The result was 6.5% on the first ballot.

AdlT became enthusiastic about electoral activity – or at least its Paris groups did. They started to prepare for the March 1977 elections to the municipal councils by trying to persuade the Union of the Left list to support some of their demands. This failed, one of the particular stumbling blocks being nuclear power. So a coalition of groups was formed to stand candidates in all the *arrondissements* of Paris and in as many other areas as possible. This coalition (AdlT, Mouvement Ecologique, SOS-Environnement, Ecologie et Feminisme, Comité pour Sauver Paris, Comité Anti-nucléaire and Atelier Ecologique) was to be the first of many unhappy attempts by the Greens in France to come together. The clashes of personality, style and strategy that emerged in 1977 were to dominate the movement in France for the next ten years. And although the results of these elections were to inspire Greens in other countries to take the electoral plunge, the lesson of the French failure to exploit their success was unfortunately not always learnt well enough.

The dominant groups in the coalition were Amis de la Terre, Mouvement Ecologique, and SOS-Environnement. Mouvement Ecologique (ME) grew out of the 1974 René Dumont presidential campaign and brought together most of the regional and local associations (including Ecologie et Survie.[3] SOS-Environnement were a coalition of conservationists, transport users and handicapped people who had come together in 1974. They found that direct action such as sitting down on motorways or railway lines, combined with electoral participation, was an effective way of attracting public attention to their grievances. They formally became a political party in May 1977.[4]

The 1977 campaign focussed on the same issues that AdlT had highlighted in 1976. It also had the double objective of forcing other parties to take up a position on environmental questions and of illustrating how the Green vision of local self-government might work. In order to distiguish the 'real ecologists' from the 'opportunists' (who had already made their presence felt in the cantonal elections the previous year) AdlT elaborated *la Charte de Saint-Omer*, which outlined a minimum programme under six headings: liberate the community, protect life, another way of working, consume better, reduce inequalities, help for the Third World. All the coalition groups accepted this with the exception of Mouvement Ecologique, which produced a different programme that included more elaborate references to population, species diversity, human rights, exploitation of the Third World and the arms race.

The campaign seemed to be well on the way to achieving its first objective even before the first ballot took place. The mayoral candidate for the united left parties held a press conference on 10 March to publicise the concessions he would make to Paris-Ecologie should they back him in the second round. He pledged that private cars would be reduced in Paris, 10% more streets would be allocated for markets, pedestrians, gardens and buses, 170 acres of private and government-owned parks would be opened up, a pollution control agency would be established and municipal aid would become available to small industries and craftsmen.

The result of the first round saw an average of 10.13% in Paris with top scores of 13.8% in the 5th and 6th *arrondissements* and 13.1% in the 7th. Elsewhere in France first-round percentages were consistently above 5%, and although it is difficult to distinguish the 'real' from the 'opportunist' ecology candidates, Les Verts claim that about 30 candidates were ultimately elected.[5]

Although Paris-Ecologie had agreed it would not advise its voters how to vote on the second ballot, Brice Lalonde made a very muddled statement on 17 March in which he 'did not blame the left for the state of Paris but did blame it for not doing anything about it.' He described the left as 'least bad'.

In the end Paris elected Jacques Chirac's list and its leader became mayor.

Even though he was under no obligation to do so, Chirac then made an interesting gesture towards the ecologists. A law passed at the end of 1975 concerning the administration of Paris had recommended that Commissions d'Arrondissements (neighbourhood councils) be established from people representing the community and local organisations. The new mayor of Paris offered one seat on each council to an ecologist. Although Paris-Ecologie accepted, it proved unable to sustain any active participation in hands-on local politics. In the end it was only SOS-Environnement who sat on some of the councils, and even they had given up by November 1977.[6]

Despite their very favourable results, the ecologists failed to build on them. The coalition broke up and arguments took place over the validity of contesting elections in the first place. Tension was worst between the provincial groups and the Paris groups which had been seen to dominate, especially through the now overt personal ambitions of Brice Lalonde. In Lyon, Philip Lebreton unilaterally formed Ecologie 1978 in preparation for the legislative election due that year. Amis de la Terre and Lalonde contested this initiative and laid down conditions for their participation. These were refused and Ecologie 1978 joined forces with SOS-Environnement. Consequently the ill-coordinated campaigns in 168 of the 490 constituencies for the 1978 legislative elections proved disappointing. According to Les Verts, Ecologie 78 polled 499,792 votes, an average of 4.4% where they stood, but accurate interpretation of the results for these elections is difficult.

Things looked better again when Solange Fernex headed the list Europe-Ecologie for the first direct elections to the European Parliament. Although Amis de la Terre boycotted the campaign she was supported by a wide number of groups. Her national score of 4.7% with 888,134 votes was the highest of all the European Green parties and she scored 10.6% in her own area of Alsace, the Haut-Rhin.[7]

In Dijon on 21 November 1978 the majority of Europe-Ecologie's candidates and workers decided to turn the Mouvement Ecologique into the Mouvement d'Ecologie Politique (MEP) and concentrate on electoral politics. At the same time negotiations started for the presidential elections of 1981. Jean-Claude Delarue, president of SOS-Environnement, put his name forward but the majority of MEP were not enthusiastic. Lalonde appeared on the scene and after a series of ballots, on which only he and Lebreton from Lyon appeared and which were hotly contested as being undemocratic, Lalonde was selected as presidential candidate. A final but unsuccessful attempt by Lalonde's detractors was made to persuade Jacques Cousteau, the famous marine biologist, to accept the nomination of the ecologists.

In the event Lalonde's 'Aujourd'hui Ecologie' campaign scored a very gratifying 3.9% with a total 1,122,445 votes in the first round. Furthermore the ecologists held the balance of votes between the blocs of right- and left-wing parties and were courted by both sides before the next round. The Socialist candidate, François Mitterand, affirmed his intention to have a moratorium on the nuclear power programme and hold a public debate on its future, but Lalonde, firmly guided by the people around him, counselled his voters to choose between the second-round candidates according to their response to the 12 key demands of the ecologists.[8] It has been suggested that Lalonde might have been able to negotiate some more concrete concessions from Mitterand at this point but this is probably wishful thinking. The subsequent performance of the Socialist government makes it unlikely that any promises would have been kept. Detailed examination of the voting patterns for these elections reveals that the vote went down in some of the ecologists' traditional strongholds – Alsace, Manche and Paris – although it went up significantly nationwide.[9] This illustrates the dilemma facing the French Greens, a need for a charismatic leader to attract votes yet difficulty in finding one acceptable to the movement.

Indeed, after the presidential elections, at the very moment when the members of the movement should have been looking and talking outwards, they turned inwards and began to argue. Already the strains between Lalonde and his supporters and the MEP were at breaking point, and the end of the campaign was marked by grave accusations followed by a court case over large sums of money that some members felt Lalonde was unable to account for satisfactorily. When President Mitterand dissolved parliament and legislative elections were called for June, the Aujourd'hui Ecologie campaign, using the same programme, only managed 157,037 votes in the 81 (out of 491) constituencies it was able to contest, although its average vote where it stood, 3.6%, was not much down on the presidential elections.

The next few years were marked by deepening rifts within the MEP. In December 1981 Les Verts – Confédération Ecologiste was founded by some members of AdlT and some regional ecological groups. This prompted a further split of AdlT at their May 1982 annual general meeting between those who wanted to dissolve AdlT completely into the Confédération and those who wished it to continue. In the end AdlT moved back into its original field of pressure-group work and those members interested in political activity went to the Confédération. Then, in November 1982, another party, Les Verts – Parti Ecologiste, was created by the remaining members of MEP.

During this troubled period elections were contested under the old two-round system: in the cantons in March 1982 and to the municipal councils in March 1983. Although the minister of the interior posted the results polled by candidates using the word *écologiste* in their title chastely apart from the left and right political blocs, it was often unclear what these candidates actually stood for. For example, 550 seats were officially accorded to ecologists in 1983 but the two Green parties were never quite sure how many belonged to them.

It was the approach of the 1984 elections to the European Parliament that forced the two parties to consider formal reunion. The process was triggered when both held annual general meetings 40 kilometres apart on the same weekend in November 1983. Guests invited from the other European Green parties to address both groups at the same time were obliged to point out the rather strange diplomatic (not to mention physical) dilemma in which they found themselves. After a painful struggle a single new party was founded on 29 February 1984 in Clichy. Called Les Verts – Confédération Ecologiste, Parti Ecologiste (it eventually dropped all but the first two words of its name) the new party plunged into what was to be, for them, a catastrophic European election campaign.

All started well however. Opinion polls in the early months of 1984 indicated a support of between 5% and 7% for the Europe-Ecologie list.[10] As the elections were to be held under a system of proportional representation with 5% as the threshold, Les Verts seemed assured of at least 4 seats. On the strength of this anticipated result (and therefore full reimbursement of their expenses) they borrowed considerable sums of money from the German and both Belgian Green parties to finance their campaign, and incurred substantial debts in France as well.

Then disaster struck in the shape of a new list called Entente Radicale Ecologiste (ERE — Radical and Ecological Accord). Heading this list were Olivier Stirn, François Doubin and – Brice Lalonde. Stirn had left the Giscardian UDF to form his own Centre Radical party and Doubin was a member of the Mouvement des Radicaux de Gauche (MRG — Left Radical Movement).

Lalonde had written to the Clichy 'unification' meeting of Les Verts confirming that he was still a candidate for the European list which he would be happy to lead under certain conditions. One of these was that the policy of 'immediate unilateral disarmament' was watered down because it was 'naive and dangerous'. This ended any hope Lalonde might have had with Les Verts, who had never forgiven his past behaviour, particularly in the 1981 presidential elections. They nominated a veteran anti-nuclear campaigner from the northwest of France, Didier Anger, to top their list for Europe. However, failing to tuck Lalonde and his personal ambition somewhere into their list was to prove a tactical error.

The Socialist party had contested the 1981 elections as part of a 'united left' grouping along with the Communist party, the MRG and the PSU. But as the European elections were to be under a proportional voting system the left felt it would maximise its vote by contesting them as separate groups. To this end, in October 1983, Jean-Michel Baylet, president of the MRG, received the approval of President Mitterand for his intention to establish a list to 'reconstruct the centre left' (*Le Progrès*, 21 May 1984). Whether the recruitment of Lalonde to this list was part of the plan or merely a lucky bonus to the strategy of the left remains unsubstantiated, but its effect on Les Verts was very clear. Their opinion poll rating dropped dramatically (*Le Monde*, 11 June 1984) and their final result was 3.36% – 680,080 votes.[11] Little consolation was to be gained from the fact that ERE polled less – 3.31% and 664,403 votes. Stirn, Doubin and Baylet all received some political preferment at a later date. Lalonde, on the other hand, was awarded a 5-minute tv show that went out late each evening. It was called *Une bonne nouvelle par jour* (A piece of good news every day). As the protocol of the programme obliged the man who styled himself Monsieur Ecologie to ignore bad ecological news, Lalonde's political suicide was viewed by the movement to be complete. The programme was taken off after a few weeks.

Although the finances of Les Verts were in a parlous state after these elections, the party stayed together and worked on its organisation and communication network. The 1985 cantonal elections were again difficult to analyse because it was not clear which candidates belonged to Les Verts and which did not. The official figures announced 91,600 votes for the ecologists with no seats gained. (*Le Monde*, 14 March 1985.) Les Verts claimed they had 170 candidates, offered support to 46 others and obtained at least 5% in over 100 cantons. Top scores were in Alsace again, at around 14%.

The sinking of the Greenpeace ship Rainbow Warrior in July 1985 provoked one of France's biggest political scandals of recent years. The affair was exposed by an unprecedented bout of investigative journalism by some French newspapers and resulted in the resignation of the then minister of defence Charles Hernu. However Les Verts could do little more than deplore the incident. To their fury the press preferred to canvass the opinion of Brice Lalonde who, as a friend of the president of Greenpeace, had made several trips on Greenpeace ships. A long interview with Lalonde in November 1985's issue of *Lui* magazine was prefaced by a coy photograph of him cuddling a model of the Greenpeace ship.

Despite this distraction, the minds of Les Verts were already turning to the March 1986 elections to the National Assembly and the newly established regional councils. Both elections were to be conducted for the first time under a system of proportional representation. But even before the campaign had properly started Lalonde was again posing problems. He began in the northern town of Lille in November 1985 by publicly calling Michel Rocard (ex-PSU leader and at that time minister for agriculture in François Mitterand's government) to quit the Parti Socialiste. He, Lalonde, would then 'call the ecologists' to join with Rocard and himself on a new list. In the same speech Lalonde indicated that he had found little evidence of radioactive pollution on the island of Mururoa where the French conduct their nuclear tests and that the presence of France there was justified. He also repeated his belief that unilateral disarmament 'was 'stupid' (*Nord-Eclair*, 10 November 1985). By interesting coincidence, Les Verts were also in Lille holding their annual meeting and they roundly criticised Lalonde for continuing to speak on behalf of the French Green movement.

At this point it becomes difficult to decide whether Lalonde's next move was motivated by spite, blind personal ambition or more complex political motives. He was certainly viewed as politically untouchable, even by the other parties preparing lists for these elections. Lalonde contested a constituency in Lyon in opposition to the man who had hounded him most over the 'missing funds' in 1981, Jean Brière. Brière scored a terrible 1.2%, Lalonde slightly more with 1.4% (*Combat Nature* 72, May 1986). The damage done was greater than a simple split vote in Lyon because Les Verts nationally and in Lyon ended up by concentrating more on attacking Lalonde than on promoting their own programme.

However the failure of Les Verts to obtain any seats in the National Assembly in these elections cannot be blamed entirely on Brice Lalonde. The party managed to stand candidates in only 28 of the 96 constituencies for the Assembly and was present in only 49 of them for the elections to the 22 regional councils. The average results were 2.4% where they stood in the legislative elections and 3.4% where they stood in the regions. The highest legislative scores, in Alsace (3.7%) and the Manche (3.8%), fell far short of the 5% threshold. However it was in these two areas that Les Verts did gain their only three regional councillors – Didier Anger with 5.5% in Manche, André Buchmann with 5.7% in Bas-Rhin and Antoine Waechter with 6.5% in Haut-Rhin.[12]

Obviously years of in-fighting and accumulating debts had done much to make sure that it was a very weakened party that went into these crucial elections (the electoral system was then returned to its original two-round system by the incoming government of Jacques Chirac). But because they have succumbed to, or been unable to rise above, the French tradition of conducting politics around personalities rather than ideas, the programmatic development of Les Verts has remained rather weak. The manifesto used for the 1986 elections was, in many ways, less attractive than the brief one used by Mouvement Ecologique in the elections of 1977. And while voters in the 1970s warmed to the sloganeering of the Greens, in the 1980s they now wanted to hear precisely *how* the Greens planned to achieve their objectives. The internal struggles of Les Verts had been so preoccupying that they had failed to move with the times. Again echoing

traditional French politics, Les Verts have also been dominated by very strong male personalities. Their style of
working has created an atmosphere that does little to attract
women. The most famous example of this occurred during a
furious debate at the party's 1984 annual general meeting in
Dijon, when one of their executive shouted that it was 'better
to violate a woman than the statutes'. He is still in post and
the 1986 programme did not contain one policy referring to
the condition or status of women.

Future Prospects

In harmony with the cyclical nature of French history the
story of Les Verts has in a way returned to where it started.
The first electoral initiative came from Ecologie et Survie,
and 12 years later one of its founder members, Antoine
Waechter, is trying to provide a new focus for a party
desperate for the national leader that the French political
scene demands. In selecting Antoine Waechter as candidate
for the 1988 presidential elections, Les Verts hoped that any
lack of charisma Waechter may suffer compared to Lalonde
would be compensated for by his trustworthiness, programmatic steadiness and commitment to hard work.

Also anxious to avoid repeating past errors, the party put
its candidates for the 1988 presidential elections through a
series of regional 'primaries'. The results of these were a
support of 58.8% for Waechter, 28.7% for Yves Cochet and
12.5% for Jean Brière. These percentages represent pretty
accurately the factions within Les Verts. Cochet, who was
the party's main hope for a seat in parliament in 1986, and
Brière, an ex-communist with an addiction to long, confused,
apocalyptic analyses of the ills of society, have both been
attracted by the development of an Arc-en-ciel (Rainbow)
coalition of the very many small alternative left groups in
France, in the belief that Les Verts stand their best chance in
such a grouping.

However, most of the party has viewed the Arc-en-ciel
initiative with suspicion. Not only have the small left groups
in France a very long history of forming and reforming in
different shapes, but their declining electoral fortunes make
them an unattractive political partner. There have also been
suggestions that the Socialist party has encouraged the

Arc-en-ciel initiative because it is intent on mopping up Les Verts in the same way it mopped up the PSU 15 years ago.

At their annual general meeting in Paris on 21-22 November 1987, Les Verts elected to their national council a predominance of people supporting the political position of Waechter. Waechter wished to present a very distinct picture of Green politics to the French electorate during the presidential elections but he quite openly viewed this as simply the first stage in the 1989 elections to the municipal councils and the European Parliament. For the first time the party has found itself embarking on a long-term, widely-agreed political strategy that is directed towards the *public* rather than towards other political parties or factions in the Green movement.

In the first round of the presidential elections, Waechter polled a respectable 1,14 5,502 (3.8%), similar to the result of Brice Lalonde in 1981. He received considerable attention from the media and advised his voters to vote in the second round for whoever they judged most likely to favour Green policies. Phase one of Waechter's strategy was felt to have been satisfactorily accomplished. However, celebrations over the renaissance of Green politics in France were cut short.

Judging his results in the presidential elections to have been sufficiently good to guarantee his party an absolute majority should they be replicated in a parliamentary election, President Mitterand dissolved parliament and called new elections immediately. When the new prime minister, Michel Rocard, announced his government, who should be secretary of state for the environment but Brice Lalonde. Although ministers resign their seats on being appointed (*suppléant* takes over), it is desirable but not essential that they should have evidence of public popularity – i.e. have won an election! (Les Verts decided to boycott these parliamentary elections. Not only would it have been very expensive to contest them but, under the French electoral system, the party's results would inevitably have been disappointing.)

Reactions among Les Verts to seeing the man still popularly perceived as Monsieur Ecologie holding a junior post in a pro-nuclear, highly technocratic, very un-ecological government are mostly ones of dismay and depression. As one long-time, hard-working activist bitterly pointed out: 'All our years of work have basically been a waste of time. While we have been campaigning on the ground, he {Lalonde} has been doing the *salons* of Paris. In our political system, you have to admit that his strategy has been the right one.'

However, Les Verts are nothing if not resilient. They know that the growing number of French people who are sensitive to mounting environmental problems belong to groups that are predominantly locally based, and that much of the fall-off of support for the French Green political movement over the years can be explained by many grassroots supporters becoming disillusioned by the posturing of some of their national representatives. They also know that the movement must bear a lot of the blame for leaving the way clear for Lalonde to become the yardstick for Green politics in France.

The French have a tradition of lionising intellectuals, whose ideas and sayings are discussed with equal passion in Parisian cafés and provincial bars, and many would agree that there is an intellectual void in France just now. It is unfortunate therefore that the debate about Green ideas in France remains fossilised in the early 1970s and is rarely conducted in public. The reasons for this do to some extent lie with Les Verts themselves in that they do not have a strong theoretical base and publish very little; expanding *public* awareness of Green ideas is not given a high priority. But it is also true that very many of the recent flood of German and English books that have extended the thinking of the movement elsewhere are unavailable in France.

The appointment of Lalonde has stimulated several Greens in France to consider ways in which they might capture the intellectual high ground for Green ideas in order to trigger serious public debate over them, and Waechter remains intent on his strategy of revitalising local Green politics while keeping the party's national activities coherent and outward-looking into the 1990s. It remains to be seen if Les Verts can shake off the yoke of French history and political tradition which has proved such a handicap to the French Green political movement after such inspiring and promising beginnings.

Notes

1 Philip Davies, *Nuclear France: Power At Any Price?*, Friends of the Earth, London, 1986.
2 *Combat Nature* 78, August 1987.

The PSU is a small left-wing party which was established in 1960 but never gained much electoral support. It did, on the other hand, attract a lot of intellectual respect through its attempts to redefine 'authentic socialism'. In 1972, the Socialist party mopped up many of the PSU's ideas and in 1975 it also recruited the party's charismatic leader, Michel Rocard. Since then the fortunes of the PSU have been in decline and most of its early radical ideas, which once attracted quite a lot of ecologists, have been recycled by the traditional Socialist party. In tune with this strategy towards the PSU the Socialist government elected in 1981 made another leader of the PSU, Huguette Bouchardeau, minister for the environment. The story of the PSU is a particulary good example of how the Socialist party deals with any perceived threat to its political territory.

3 Les Verts : Parti Ecologiste leaflet, 1983.
4 C. Journès, 'Les Ecologistes, l'Etat et les Partis', in P. Bacot & C. Journès (eds), *Les Nouvelles Idéologies*, Presses Universitaires de Lyon, 1982.
5 *Combat Nature* 28, n. d.
6 For a comprehensive treatment of these elections see Athleen Ellington, *From Pressure Group to Party, Les Amis de la Terre in the Paris Municipal Elections March 1977*, M.A. thesis, University of London, June 1979.
7 *Combat Nature* 45, June 1981.
8 *Le Monde*, 28 April 1981.
9 C. Journès, op. cit.
10 *Le Monde*, 11 June 1984.
11 *The Times Guide to the European Parliament*, Times Books, 1984.
12 Les Verts, election results, March 1986.

Main Party Publications

Sauve qui peut la Forêt, 1985 (acid rain).
Le Chômage: Partage du temps de travail et des revenus, 1985 (employment).
1986 General Election Manifesto, *La Choix de la Vie*.
Sortir du nucléaire, 1987 (exit from nuclear power).

Vert Contact is the national party newsletter.
Combat Nature, BP 3046, 24003 Périgueux Cedex, quarterly journal of local activists covers the activities of Les Verts.
Silence, 4 rue Bodin, 69001 Lyon, monthly green/alternative journal .

Studies of Les Verts

BRIDGEFORD J., 'The Ecologist Movement and the French General Elections 1978', *Parliamentary Affairs*, 1978.

McDONALD J.R., 'Environmental Concern and the Political Process in France: Patterns of the 1981 Elections', *The Environmental Professional*, 1982.
JOURNÈS C., 'Les Ecologistes, l'Etat et les Partis', in BACOT P. & JOURNÈS C., (eds), *Les Nouvelles Idéologies*, Presses Universitaires de Lyon, 1982.

Address

Les Verts
90 rue Vergniaud
75013 Paris

tel: (33) 1 45899911

Organogram: Les Verts

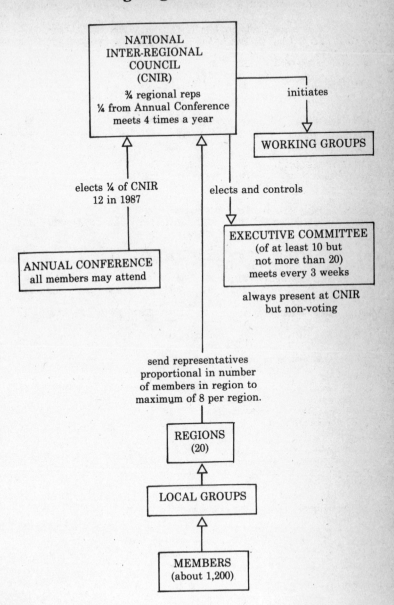

NATIONAL
INTER-REGIONAL
COUNCIL
(CNIR)

¾ regional reps
¼ from Annual Conference
meets 4 times a year

initiates

WORKING GROUPS

elects ¼ of CNIR
12 in 1987

elects and controls

ANNUAL CONFERENCE
all members may attend

EXECUTIVE COMMITTEE
(of at least 10 but
not more than 20)
meets every 3 weeks

always present at CNIR
but non-voting

send representatives
proportional in number
of members in region to
maximum of 8 per region.

REGIONS
(20)

LOCAL GROUPS

MEMBERS
(about 1,200)

Election Results

	NATIONAL (Assembly)[1]				PRESID-ENTIAL[2]		EURO-PEAN[3]	
	1988 Jun	1986 Mar	1981 Jun	1978 Mar	1988 Apr	1981 Jun	1984 Jun	1979 Jun
8 National Front (FN)	**1**	**35**						**10**
	9.8	*9.7*			*14.4*			*11.0*
Other Right	**13**	**14**	**11**	**3**				
		3.9	*3.1*	*3.2*		*3.0*		
7 Gaullists (RPR)	**128**	**145**	**88**	**150**				**26**
		21.2	*20.9*	*22.6*	*19.9*	*18.0*		*27.9*
							41	
	40.4						*43.0*	
6 Giscardians (UDF)	**130**	**129**	**63**	**138**				**15**
		18.8	*19.2*	*21.4*	*16.6*	*28.3*		*16.2*
3 Socialist Party (PS)	**276**	**208**	**285**	**113**			**20**	**21**
4 Left Radicals (MRG)	*37.5*	*31.4*	*37.8*	*24.7*	*34.1*	*25.8*	*20.8*	*23.4*
Other Left		**7**		**1**				
	0.3	*2.8*	*1.9*	*6.2*	*4.1*			
1 Communist Party (PC)	**27**	**35**	**44**	**86**			**10**	**19**
	11.3	*9.7*	*16.1*	*20.6*	*6.8*	*15.3*	*11.2*	*20.4*
10 Greens (Les Verts)		*1.2[4]*	*1.1[4]*	*2.2[4]*	*3.8*	*3.9[5]*	*3.4*	*4.7 [7]*
11 Miscellaneous							*10.6[6]*	*8.4*

Key: **Seats** in bold, *Percentages* in italics.

References

SMITH Gordon, *Politics in Western Europe*, Heinemann, 1984.
The Times Guide to the European Parliament, Times Books, 1984.
Le Monde Dossiers et Documents.
Les Verts documentation.

Notes

1 1978, 1981 and 1988 percentages are after first ballot, seats are after second ballot. In 1986 the election was held under a PR system with regional lists.
2 Percentages are given for first ballot. Only the two leading candidates contest second ballot. In 1981, François Mitterand, the Socialist candidate, became president after obtaining 51.75% of the vote against Valéry Giscard d'Estaing. In 1988 he was re-elected, obtaining 54% against the RPR candidate, Jacques Chirac.
3 European elections are conducted under a PR system with a national list.
4 These percentages are nationwide. Les Verts did not stand in every electoral constituency. In 1978 they polled an average of 4.4% in the 168 constituencies (out of 490) where they stood. In 1981 the average was 3.6% in 81 of the 490 constituencies. In 1986 they polled an average of 2.4% in 28 of the 96 constituences under a PR system with regional lists.
5 Les Verts contested the 1974 presidential elections polling 1.3% in the first ballot.
6 This percentage contains the 3.3% polled by the ERE list of Olivier Stirn, François Doubin and Brice Lalonde.
7 Les Verts officially boycotted this election.

7: WEST GERMANY *Die Grünen*

Area: 248,706 sq. km.   *founded: 12/13 January 1980*
Population: 61 million (1985)   *members: 43,500*
Density: 245 per sq. km.

Member: UN, OECD, European Communities, NATO, WEA
Language: German
GNP per capita: US $10,670 (1984)

Background and Electoral System

Although the German people have inhabited central Europe since ancient times, a national state was formed comparatively late. At the time of the French revolution in 1789 there were more than 300 German principalities and when Germany was eventually unified in 1871 this was under the most militaristic of those petty states – the kingdom of Prussia. As the German empire grew through military might it also became prosperous, and while a parliament was created, this Reichstag served largely as window-dressing. Bismarck is said to have told the parliamentarians that the decisive factors in the lives of nations were 'not speeches and majority resolutions but iron and blood'.

The rise of the Nazi party after the First World War and the almost unchallenged power of Adolf Hitler have been the subject of much study. The mixture of fear, doubt, loyalty and resignation that caused ordinary Germans, soldiers and civilians, to remain more steadfast behind Hitler than they did behind the kaiser in the First World War may be difficult to understand today, but it has without doubt greatly coloured subsequent developments in both East and West Germany.

To a great extent the constitution of the Federal Republic of Germany established after the Second World War was aimed at preventing a possible repetition of the errors of the Weimar republic and the Nazi experience. Considerable power was devolved to the eleven *Länder* (States) so that the failure of any one *Land* would be less likely to damage the whole. The upper house or Bundesrat (federal council), made up of members of the *Länder* governments, has absolute veto over any decision taken by the directly elected lower house, the Bundestag (federal diet). A *Grundgesetz* (basic law) guarantees rights which are legally binding on the legislature, executive and judiciary. It also provides safeguards over the use of emergency powers.

The Federal Republic of Germany became a sovereign state in May 1955. However, West Berlin remains occupied by the British, Americans and French so, although it is administered like the other *Länder*, it is not formally incorporated into the Federal Republic. Representatives elected to the federal parliament from West Berlin may take their seats but are not allowed to vote.

German elections are conducted under the additional member system of proportional representation. Electors have two votes, one for a candidate in the constituency and one for a party list. Half of the 496 seats in the Bundestag are allocated to candidates elected from the constituencies by simple majority, and the remaining seats are allocated proportionally to party lists in the *Länder*. All parties obtaining either three directly elected seats or 5% of the national vote are eligible for this allocation.

Each independent candidate standing for election in a constituency requires the endorsement of 200 registered electors, but establishing a party list is a bit more complicated. Unless the party has held more than five seats in the previous parliament it requires the endorsement of 1% or 2,000 (whichever is less) of the *Land* electorate. For European elections parties may choose to establish either *Länder* lists or one national list. These lists again require 2,000 signatures, or 4,000 if the party does not have at least five seats in the appropriate parliament. Parties also have to fulfil a certain number of conditions set out in a special law on political parties passed in 1967. This includes having to give evidence of seriousness of purpose, judged by size and stability of the organisation, number of members, statutes, political programme and so on. However the 1967 law was only intended to discourage frivolous candidates, not to judge a party's programme or political style: only the Federal Constitutional Court has the power to actually ban a party.

The 1967 law also provides for a 'refund' of election expenses to all parties polling more than 0.5%, calculated according to their share of the vote. As the kitty for this is established by multiplying the number of people entitled to vote by 5 Deutschmark (3.5 DM before 1983), this 'refund' is more in the nature of a windfall. Because Die Grünen run extremely modest election campaigns compared to the other parties they are now thought to be the 'richest' party in West Germany.

Factors Influencing the Development of Green Politics

The all-out commitment to industrialisation in West Germany since the war has created amazing levels of pollution and natural spoilation. A quarter of the country is covered by trees, yet by the 1980s it was known that about half of them were dying from diseases attributable to chemical pollutants. The media gave the devastation much publicity and this horrified a people with a long culture of romantic naturalism. During the 1970s considerable opposition also developed to several large-scale projects such as the nuclear power plants at Wyhl in Baden-Württemberg and Brokdorf in Schleswig-Holstein, a nuclear waste reprocessing plant at Gorleben in Lower Saxony and a new runway at Frankfurt airport.

At the heart of Germany's campaigns to protect the environment are the *Bürgerinitiativen* (Citizens' Initiatives) whose federal umbrella organisation recorded over 1,000 member groups in the mid 1970s. These groups grew up gradually over the 1950s and 1960s across a multitude of local issues, and to be active in them was considered a proper expression of civic pride.

As the campaigns moved from very local issues to issues of broader concern, particularly over the siting of nuclear power stations, it eventually became clear to ordinary people that protecting the environment cut across existing political loyalties, highlighted dubious democratic processes and called into question the very direction of West German society. The experiences at Wyhl in 1975 were typical.

Farmers were worried about the effect of radiation on their products and local people resented the damage to their countryside, but they were all shocked to discover that both the state president and the economics minister of Baden-Württemburg were on the boards of companies applying for the contract to build the power plant.[1]

Die Grünen have been called the 'watermelon party' – green on the outside but red on the inside – and the debate about whether the Greens are simply socialists with a green stripe or a new political force altogether goes on inside as well as outside the party. The role of the left in the development of Die Grünen and the reaction of the party to the left need to be understood in the context of Germany's history.

The Social-Democrat party (SPD) and the Communist party (KPD) were founded in 1875 and 1918 respectively and banned by Hitler in 1933. They were both reinstated after the Second World War but the Communist party was again banned in 1956, this time by Adenauer. The SPD went on to shed its Marxist image and develop a brand of politics that meant it was able to form a 'grand coalition' with the right-wing Christian-Democrats (CDU/CSU) in 1967 and then, two years later, a government with the minority liberal Free Democrats (FDP).

By this repositioning the SPD alienated much of its left wing. They took mostly to *Äusserparlamentarische Opposition* (ÄPO — extra-parliamentary opposition), though some joined the reformed Communist party, which was legalised again as the DKP in the context of chancellor Willi Brandt's policy of detente with Eastern Europe.

Among the best-known groups of the ÄPO were the various K-groups, mostly fundamentalist communists inspired by Mao Zedong; the Red Army Fraction, who turned to terrorism; and the 'Spontis'. The Spontis took a more anarchist aproach to politics and were inspired by the Italian spontaneist movement of the 1960s. They are fond of satirical sayings, apparently superficial but containing very serious messages. A favourite is: 'Marx is dead, Lenin is dead, and I'm not feeling too well either.' Others include: 'Germans leave Germany and then there will be peace,', 'God knows everything but says nothing, I know nothing but say everything,' and 'The Communist party is the foreskin of the working class, when things get serious it draws back.'[2]

Partly in reaction to the 1968 student movement and its

declared intention to 'march through the institutions', the SPD government began a campaign against the left which included the notorious *Berufsverbot* (job prohibition), a policy of not employing activists (or former activists) from leftist organisations for any government jobs, including teaching posts. This behaviour from the main party of the left, which seemed to have forgotten the days when it was discriminated against itself, put the SPD beyond the pale for many people. Perhaps inevitably, the non-violent 'alternative' left became more entrenched than discouraged and flourished in an atmosphere of opposition to all established political parties.

The founders of Die Grünen, conscious of past discrimination against social groups in Germany, were determined that the new party would be inclusive of as many disenfranchised groups as possible, and they saw the 'alternative' left as effectively disenfranchised.

It would be wrong, however, to assume that the 'alternative' movement in West Germany is uniquely the terrain of the extra-parliamentary left. Although focussed in the bigger cities such as Frankfurt, Hamburg and of course West Berlin, people involved in 'living alternatively' reflect a broad spectrum of political, social and economic backgrounds and their projects and activities cover a very wide range. Doctors and lawyers have established collectives, thousands of self-help groups have grown up covering everything from practical solutions to child care to drug abuse and homelessness, and spiritual renewal movements flourish. New lifestyles are being tested in communes, and there are innumerable initiatives for environmental protection and renovation. The 'subculture' has its own newspapers and publishing houses, its own theatre groups and rock bands, and the goods and services it demands have created many new businesses and cooperatives. (Indeed so 'established' has the 'alternative' scene become that it is now experiencing the same problems and constraints as mainstream businesses and activities – growth and merger have become prerequisites for survival. A growing number of projects require public money to keep going and many are now dependent on funding from Die Grünen, who put much of their income into *Ökofunds* which are administered at State level to acceptable projects.)

As in other West European countries the peace movement in West Germany is made up of a variety of groups, not all of whom share the same definition of 'peace'. The *Ostpolitik* of the SPD/FDP governmental alliance of the early 1970s lulled many Germans into believing that disarmament and peace matters were 'in good hands'. So much so that when the famous 'twin track' decision was taken in 1979 to place cruise and Pershing missiles in Europe, the German peace movement had to be shaken awake by their colleagues in other countries. The growing Green movement and its interest in electoral politics at this time did much to loosen the grip of the traditional left political groups on the peace issue and they were eventually able to claim the 'peace party' title for themselves. One of the parties in the SPV-Die Grünen electoral coalition of 1979, the Aktionsgemeinschaft Unabhängiger Deutscher (AUD — Action Community of Independent Germans), was a party with a long tradition of neutralism, and two people who played major roles in the founding of Die Grünen, Petra Kelly and Roland Vogt, consistently argued the intimate relationship between peace and ecology.

Without doubt the West German electoral system has played an important role in the development of Green politics in West Germany. Voters have felt able to use their second vote (for a party list) to 'see what the Greens can do', knowing that a freak result giving a relatively unknown party a majority would be impossible. They have also been able to give the new brand of politics a chance to prove itself not only on local councils but also in the *Länder* parliaments. Between 1979 and March 1983, when they eventually entered the Bundestag, Die Grünen enjoyed steadily improving results locally, gaining many seats on local councils and in three State parliaments – Baden-Württemberg in 1980, Lower Saxony and then Hesse in 1982. Their first attempt at the federal elections in 1980 showed, by comparison, a disappointing result of 1.5%. Certainly the confrontation between the then chancellor Helmut Schmidt (SPD) and the flamboyant right-wing Bavarian Franz-Josef Strauss (CDU/CSU) dominated the elections, persuading many to opt for the SPD as the lesser evil, but the 'not yet' message from the voters to the Greens might well have been issued even in a more low-key election.

The considerable executive power held by the *Länder* parliaments also meant that the entry of the Greens attracted considerable publicity and interest, particularly in Hesse where Die Grünen held the balance of power after September

1982. The extensive coverage given to the fierce arguments that took place over the conditions under which the Greens would 'tolerate' an SPD government meant that by March 1983 most Germans had at least some idea of the issues that interested the party.

Of significant importance to the beginnings of Die Grünen is the cash that can be gained through contesting an election. The generous financial payments to parties were extended to the first direct elections to the European Parliament in 1979, which were run on simple State or federal lists. So when the electoral alliance of groups that eventually evolved into Die Grünen gained 3.2% of the vote in these elections they obtained 4.8 million DM. Having run a 'shoe-string' campaign costing about 300,000 DM, this meant a clear profit of 4.5 million DM — a considerable sum of money that was used to establish local parties and the national party infrastructure. The French Greens, by contrast, who scored a larger national vote of 4.7%, incurred large debts which overshadowed their future development (see Chapter 6).

It has not only been disaffection with the established political parties that has motivated so many people in Germany to move into informal economic and social structures or to champion the causes of peace, human justice and a healthy environment. There was also a growing revolt against the values and objectives of the formal, well regulated but ruthlessly modernising and impersonal West German society. Young postwar Germans were offered material compensation for the ghastly historical error of Nazism, and part of the disillusionment of the youth of the late 1960s and 1970s can be attributed to a generation coming to terms with their country's history and finding the compensations offered by their parents' generation not just inadequate but inappropriate. They see the Green movement and Die Grünen as a way of refreshing the pages of Germany's history book, with their generation taking on the heroic role of assuring an ecologically sustainable future for all generations to come.

Early Years (1977-1983)

When *The Times* announced a clear victory for Helmut Kohl and his Christian-Democrat/Liberal coalition in the March

1983 elections to the West German parliament, it followed its headline with a boldly emphasised 'Greens heading for Bundestag'. Like many newspapers, *The Times* devoted nearly as many column-inches to the 5.6% and 28 seats won by Die Grünen in those elections as it did to reporting the end of 13 years of a Social-Democrat-led majority in the Bundestag. But however it may have appeared to the outside world, Die Grünen did not become a success overnight. That result in March 1983 came after six years of steady but frequently difficult development for the West German Green party.

Between 1977 and 1979 modest, but nevertheless cumulatively important, electoral gains were made by small parties standing on peace and environmental issues in local elections all over Germany. But behind the election results fierce arguments were going on between these different parties, which had sprung up from all points of the left/right political spectrum. Coalitions, splits and new mergers took place amid accusations of infiltration by the far right or left, as clashing parties and groups sought to make electoral pacts.

For most of this period, the mainstream of the anti-nuclear and environmental movements looked on with deep suspicion. On the whole they felt that these attempts to give voice to their concerns through a political party smacked more of opportunism than anything else. Many felt that a move into party politics would be a regressive step, but at the same time they could propose no other strategy for their movement which was undeniably at a crossroads. Traditional pressure-group activity was simply not producing satisfactory results. When some citizens' groups did try taking their environmental protests to local elections they gained a few seats and this encouraged them to come together and eventually form State-wide parties.

It was the June 1979 elections to the European Parliament and the financial gains that could be made by standing in elections which began to turn people's minds to a nationwide environmental party. One of the first local Green parties to be founded (in 1977 in Lower Saxony), the Grüne Liste Umweltschutz (GLU — Green List Environmental Protection) had already taken steps towards establishing a national party by influencing the development of GLU parties in other states – Hamburg,   Hesse,   North-Rhine-Westphalia, Rhineland-Palatinate and Baden-Württemberg. Activists in the GLU came principally from nature protection groups but the party had also managed to attract a growing number of members from groups concerned with social issues.[3] Then, on 12 July 1978, Dr Herbert Gruhl, ex-member of the Christian-Democratic Party (CDU), author of *A Planet is Plundered*[4] and coiner of the famous slogan 'neither left nor right, we are in front', founded the Grüne Aktion Zukunft (GAZ — Green Action Future) with the express intention of setting up a national Green party.

Gruhl's initiative startled the small parties who were battling it out in the *Länder* and some other groups who were beginning to contemplate taking up electoral politics. These included members of the Bundesverband der Bürgerinitiativen (BBU — Union of Citizens' Initiatives), an umbrella organisation of anti-nuclear and other ecological activists. Talk of the possibility of a new political party made other groups prick up their ears too. Particularly interested were the anthroposophists (followers of Rudolph Steiner), members of the Free International University who were considered as belonging to the 'non-dogmatic' left, some 'Sponti' and anarchist groups as well as some disillusioned members of the Social-Democrat party (SPD).

Meetings held to establish some unity between the left and right Green parties and the non-party groups were not immediately successful. Eventually, in February 1979, GAZ and GLU agreed to contest the European elections in coalition with the Grüne Liste Schleswig-Holstein (GLSH) and the Aktionsgemeinschaft Unabhängiger Deutscher (AUD), which since its foundation in 1965 had been mostly active in southern Germany, and had adopted ecological issues in the 1970s. The Sonstige Politische Vereinigung Die Grünen (SPV-Die Grünen – Alternative Political Alliance, The Greens) was founded on 16-17 March 1979 by 500 delegates at a meeting in Frankfurt-Sindelfingen.

Two members of the executive of the BBU, Roland Vogt and Petra Kelly, joined SPV-Die Grünen at this time, and it also received support from a number of well-known intellectuals and activists, including Heinrich Böll and Rudi Dutschke. Noticeably absent from this new political formation were the Bunte Liste : Wehrt Euch! Initiativen für Demokratie und Umweltschnutz (BLW — Multicoloured List : Resist! Initiatives for Democracy and Environmental Protection) from Hamburg and the Alternative Liste für Demokratie und Umweltschutz (AL — Alternative List for Democracy and Environmental Protection) from Berlin. These were parties that had grown up under the influence of the Kommunistischer Bund (KB — Communist League).

Two major issues, a nuclear-free Europe and a Europe of regions, made up the platform of SPV-Die Grünen in the 1979 European elections. The result was 3.2% of the vote and 4.5 million DM in the bank.

The cash was used to set up national and State offices, and many new members and activists were attracted by this new force in German politics. Membership rose to about 10,000 by the end of the year. The Multicoloured and Alternative Lists became interested again and many of the small communist 'K-groups' dissolved as intense discussions opened over a possible cooperation. The left/right arguments now broke on the national scene and dominated a series of meetings and seminars that preceded a congress at Offenbach in October 1979. Although this congress was supposed to come up with a programme for the new national party, argument raged not only over a contentious economic programme but also over whether membership of a united Green party could be compatible with membership of other parties. In the end, a compromise was reached whereby the decision was left to the local branches.

It was the Offenbach congress that resulted in the famous 'four pillars' on which the party stands. Most of the assembly wanted the new party to represent other possibilities to either socialism or capitalism but the left-oriented delegates insisted on socialism and were reluctant about adopting non-violence as a fundamental principle. The meeting became steadily more heated and frustrated. August Haussleiter:

> I myself had been almost desperate with the situation because there were 3,000 people screaming their own positions in the convention hall. This person kept saying, 'Don't give up. Don't give up. They're getting tired.' Although agreement seemed impossible, I took a piece of paper and wrote four words on it: ecology, social responsibility, grassroots democracy, and non-violence. Then I called Gruhl (leader of the conservatives) and Reents (leader of the left) into the room where the journalists were and said 'Sign.' We then went back into the convention hall and announced, 'We have a programme.'[5]

These four pillars are now legendary and often quoted as the key to Die Grünen's success. However, it has also been suggested that, because they can be interpreted very broadly, and, even more importantly, separately from one another, they may one day prove too fragile to support the huge and variegated body that has to stand on them. Helmut Lippelt, a historian from Lower Saxony and present member for Die Grünen in the Bundestag, reckons that the real glue that held Die Grünen together in the early days was 'Success!'

The pressure under which those first uniting principles were established was also reflected in the founding congress of Die Grünen which took place in Karlsruhe on 12-13 January 1980. Lukas Beckmann, the first national office manager and subsequently a speaker on the *Bundesvorstand* (national executive committee), caused the clock in the hall to be stopped several times so that delegates would not leave for their trains before the constitution was finally approved:

> The Karlsruhe congress engineered what many had perceived as impossible: the merging of the more conservative forces such as the GLU and AUD which had so far spearheaded the efforts to set up Green parties at *Länder* level and the 'alternative' and 'multicoloured' lists with their background of 'new left' politics and, in particular, the participation of avantgarde communist parties such as the KB and KPD.[6]

Although the party only scored a modest 1.5% in the 1980 federal elections, the build-up of electoral successes in local councils continued. At *Länder* level Die Grünen passed the magic 5% barrier first in Bremen in October 1979, gaining 4 seats. Then came 6 seats in Baden-Württemberg in March 1980; 9 in Berlin (Alternative List) in May 1981; 11 in Lower Saxony in March 1982, 9 in Hesse in September 1982 and 8 in Hamburg in December 1982. After another great struggle with the 'mosaic' of their economic programme at a delegate congress in Sindelfingen in January 1983, Die Grünen eventually entered the West German Bundestag in March of that year with 28 seats (including one non-voting representative from West Berlin). As the *Times* leader of 8 March put it:

> ...the {West German political} system will probably benefit from the presence for the first time in

the Bundestag of the environmental, pacifist
Greens. Their 27 members will represent a whole
swathe of young people and intellectuals who felt
they had no political home in the traditional
parties, and their ideas and unconventional methods – even their dress – could bring a welcome
breath of fresh air to the political scene.

Although they were not the first Green party to gain
representation in a national parliament (the Swiss Greens
won their first seat in 1979, and Ecolo and Agalev won a total
of nine seats in the Belgian Senate and Chamber of Representatives in 1981), Die Grünen attracted the most attention.
However the interest of the outside world concentrated
mainly on the intense internal arguments that were going on
within the party. Finding themselves in opposition alongside
the SPD instead of in opposition to it meant that Die Grünen
had to elaborate new political strategies at a national level.
Hard enough for any new political party, but particularly
hard for one committed to a new style of doing politics that
included inviting the press into all their meetings. Die
Grünen literally chose to conduct their adolescence in
public, with the bitter debates between rival points of view
becoming a matter of passionate absorption to protagonists,
friendly and hostile observers and professional commentators alike.

The strategy debate came to concentrate around the fact
that Die Grünen held the balance of power in the *Land*
parliament of Hesse after the elections of September 1982.
The party refused to contemplate any coalition with or
tolerance of an SPD government. Although Die Grünen lost
two seats in fresh elections in September 1983 the deadlock
was not resolved. Earlier the same year in Hamburg, the
Grüne Alternative Liste (GAL) had already found itself in a
similar situation. They offered to tolerate an SPD government but on conditions that the SPD found impossible to
accept. This time a second election in December 1982 saw the
Greens lose a seat and the SPD gain an absolute majority.
The result in Hamburg, along with their own drop in the
polls, encouraged the Hesse Greens to accept conditions for
'tolerating' an SPD government in the State at their October
1983 conference. They were certainly also influenced by
opinion polls that pronounced the electorate in favour of
such a step.

Die Grünen split into two factions over this strategy and
the argument was even supplemented by a dispute as to
whether it was a good thing to have different factions within
the party or not! Because the story of Die Grünen has been
dominated by this internal tussle and because the German
Greens offer only a more flagrant example of the debates that
go on in all the Green parties, it is worth looking at them in
more detail.

The Factions in Die Grünen

Although there is a fondness for mixing all the factions (also
called currents or tendencies) together and then spreading
them out onto one straight line, this is a confusing and
inaccurate way of looking at the internal dynamics of the
party. It is perhaps easier to think of them as three overlap-
ping but different layers:

1) the strategy debate between Fundis (fundamentalists)
   and Realos (realistic reformers);
2) the left/right political currents;
3) the special interest groups.

1. The Strategy Debate

Fundis are to be found throughout the party, but they are
particularly noticeable on the State and national committees
and executive bodies. They are also in the parliamentary
groups but as a minority. They believe that the party must
avoid anything that would undermine the broad critique that
Greens have brought to bear on industrial society and often
argue that the major parties resemble each other more than
either of them resembles the Greens. They view any compromise with another party as legitimising 'politics as usual'
and delaying the moment of radical change required by the
logic of Green politics. As Rudolf Bahro graphically put it in
Hamburg in 1984, compromise means 'cleaning the dragon's
teeth and wiping away its excrement'.

But not all fundamentalists arrive at their strategy position for the same reasons. Bahro, exiled from East Germany
in 1979 after two years in prison, immediately joined Die

Grünen and went on to inspire Greens everywhere. The logic of his thinking and writing led him to identify the personal and spiritual revolution that a shift to a Green way of life would require. However, the trail of Bahro's intellect also led him to make that perfect circle of logic that can repel rather than embrace reality. His fundamentalism takes the form of asking society to take a heroic and collective plunge into profound change, guided by faith.

Petra Kelly, perhaps the most famous member of Die Grünen, is also driven by a deep spirituality and a commitment to the personal dimension of politics. She is described by people of all opinions as a 'real fundamentalist', unprepared to compromise on the key life and death principles that were established when Die Grünen was formed and when she coined the celebrated description of an 'anti-party party':

> There is not a little bit of cancer or a little bit of malnutrition or a little bit of death or a little bit of social injustice or a little bit of torture. It does not help us in any way if we begin accepting lower and safer levels of, for example, radioactivity or lower and safer levels of, for example, lead or dioxin. We must speak out clear, loudly and courageously, if we know that there are no safe levels.[7]

Her position is that Die Grünen should only work with 'truly ecological partners' who are genuinely committed to 'new and radical and non-violent and feminist as well as pacifist approaches'. She does not see that the SPD falls into this category yet.

Another fundamentalist, Jutta Ditfurth, one of three speakers on the party's national executive committee, puts it like this:

> Reformism, in its Green-Socialdemocratic form, starts out from the assumption that there will be no radical break in our society. The time for revolution is past, so the illogical conclusion is drawn that reformism is the only option. This is pretty sloppy political thinking. For any serious analysis must take into account the fact that every variant of reformism has proven itself historically bankrupt.[8]

Fundamentalists also worry about losing contact with the activists in the broader movement and the danger of losing their radicalism in the softening environment of parliamentary posts – a fate suffered by many '1968ers' all over Europe. Manfred Zieran feels that it doesn't matter if Die Grünen are in parliament or not. 'What counts is the existence of a strong social opposition movement which has broken with present consciousness. Then the space will exist in which things can be changed in a legal or parliamentary fashion.'[9]

Realistic reformers, or Realos, argue that the advanced stage of the developing global crisis requires action within the existing power structures. 'No one can say how we are to manage a revolution, or even a small-scale social transformation.'[10] To maintain a self-righteous attitude and oppositional attitude towards politics will condemn the Greens to the sidelines while the more powerful and well-established interests continue to destroy the environment and undermine the social fabric for the short-term goals of industrialism. Realos say that they don't just want to be against polluted rivers but they want to set about cleaning them up. They acknowledge that many people accept that the Greens have been asking the right questions, but reckon the time has come for them to start providing some answers. According to opinion polls Realos are in the majority in the party and they inevitably predominate in the parliaments at both *Land* and national level.

Their best-known spokespeople are Joschka Fischer, formerly of the Sponti movement and from 1985 to 1987 Minister for Environment and Energy in the Hesse parliament, and Otto Schily, a lawyer famous for his support of civil liberties in the 1970s who was re-elected to the Bundestag in 1987. These two are now known as 'Superrealos' and they have recently been questioning their party's commitment to taking West Germany out of NATO and advocating things like courting the 'yuppie' vote and investigating Green capitalism; all in order to keep the SPD looking to the Greens for its coalitions instead of rightwards towards the Liberals (FDP). This they feel would marginalise the Greens for ever. Otto Schily has described the Greens as natural junior partners of the SPD:

> Some sections of the Greens underestimate the dangers of a shift to the right, as is clear from their

formula of the lesser evil, and they underestimate the dangers of a conservative foreign and security policy. We must take into consideration what effect our rejection of a realistic left coalition perspective would have on the right and how this would clear the terrain for rightist policies.[11]

Less extreme Realos believe that such compromise towards the SPD is not necessary and that a clarification and elaboration of Die Grünen's policies, particularly in difficult and sensitive areas such as economics and defence, is what is needed. Christa Vennegerts, one of the speakers of the Bundestag group, feels this would restore the party to its vanguard role and cause the other parties to reorientate towards the Greens. All Realos agree that the the time has come for 'constructive' politics and they condemn the simplistic 'oppositional' stance of the Fundis.

2. *The Left/Right Political Currents*

The second layer of political currents is to be found spread, rather unevenly, over the Fundi/Realo strategy spectrum.

The absorption of people from a background of left politics into Die Grünen has had both positive and negative results. The many groups active on the political terrain to the left of the SPD during the 1960s and 1970s had not managed to organise themselves enough to gain parliamentary representation. So when Die Grünen was founded they were anxious not to be excluded from any successful political grouping that did occur. Many found working in the Green party hard going, especially if they came from the more dogmatic K-groups, but they were able to make the 'transformation' because they genuinely sought a new and relevant political and personal philosophy. They definitely brought valuable political experience to the new party. Wilhelm Knabe, a speaker of the federal executive until 1984 and since 1987 a member of the Bundestag, puts it like this:

From a practical point of view, the chief lesson for the ecologists was organising – how to organise a conference, a demonstration, or a boycott. A great deal was learnt in this area. They also emphasised

> the role of capital in environmental destruction.
> And from us they learned that external rela-
> tionships between people and nature have a great
> effect, that not everything can be explained by
> internal, societal forces. In addition, I think many
> people from the K-groups found it a relief – in fact,
> a pure psychological release – to be able to be *for*
> something.[12]

Others either had more difficulty in making the philosophical
shift or had no intention of doing so. The Z-fraction (Marxists
who had split away from the Communist League) organised
in 1980-81 within Die Grünen around a newspaper called
Moderne Zeiten with supporter groups called Socialist Political Initiatives. In their founding declaration they saw their
task as 'keeping open the possibility of constantly making
new links with the grassroots movements' and 'fighting
against any tendency towards bureaucratisation or cooption by the bourgeois state'.[13] They saw class-conscious-
ness as being at a very low ebb in Germany and that a way of
changing this would be via Die Grünen.[14]

In 1981 the party held a tribunal to hear evidence against
this group remaining in the party but this ruled in their
favour, a decision felt to have been subsequently justified by
the success of the Hamburg Greens in a broad left alliance
known as the Green-Alternative List (GAL), and of the Berlin
Greens with the Alternative List (AL). One of the people who
argued passionately against the expulsion of the Marxists at
this tribunal was Petra Kelly. Her experience in the Bundestag *Fraktion* has subsequently caused her to change her mind
as, like many people in the party, she became increasingly
uneasy about the efforts of the left-wing activists to pull the
party frankly into a position 'left of the SPD':

> The former Communists became critical of Marx,
> left their tradition and came to us – but many
> never really left behind their loyalty to that group.
> In times of crisis it is stronger than their loyalty to
> the Greens, and it is sometimes brutal. They make
> everything subservient to it and refuse to look at
> the cause of a conflict, convincing themselves
> instead that it is another group who is causing
> them to struggle. Sometimes they create an artifi-
> cial struggle that does not even exist.[15]

Thomas Ebermann, at present member of the Bundestag, and Rainer Trampert, who left his job as speaker on the federal executive to work with Ebermann in 1987, are the main spokespeople for this group. Both are from Hamburg and both came from the Communist League. Although they have difficulties with the phenomenon of Rudolf Bahro, many of the Marxist-oriented left are in favour of the strategy of fundamental opposition. Trampert and Ebermann emphasise that the parliamentary existence of Die Grünen must only be an expression of 'irreconcilable opposition to and critique of existing conditions'.

Another main spokesperson for the left is party speaker Jutta Ditfurth. Her statements suggesting that the freeing of terrorists would be not pardon but justice caused an uproar, with even her supporters reduced to excusing it as simplistic and exaggerated. Co-speaker Regina Michalik went further when she asked for a 'broad show of unity' with the Autonomen group who shot at policemen during a demonstration at Frankfurt airport, killing two and wounding nine more.[16]

There is deep disagreement among the Marxist-oriented Greens about how to win the theoretical debate within the party, some favouring a sort of 'bunker' policy – holding on to certain posts and trying to lead the theoretical debate from there – and others preferring to seek to establish a new 'revolutionary bloc' made up of eco-socialists from inside and outside the party. This tactical confusion is comparable with the sectarian squabbles that prevented the small left-wing groups from coming together before the Greens came on the scene.

Other 'eco-socialists' of more social-democratic flavour, many from the SPD, see 'compromise and integration', the strategy of the Realos, as the best way forward.

The eco-libertarians form a very much smaller political current within Die Grünen but bring to the Green canvas, like the eco-socialists, a paint-brush dipped in a different ideological pot. They are particularly influential in Baden-Württemberg. The eco-libertarians attack the heritage and ideological baggage that many socialists have brought to Die Grünen and by doing so have become labelled the right wing of the party. Their programme tends towards the 'value conservatives' (so called to distinguish them from the customary 'structure conservatives') whose best-known spokesman was Herbert Gruhl. He left Die Grünen, along with

several others, disaffected by the decision not to expel the
Communists and by the eventual adoption of what was seen
as an 'impossible' economic programme.

Gruhl founded another party called the Ökologisch-
Demokratische Partei (ÖDP — Ecological Democratic
Party) which never attracted much support. The eco-
libertarians, while regretting the loss of the value conservative dimension in Die Grünen, represent a more centrist-
liberal approach to politics. They claim not to identify with
either the Realo or Fundi strategy but say in their declaration published in the *Tageszeitung* of 7-8 March 1984:

> For ecological politics we need to be relaxed and
> patient. There is no fixed image of the kind of
> society we seek. We want to create the conditions
> in which it will be *possible* to think realistically
> about fundamental social change...democratic
> change can only come about through com-
> promise...to take part in parliament is meaningful
> only if what we want to achieve is a reform of
> existing conditions.{Therefore the Greens}should
> have no fear or hesitation in entering into negoti-
> ations, and not only with the SPD {because} a
> privileged link with social democracy {must be
> rejected}.

3. Special Interest Groups

Most members of both the party committees and the parliaments have one or more special interest that they pursue
from their posts. They link to outside movements either
directly or with other like-minded members in various
working groups. This brings a richness of experience into the
party which is not always used to the full. The *Länder* have
their own working groups which send delegates to national
working groups. But as these groups have been unable to
provide the sort of back-up needed by the national parliamentarians, the Bundestag 'fraction' have been obliged to establish their own research and policy development groups.
Bringing together what are sometimes conflicting opinions
on the various topics for, say, election manifestos, remains a
difficult task, and the end result frequently bears the mark of

unhappy compromise.

One special interest group which has managed to make considerable impact on both party style and programmatic content is that of women. Several conferences devoted to women's issues have been held, a *Feminat* of six women headed the national parliamentary group in 1984 and all but one of the *Länder* lists for the 1987 elections to the Bundestag were headed by women. The exception was in Hamburg where the success of an all-women list for the State elections in November 1986 put the local party into a generous enough mood to give their number one spot to a man – Thomas Ebermann. The result of these elections was a Green parliamentary 'fraction' of 25 women and 19 men, the first time in German history that any parliamentary group has had a majority of women.

In collaboration with feminist lawyers the Bundestag women's group has prepared a detailed proposal for legislation on women's discrimination which received its first reading in the 1987-88 parliamentary session.

Die Grünen after 1983

Behind the dramatic reporting of Die Grünen's internal conflicts the first Green representatives in the Bundestag were judged to have been industrious and to have used the possibilities available to them with reasonable success.[17] They set out to compete with the SPD for the title of 'genuine' opposition party and to use the Bundestag as a forum for explaining Green politics to the people at large. They were also very conscious of their pre-election commitment to give representation to minority groups who were otherwise deprived of a lobby. This role was summed up in the image of the parliamentarians being the 'kicking leg' of the movement in which the other leg was firmly planted.

Legislative success has been limited to the passage of a bill to prohibit the importation of meat from a threatened species of turtle, but the number of bills presented by Die Grünen, along with a large number of verbal and written questions, influenced debates both within and outside of the parliament. If unsatisfied with parliamentary responses then the 'fraction' simply held a press conference to put its own view.

This system worked well until the mid-term rotation of

parliamentarians took place. It was preceded by a stiff debate in the party about the wisdom of the rotation principle which was intended to avoid undue concentration of power in one person. It was argued that rotation only shortened the term of power, which remained absolute, and did not prevent people remaining in powerful positions by skilful sideways moves within the party. There was also the problem of 'wastage' of experienced people. The intention was that each rotating team should work as assistants to the sitting MPs. In the event this proved difficult, as many people had to consider their pre-election jobs which could only be held for them as long as they were actually sitting as a member of parliament. The party decided that MPs who had been elected under the principle of rotation must rotate, and in the Bundestag all but Petra Kelly did so. However, out of the seven Die Grünen members of the European Parliament, elected in 1984, only two rotated on time, and a third did so eventually. Mid-term rotation has now been abolished and eight of the Die Grünen MPs elected in 1987 are in their second term.

The effect of mid-term rotation on the first Green Bundestag group was significant. For example, the press, who had showered attention on the 'stars' of the first two years, lost interest in the new and inexperienced faces and began staying away from the routine open meetings and even press conferences. This weakened the 'kicking leg' function of the 'fraction'. A great success of the first parliamentary session, however, was the role of Otto Schily in the investigations into the Flick scandal. It remains one of the best examples of how elected Greens can puncture the protective political cushion and expose to the critical gaze of ordinary citizens the corrupt relationship that many major industries have with government and the political process. In this case tax irregularities of a big industrial concern involved substantial payments to political parties, and Schily employed his considerable legal skills to effectively force the SPD to reject attempts to whitewash the matter and oblige Chancellor Kohl to cancel his amnesty for the main culprits. Resignations included the economics minister Count Lambsdorff who was prosecuted for his involvement.

However, the first term of Die Grünen in the Bundestag was somewhat overshadowed by events in Hesse. With hindsight, it is interesting to compare the strategy of the SPD in Hesse with their national strategy up to the 1987 elections to the federal parliament. Despite obviously deep arguments about how to deal with this troublesome new party and its effects on SPD policy and strategy, the SPD acted with considerable subtlety if not always with success. They exploited the considerable talents of some of their younger politicians, like Oskar Lafontaine in Saarland, to great effect, and managed on the whole to use the 'fundi' position of their leader Johannes Rau as a foil for the 'realo' position adopted towards Die Grünen by Holger Börner in Hesse and his colleagues such as Lafontaine, Gerhard Schröder in Lower Saxony and Björn Engholm in Schleswig-Holstein. By comparison Die Grünen deployed their differences like cudgels, and on themselves rather than on the opposition.

After the deadlock between the parties had not been resolved by the September 1983 elections to the Hesse parliament, Die Grünen and the SPD entered into long negotiations over a 'toleration' agreement. Die Grünen certainly wished to use what became known as the 'experiment' in Hesse in a positive way, but the SPD were equally keen to use it as a way of discrediting Die Grünen. However, outside pressure on both parties to stick with the negotiations and to form a partnership grew – from opinion polls and from the press (both alternative and establishment). Election results from other *Länder* added extra incentives to go ahead. In March 1984 in Baden-Württemburg Die Grünen increased their vote from 5.3% to 8%, winning 9 seats in the *Land* parliament, while the SPD vote remained stable and the FDP and CDU votes dropped. In June, the Hesse Greens voted to pass the SPD budget and elect Börner as prime minister. This 'toleration' agreement broke down in December over a decision to subsidise the expansion of the Nukem/ Alkem nuclear enrichment plant in Hanau. However, immediate negotiations were started over a full coalition.

In the meantime the party's steady electoral gains continued. Die Grünen entered the European Parliament with 8.2% and 7 seats in June. In the autumn local elections the party crossed the 5% barrier for the first time in Saarland and Rhineland-Palatinate, and won 8.6% in North Rhine-Westphalia – promising results from three of the four remaining *Länder* where the Greens had yet to enter the State parliament.

But the elections to the State parliaments in Saarland and Berlin in March 1985 brought mixed results for Die Grünen. In Saarland where a toppling of the CDU was on the cards, SPD leader Oskar Lafontaine made a pre-election coalition

offer to the Greens announcing that 'progress has a name...it
is called eco-socialism'. Although the Saarland Greens did
produce a toleration proposal for Lafontaine, its flabbiness
only inspired him to go for an all-out majority with a 'work,
peace and environment' campaign. His 49.2% gave the SPD a
majority of seats in the Saarland for the first time and Die
Grünen polled a miserable 2.5%. In Berlin, the Alternative
Liste also offered terms for their toleration of a possible SPD
government. This time their tough nature made it easy for
SPD leader Hans Apel to refuse them. In this case, however,
the SPD share of the Berlin vote fell by 5.9% to a postwar low
of 32.4% while Die Grünen nearly doubled their vote to
10.6%, gaining 15 seats. This meant that the CDU stayed in
government with 46.6% supported by the 10.4% of the FDP.

If Holger Börner had any difficulty in interpreting these
results he got a clearer message from the local elections in
Hesse which were also held at this time. His party made up
ground lost to the CDU five years before and Die Grünen
increased their vote by over 5% to 7.1%. On several local
councils in Hesse 'red-green' coalitions had already fun-
ctioned for some time. In May 1985 Börner offered Die
Grünen a coalition which included the post of minister for
environment and energy.

Die Grünen were deeply divided over whether this coalition should take place and the debate raged over the summer.
An election to the *Land* parliament of North Rhine-
Westphalia, also in May, did nothing to clarify matters. Led
by Johannes Rau himself, the SPD in North Rhine-
Westphalia went for a no-compromise win and a strong
attack. He was greatly assisted by two own goals from Die
Grünen. Firstly they produced a 400-page manifesto containing the full range of views and divisions within the State
party. Buried within this programme was a resolution to
legalise sex between adults and children. Although a congress was quickly called to remove the offending resolution
the damage had been done. At the same time two members of
the Bundestag, Antje Vollmer and Christa Nickels, sent a
letter to Red Army Fraction prisoners on hunger strike. A
genuine if naive gesture according to Otto Schily, but again
damaging to the party. The SPD scored a 52.1% victory in
North Rhine-Westphalia and Die Grünen languished below
the 5% mark with 4.6%.

A party conference at Hagen in June produced a lot of
'position taking' but no serious analysis of what had hap-

pened in Hesse or elsewhere. Bahro left the party in despair. In September 1985 a demonstrator, Günter Sare, was killed during an encounter with police water-cannons at an anti-fascist demonstration in Frankfurt, and when the Hesse party agreed to the coalition terms one month later, party speaker Jutta Ditfurth issued a furious statement on behalf of the federal and executive committees of the party which had both rejected the terms of the coalition. 'Only 18 days after the murder of Günter Sare by police the Greens in the State parliament of Hesse have decided to go into coalition with the SPD, to join sides with the rulers.'[18]

Under the coalition agreement for matters concerning the environment, waste disposal/recycling, energy, water, conservation and emission control were brought together under one ministry for environment and energy. Die Grünen were to have the minister's post (taken by Joschka Fischer, until then member of the Bundestag), and one secretary of state in the ministry. Attempts to negotiate a minister for women's affairs had failed, but a secretary of state post was created with a department and budget to deal with women's affairs. This post was taken by Marita Haibach.

When Fischer was finally sworn in on 12 December 1985 reactions varied. Even his detractors in Die Grünen had to admit that 'if anyone could handle the challenge then it's Joschka', and the Berlin alternative paper *Tageszeitung* remarked jubilantly, 'The long march through the institutions – one made it ' (11 March 1985). However, many people were doing calculations on their fingers as the next elections to the Bundestag began to loom. The prospect of Die Grünen holding the balance of power there had to be taken seriously. Johannes Rau carefully distanced his party from the Hesse 'deal', a strategy he maintained remorselessly right up to the January 1987 elections. The CDU/CSU government's spokesman in the Bundestag, Alfred Dregger, announced: 'A red-green alliance in Bonn would mean...inflation, unemployment and state bankruptcy.' With less finesse, FDP representative Dieter-Julius Cronenberg likened the entry of Die Grünen into government to letting 'bacteria into the bloodstream'. Industry hit the nail more accurately on the head when one spokesman commented: 'When the Greens exploit the environmental law to its full stops and commas, it's going to be torture.'[19]

At the Offenburg conference held 13-15 December the Fundi faction had their revenge for what they saw as the

Hesse 'coup'. A mid-conference trip to join a demonstration against the building of a nuclear waste reprocessing plant at Wackersdorf brought delegates back to the roots of their protest. On returning to Offenburg, a Fundi-dominated party executive was confirmed by 468 votes to 214.

Only in comparison to 1985 could 1986 be seen as a quiet year for Die Grünen. The warring factions did become reasonably amicable, taking note perhaps of opinion polls that placed the party on the borderline of 5%. A conference at Hagen in February was remarkable for its harmony. An appearance by Hans Janssen of IG-Metall represented the first formal recognition of the party by the hitherto hostile trade unions. A 'detoxification' and waste treatment programme for the chemical industry was approved.

Then came the accident at Chernobyl. The SPD ended its wavering over nuclear power and even the FDP voted for a 'review' of the country's reprocessing industry, including Wackersdorf, where violent clashes had again taken place between police and demonstrators.[20] At the Easter conference at Hanover the Fundis won the day again and voted to end all use of nuclear power immediately and to terminate the coalition in Hesse. Even Joschka Fischer was moved to announce that the accident had made a closedown of the nuclear industry a matter of emergency. But the conference also recognised that concrete steps needed to be worked out in order to carry achieve this.

SPD leader Gerhard Schröder began his preparations for the June 1986 elections to the Lower Saxony parliament early and they included negotiations over a possible coalition with Die Grünen. Opinion polls were showing that 80% of the population wanted to end the nuclear programme and every party was convinced that Die Grünen would reap most of the electoral benefit from Chernobyl. The SPD wanted to be sure that it didn't miss out. The CDU was so convinced of the threat to its majority in Lower Saxony (and conscious of the impending national elections) that it mounted a hard and dirty election campaign. This included releasing a list of personal details about Green party officials, all obtained from the extensive West German police files, initiating for the first time a debate about the party's programme in the Bundestag and publishing huge posters headed 'The SPD wants to cooperate with these people'. The posters listed some of Die Grünen's policies distorted in such a way to imply that the Greens were enemies of peace and freedom, wanted to encourage pollution, drug taking, anarchy, release of dangerous prisoners, leave Germany defenceless and so on. They were called 'agents of Moscow', and 'like ETA in the Basque country' with political and military wings.[21] When Schröder saw the tack of the CDU campaign he swiftly backed off from any suggestion of a coalition with Die Grünen. The campaign worked. Although they lost over 6% the CDU were able to scrape a majority with the FDP who retained their 9 seats. The SPD upped its score by 5.5% to 42.1% and the 'Chernobyl effect' for Die Grünen was reduced to a meagre 0.6% increase which allowed them to keep their 11 seats in the *Land* parliament.

The sobering experience of Lower Saxony put all factional squabbles firmly onto the back burner. Long inconclusive debates continued but, although prominent members of both factions used their access to the media to put across their point of view, it was clear that no decision would be made about any coalition at national level until after the election had taken place.

Elections to the Bavarian parliament in October gave the party a boost. The Christian-Democrats (CSU in Bavaria) were considered to be in an unassailable position yet Die Grünen entered the parliament for the first time with a gratifying 7.5% which gave them 15 seats. The following month, an all-woman slate of the Green Alternative List (GAL) won 10.4% and 13 seats in Hamburg. The SPD lost nearly 10% of the vote there and also, by a whisker, control of one of their most important strongholds. With no hope of either CDU or SPD forming a coalition with the Greens new elections were programmed for after the national elections. For these, opinion polls rallied for Die Grünen but not for Johannes Rau and the SPD. In the face of the Bavaria and Hamburg results, Rau's claim that the SPD could win an outright majority in the elections to the Bundestag began to look a bit thin.

In the end, the national elections on 25 January 1987 saw the CDU/CSU remain the main political grouping in the Bundestag but with a drop in its support of 4.5% that surprised them. The SPD lost a few seats too but were grateful not to lose more. Both smaller parties gained in this election, the liberal FDP with 9% and 46 seats and Die Grünen with 8.3% and 44 seats (including 2 from Berlin).

Almost immediately the 'toleration' agreement between the warring factions inside Die Grünen broke down. In

Hesse, in February, they pulled out of the coalition with the
SPD, again over the Nukem/Alkem plant, forcing new
elections which were held in April. The SPD vote slumped,
letting a CDU/FDP coalition take power. The vote for Die
Grünen, on the other hands, soared to 9.4% and 10 seats, with
Fischer obtaining a personal vote of 23% in Frankfurt. The
following month new elections were also held in the
deadlocked city of Hamburg. There Die Grünen's vote fell to
7.1% and they lost 5 seats but the SPD were able to form a
governmental coalition with the FDP. Also in May the
Greens made it into the *Land* parliament of Rhineland-
Palatinate for the first time with 5.9% and 6 seats. Infinite
interpretations could be put on these results and indeed they
were.

Although the pressure to decide nationally about a
strategy of coalition with the SPD was off, Die Grünen clung
to this debate for dear life, using it more than ever as a
smoke-screen for the deeper and more serious divisions
within the party. Arguments grew in intensity and some of
the main protagonists like Schily, Fischer, Trampert and
Ditfurth resorted to hurling personal insults at each other
through the media. In the autumn the party's conference at
Oldenburg faced three main options for a foundation that
would, on behalf of the party, receive substantial government
funds available to such political research foundations. One
came from a women's group, another came from a coalition of
four *Land* parties who had formed their own foundations to
receive similar funds available at State level, and another
from the Heinrich Böll Foundation. This last foundation,
named after the late author who had supported Die Grünen
from its earliest days, brought together a large number of
'critical-left' intellectuals. The debate and the ultimate
decision to choose no one foundation but to ask them to
amalgamate caused a great deal of alarm in many parts of the
party. Petra Kelly described it as 'tantamount to a declaration of intellectual and political bankruptcy'.[22]

The September elections in Schleswig-Holstein and
Bremen stoked the conflict. In the former state the SPD
became the biggest party but the CDU were able to hang on to
power in coalition with the FDP who increased their vote
from 2.2% to 5.2%. Rigidly opposed to any coalition, Die
Grünen stayed out of the parliament with 3.9%. In Bremen,
which had seen the first entry of Die Grünen into a State
parliament in 1979, the Greens nearly doubled their vote to

10.2% and ten seats. Once again the FDP more than doubled its vote, this time to 10%. The CDU lost nearly the the same percentage but the SPD needed no help to govern with its 50.5% of the vote, a mere 0.8% down on last time. A new party, the neo-Nazi Deutsche Volksunion, made an ominous debut with 3.4%.

Then in November two policemen died and nine more were injured by demonstrators at Frankfurt airport. The killer(s) came from the Autonomen (Autonomists) – a collective noun for the occasionally violent groups living mostly in the 'alternative' areas of Frankfurt, Hamburg and West Berlin. The reaction of the different factions in Die Grünen revealed the florid differences between the hard-line left and the rest of the party. The first group, represented by Thomas Ebermann in the Bundestag and Jutta Ditfurth on the party executive, were unable to produce a condemnation of the killings, and appeared equivocal about Die Grünen's commitment to non-violent protest. The rest of the party furiously distanced themselves from the violence with a statement that no political cause justified the taking of human lives.

1987 ended miserably for Die Grünen, with local parties coming to Bonn to demand better behaviour from their representatives. A 'crisis meeting' was held on 12 December to try to find a way out of what was no less than political and organisational paralysis for the party. Much hope was placed in a non-delegate, non-decision-making strategy conference planned for June 1988, where papers submitted by the different factions would be considered.

However the conference turned out to do little more than temporarily paper over the cracks. As it was the first non-decision-making big national conference the party had held since its foundation, a holiday mood suffused the event. The organisation of the conference (carefully renamed a 'perspective congress') did enable members of local parties to discuss a wide number of issues with their national figures in a convivial atmosphere, but it also allowed the principal gladiators (who were on their best behaviour) to shuffle around the main issue, which was the apparently unbridgable divide between not only their strategies but also their long-term political goals. On the second day of the congress an editorial in the *Frankfurter Rundschau* spoke of the huge amount of political incompatibility, personal animosity and jealousy that existed between the Ditfurths, Vollmers, Schilys and Ebermanns of the party. As no wing really wanted to compromise and there was a world of difference between the ideas of the leading Fundis and Realos that could not be bridged, the paper felt that the weekend promised to be 'a drag' (18 June 1988).

On the whole, though, the press reviewed the congress sympathetically and their reports were tinged with more than a little *tristesse* at the troubled state of the party, which is now also being touched by allegations of financial scandals. They noted that the internal arguments of the 'peace party' had effectively kept them off the political stage during an eventful year for East-West relations, and when one television camera lingered in the tent where the forum devoted to environmental politics was meeting, it found the arena nearly empty. The commentator wondered if the party had lost touch with the very essence of the values which had inspired the founding of Die Grünen.

Future Prospects

Many of the difficulties encountered by the German Green party have been impossible to resolve because the structures and the framework for handling conflict are missing. Not all conflict can necessarily be channelled constructively, but most organisations require at least a few damage-limitation mechanisms to survive serious differences of opinion or abuses of power within them. Die Grünen have a quite proper commitment to basic democracy and its implied checks on abuse of power, but the system is simply not working. Until they do face up to their organisational problems it is not likely that Die Grünen will be able to resolve their present political predicament.

Considerable power and resources are, quite rightly, devolved down to local and *Länder* parties, but the concomitant responsibility of the local parties for the representatives it elects to offices within the organisation is seriously neglected. There seem to be three main reasons for this.

Firstly, the lines of accountability for elected office holders are unclear and there are virtually no imposable sanctions (for example, the parliamentarians who chose not to rotate stayed in post, and despite a conference vote of no confidence in a member of the executive that person stayed in post until the end of his elected mandate). Secondly, the main decision-making body is the national delegate conference, but few people accept that these are representative of the party membership any more. A party rule against holding more than one mandate means that members elected to councils and parliaments become ineligible for posts within the party. This immediately disenfranchises around 6,000 obviously committed members. Many more members with full-time jobs and/or family commitments are similarly disenfranchised because taking an active role in the party means frequent attendance at often long meetings at local, *Länder* and national level. Consequently meetings and the non-professional expenses-only party bodies have become heavily peopled by those of independent means, students and the unemployed, so are no longer representative of the party at large. Tack onto this structure the fully professionalised parliamentary groups at State and national level, with their teams of experts and media-worthiness, and additional strains and jealousies become inevitable.

A third difficulty stems from the different interpretations within the party of what the *Basis* (grassroots) of the party actually is. Gene Frankland identified six definitions – the extra-parliamentary movements, the party membership, the party activists, the party's working groups, the party functionaries and/or the party's electorate.[23] To this may be added another, proposed by Peter von Oertzen – the workers of 2020.[24]

Ill-defined lines and areas of responsibility and accountability, and cumbersome decision-making processes, have been exploited by the 'professional activists' among whom are to be found the more explicitly left-wing Greens. Although still a minority in the party, they have largely succeeded in their declared intention of gaining positions of power and influence within it. In doing so they have managed to dominate the Fundi strategy position, which many Greens resent bitterly, as they would like to coordinate the two strategy approaches in a more sophisticated and variable way.

Chronic disorganisation has also fostered a lack of respect for such democratic processes as do exist in Die Grünen. More and more party representatives are taking actions and making speeches (at home and abroad) that have nothing to do with the common ground around which the party was founded, and the different opinions within the Bundestag *Fraktion*, instead of enriching it, now render it impotent.[25] The end result is that the collective voice of the party membership has been reduced to unrepresentative delegates giving emotional responses to passionate speeches at conferences instead of a considered view on well documented and argued options.

A commission set up in June 1985 to consider new organisational forms has so far failed to report. Made up of a man and a woman representative from each of the *Länder* its debates have probably become a microcosm of the national one. This raises the probability that only an outside, neutral, body will be able to design an acceptable new structure for the party's organisation.

Meanwhile some attempts are being made to try to end the political stalemate. A new faction, known as the Neutralos, has been born. Their slogan is: 'This party's not for splitting,' and their objective is to return the party to the principles and common ground that made it attractive to a wide range of people in the first place. They feel the time has come to 'shave off' the extremists. Although a Neutralo slate for the party speakers' jobs in the Bundestag was rejected, that this new faction may yet be successful is suggested by a definite trend away from the old simplistic divisions. Fundis and Realos and left and right labels are giving way to complicated descriptions such as: 'Well, I suppose he's a Realo, but he's a bit left-leaning on economics, and a definite Fundi on NATO.' The Neutralos' forum at the Perspektivenkongress, and their manifesto *Aufbruch 88* (New Direction 88), attracted a lot of attention as did their proposal for using party-wide referenda as a way of resolving the impasses in the party. However the sceptical wonder how any of the conclusions of such referenda could be implemented and even doubt that an acceptable set of questions could be compiled.

Despite the obvious difficulties, the development of the Neutralo faction holds out hope that Die Grünen will start to take serious stock of its position in what could be a 10% political ghetto to the left of the SPD. If popular majorities are to be built around the ideas of the Greens, the squabbles inside *both* of the large German parties and the regular electoral gains of the centre/liberal FDP cannot be ignored by Die Grünen strategists for ever.

But as well as facing up to the steady erosion of 'ordinary' people from the ranks of the party's activists, and wrestling with crucial strategies towards the other political parties, Die Grünen will also have to address the increasing disenchantment of intellectuals, many of whom gave the party important support in its early days. Just when the press and other parties are finding it easier to ridicule and attack Die Grünen, fewer people are prepared to step forward and defend them. Although the question of the foundation was resolved at a congress in Ludwigshafen in March 1988 by creating a Rainbow Foundation Association to include the three proposals from the Heinrich Böll Foundation, for a women's foundation and a *Länder* foundation, the formula favoured by Die Grünen and the rules surrounding the allocation of money in such foundations (about DM 75 million in this case) might well be a recipe for further deadlock. There is also a danger that the famous social movements which gave birth to the party are now reduced and weakened. It is not clear whether this is part of the natural cycles of such movements or a terminal decline, and whether it will affect the regular 7-8% that the party is at present getting in the opinion polls. Certainly the number of groups that are dependent on the *Ökofunds* from Die Grünen to finance their activities and projects is growing. This puts the party in a position of patronage – something they say they despise in others.

It is true that the difficulties faced by Die Grünen seem overwhelming when listed in this way. But as these are roughly what any Green party can expect should it win a significant number of seats in a national parliament they merit close examination. The way the German party handles its transition from an adolescent to a mature party without losing its radicalness is of intense interest to its counterparts in other countries. However, before any problem can be properly treated it needs to be diagnosed correctly. This Die Grünen have so far failed to do.

Notes

1 The story of the Wyhl campaign is told in Wolfgang Sternstein, *Uberall ist Wyhl* , Haag und Herchen, Frankfurt, 1978.
2 W. Hau, *Sponti-Sprueche*, Eichborn, Frankfurt, 1982.
3 Werner Hülsberg *The West German Greens*, Verso, 1987, p. 82.
4 Herbert Gruhl, *Ein Planet wird geplündert*, Fischer, Frankfurt, 1978.
5 Fritjof Capra & Charlene Spretnak, *Green Politics*, Paladin, 1985, p. 36.
6 Wolfgang Rudig, *Energy, Public Protest and Green Parties, a comparable analysis*, Ph.D. thesis, Manchester University, 1986.
7 Petra Kelly, 'Towards a Green Europe! Towards a Green World!,' speech to the International Green Congress in Stockholm, August 1987.

8 Jutta von Ditfurth, 'Skizzen einer radikalökologischen Position', in T. Kluge (ed.), *Grüne Politik*, Fischer Taschenbuch, Frankfurt, 1984.
9 Manfred Zieran, *Pflasterstrand* 171, 19 November 1983.
10 Joschka Fischer in *Pflasterstrand* 169, 22 October 1983.
11 Otto Schily in *Sozialismus* 11, 1984.
12 Fritjof Capra & Charlene Spretnak, op. cit., p. 21.
13 *Moderne Zeiten* 0, 1981.
14 Werner Hülsberg 'The Greens at the Crossroads,' *New Left Review* 152, July/August 1985.
15 Fritjof Capra & Charlene Spretnak, op. cit., p. 148.
16 *Independent*, 22 October 1987 and Diana Johnstone, *In These Times*, 13-19 January 1988.
17 See for example Gene Frankland, *The Greens, Parliamentary Challenges and Responses*, American Political Science Association, 1985, and Dirk Cornelsen, *Ankläger im Hohen Haus*, Klartext, Essen, 1986.
18 Werner Hülsberg, *The West German Greens*, p. 173.
19 *Time*, 11 November 1985.
20 *The Times*, 26 May 1986.
21 Werner Hülsberg, op. cit., p. 202.
22 Press Release 860/87, 23 September 1987.
23 Gene Frankland, op. cit.
24 Werner Hülsberg, op. cit., p. 118.
25 Uschi Eid, interview with author, 9 February 1988.

Main Party Publications

1983 Federal Election Programme.
1987 Federal Election Programme.
Purpose in Work – Solidarity in Life (economic policy), 1984.
Umbau der Industriegesellschaft (industrial conversion), 1986.
Der sofortige Ausstieg ist möglich – Das Sofort-Programm für den Ausstieg aus der Atomenergie (immediate exit from nuclear power).

Grüner Basis-Dienst is the national party newsletter.
Grünes Bulletin is the Bundestag fraktion newsletter.

NB: Many of Die Grünen's publications are translated into several languages. They also produce a wide range of *Infoblatts* (short policy papers).

Studies of Die Grünen

HÜLSBERG Werner, *The West German Greens*, Verso, 1987.
CAPRA F. & SPRETNAK C, *Green Politics*, Dutton, New York, 1984.
PAPADAKIS E., *The Green Movement in West Germany*, Croom Helm, Beckenham, 1984.

There are of course many other studies and articles concerning Die
Grünen. Further references may be obtained in the above books.

Addresses

Die Grünen
Colmantstrasse 36
5300 Bonn

tel: (49) 228 692021/2

Die Grünen im Bundestag
Bundeshaus
5300 Bonn 1

tel: (49) 228 16 7213 (press office)

Organogram: Die Grünen

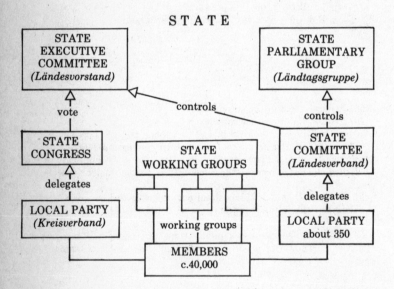

NATIONAL

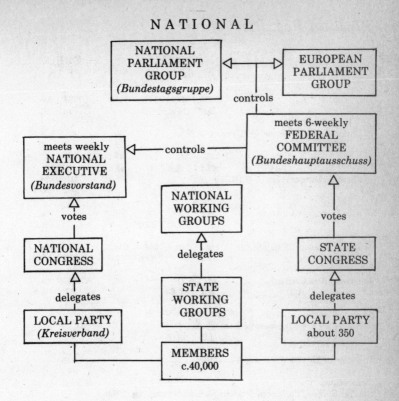

Election Results: National

	NATIONAL (Bundestag)[1]				EURO-PEAN	
	1987 Jan	1983 Mar	1980 Oct	1976	1984 Jun	1979 Jun
7 Christian-Social Union (CSU)					**7** *8.5*	**8** *10.1*
6 Christian-Democrat Union (CDU)	**223** *44.3*	**244** *48.8*	**226** *44.5*	**243** *48.6*	**34** *37.5*	**34** *39.1*
5 Free-Democrat Union (FDU)	**46** *9.1*	**34** *6.9*	**53** *10.6*	**39** *7.9*	*4.8*	**4** *6.0*
3 Social-Democrat Party (SPD)	**186** *37.0*	**193** *38.2*	**218** *42.9*	**214** *42.6*	**33** *37.4*	**35** *40.8*
10 Greens (Die Grünen)	**42** *8.3*	**27** *5.6*	*1.5*		**7** *8.2*	*3.2*
11 Miscellaneous (includes Pacifists, Women's Party, Democratic Ecology Party ÖDP)	*1.3*	*0.4*				

Key: **Seats** in bold, *Percentages in italics*.

References
SMITH Gordon, *Politics in Western Europe*, Heinemann, 1984.
The Times Guide to the European Parliament, Times Books, 1984.
Economist, 31 January 1987.

Notes
1   22 representatives from Berlin who have no vote in the Bundestag are not included in this table. Die Grünen had 1 Berlin representative in 1983, 2 in 1987.

Green Vote in Länder

	1978	1979	1980	1981	1982	1983	1984	1985	1986	1987	1988
Baden-Württemburg			Mar *5.3* **6**				Mar *8.0* **9**				Mar *7.9* **10**
Bavaria	Oct *1.8(e)*				Oct *4.6*				Oct *7.5* **15**		
Berlin AL(h)		Mar *3.7*		May *7.2* **9**			Mar *10.6* **15**				
Bremen		Oct *5.1(g)* **4**				Sep *5.4* **5**				Sep *10.2* **10**	
Hamburg GAL(i)	Jun *3.5(a)* *1.1(f)* *0.0(e)*				Jun *7.7* **9** Dec *6.8* **8**				Nov *10.4* **13**	May *7.0* **8**	
Hesse	Oct *1.1(c)* *0.9(d)* *0.0(b)*				Sep *8.0* **9**	Sep *5.9* **7**				Apr *9.4* **10**	
Lower Saxony	Jun *3.9(b)*				Mar *6.5* **11**				Jun *7.1* **11**		
North Rhine-Westphalia			May *3.0*					May *4.6*			
Rhineland-Palatinate						Mar *4.5*				May *5.9* **6**	
Saarland			Apr *2.9*					Mar *2.5*			
Schleswig-Holstein		Apr *2.4(f)*				Mar *3.6*				Sep *3.9*	May *2.9*

Key: **Seats** in bold, *Percentages* in italics.
(a) BLW - Bunte Liste Wehrt Euch, Initiativen für Demokratie und Umweltschutz.
(b) GLU - Grüne Liste Umweltschutz.
(c) GLH - Grüne Liste Hessen.
(d) GAZ - Grüne Aktion Zukunft.
(e) AUD - Aktionsgemeinschaft Unabhängiger Deutscher.
(f) GLSH - Grüne Liste Schleswig-Holstein.
(g) BLG - Bremer Grüne Liste.
(h) AL - Alternative Liste.
(i) GAL - Grüne Alternative Liste.

8: ITALY

Federazione delle Liste Verdi

Area: 310,268 sq. km. *founded: 16 November 1986*
Population: 57.2 million (1985) *members: 134 lists*
Density: 189 per sq. km.

*Member: UN, OECD, NATO, WEA and European
Communities*
Languages: Italian (German in Trentino-Alto Adige)
GNP per capita: US $6096 (1984)

Background and Electoral System

In the first half of the 19th century, the northern states of
Italy were ruled either by the house of Savoy or the Austrian
empire. Further south, Tuscany and some smaller duchies
were separated from the southern half of Italy (the kingdom
of Naples) by the papal states and Rome. Generalised
practical dissatisfaction with this arrangement combined
with nostalgia for the grand days of the Italian Renaissance
to ignite the desire for a united Italy. The principal orchestra-
tor of the *risorgimento* (resurgence), as the unifying process
became known, was Camillo di Cavour, prime minister of the
kingdom of Sardinia. Although he was to die in 1861, in the
midst of much politics, passion and battling, Italy was
considered 'made' in 1870 – at least to all except those who
considered the territories of Savoy and Nice, Trentino and
Trieste to be properly part of the Italian state. These regions
became known as *Italia irridenta* (unredeemed Italy).

But political unity did not bring practical unity or democracy to Italy overnight. To begin with only about 600,000 out
of a population of some 22 million were able to vote, in
elections to a national parliament where the politicians

seemed no less corrupt and incompetent than their predecessors in the smaller states. (Among other restrictions, the pope forbade Catholics from taking part in political life.) Consequently the revolutionary fervour that had brought about Italian unity remained unsatisfied and turned to the new socialist ideas that were stirring in the rest of Europe. Soon after suffrage was significantly broadened in 1913, the First World War dealt Italy another blow.

Italy entered the war on the side of the Allies with the objective of completing the *risorgimento*, and was disappointed with the eventual settlement which restored only Alto Adige, previously held by the Austrians. The postwar depression compounded Italy's political instability, and middle-of-the-road parties were unable to moderate the ideological rift between the now politically active Catholics and the Socialist and Communist left.

Into this chaos came Benito Mussolini, a one-time left Socialist who developed an intense nationalism while a soldier during the war. In 1919 he formed the Fascio di Combattimento from mostly ex-soldiers. Claiming loyalty to king and church, Mussolini's *squadristi* of black-shirted thugs attracted the support of property holders and patriots by violent attacks on their political enemies – Communist and Socialist (even Christian-Socialist) office bearers and their supporters. Although the Fascists gained their maximum electoral support of 35 out of 500 seats in the 1921 elections, they were able to make Italy ungovernable. The Liberal coalition government was equivocal in its dealings with the Fascists as it was not dissatisfied with their tough line towards the extreme left. Violence escalated and the king refused a belated attempt to impose martial law. When the cabinet resigned, he named Mussolini as head of a coalition government in late 1922 and gave him one year's emergency power to restore order. The violence did abate, but Mussolini went on to steadily replace the emergency powers with his own dictatorship. This was even supported by the Vatican to whom Mussolini was astute enough to restore certain powers, notably the sovereignty of the Vatican city-state and the church's authority in matters of education and marriage.

Much analysis has been made of Mussolini's Fascist movement and of movements inspired by it in other countries, but it is perhaps wisest to consider the birth and progress of Italian Fascism against Mussolini's own words:

'Fascism was not the nurseling of a doctrine worked out beforehand with detailed elaboration; it was born of the need for action.'[1]

Just as the constitution of the Federal Republic of Germany after the Second World War was written in the light of the rise to power of Hitler (one of Mussolini's most diligent pupils), so the constitution of the Italian republic, declared after a referendum in 1946, was drafted to ensure extensive democratic rights for its citizens.

The new constitution of the Italian republic came into force on 1 January 1948 and states that Italy is 'a democratic republic founded on work'. A two-chamber parliament is elected for five years. The 630-seat Camera dei Deputati (lower house) is directly elected. 315 senators are elected from the regions according to population. Each region has at least seven senators, except for the Valle d'Aosta which has one. The president, who is elected by an electoral college of the lower house, the senate and three representatives from each regional council (one from Valle d'Aosta), may nominate 5 senators from public life and, if he or she wishes, become a senator for life on retirement.

The president may dissolve both houses of parliament but a constitutional court, made up of 15 judges (five of whom are appointed by the president, five by parliament and five by the highest courts) has considerable powers. For example it decides on the constitutionality of laws and the powers of the regions, as well as dealing with any conflicts between regions or between a region and the state. The reorganisation of the Fascist party is forbidden and direct male descendants of King Victor Emmanuel are banned from Italian territory.

Locally, Italy is divided into 20 regions, 96 provinces and around 8,000 municipalities. Five regions – Valle d'Aosta, Trentino-Alto Adige, Friuli-Venezia-Giulia (in the north) and the islands of Sicilia and Sardegna – have special autonomous status, and in Trentino-Alto Adige where cultural and linguistic tensions are considerable the two provinces have powers similar to those of a region. The legislative and administrative roles of the regional councils vary but usually include such things as planning, health and education. The provincial councils are mostly concerned with the coordination and integration of regional and municipal council activity. The responsibility of the municipal councils varies greatly according to their size.

For the purpose of national elections Italy is divided into

32 constituencies. The votes which are cast for lists of
candidates are counted nationally and distributed regionally
using a system of pure proportionality based on quotients.
Special provisions are made for the redistribution of residual
votes in areas where there are linguistic minorities. Similar
rules apply for elections to the European Parliament, regional and provincial elections, and for elections to municipal
councils where the population is over 5,000. In the smaller
comuni a simple majority system is used.

Lists may be established by individuals or parties and
candidates may appear on up to three lists in one election. By
standing down, the seat is allocated to the next candidate on
the list. New lists require 250 signatures per electoral
constituency. After national and regional elections the lists
receive appoximately 1,000 lire (roughly 50p) per vote polled
and parties elected to parliament receive considerable state
funding. Rules control electoral broadcasting on public tv,
but parties may buy time on the privately owned channels.

Factors Influencing the Development of Green Politics

As in France, the Communists in Italy emerged from their
resistance activities during the Second World War with
considerable prestige and to begin with held seats in the
government. However, influenced by the Cold War, the
Christian-Democrat leader De Gasperi dismissed the Communists in 1947. In the general election of the following year,
the Communists and their left-wing Socialist allies received
only one-third of the vote after overt intervention from both
the Vatican and the United States of America. Since then,
despite being consistently the second largest party in the
lower house of parliament, the Communists have never been
part of any Italian government. Nevertheless they have
exerted considerable influence over politics in Italy. The
Christian-Democrat party (which has formed part of every
government since the war, making Italy's politics more
stable than the foreign press likes to portray them) has
carefully avoided becoming a clerical party and has consistently sought to make coalitions with parties to its left. After
1956 the Italian Communist party began to distance itself
from Moscow, which gained it increased support and respect

in Italy, and when Pope John XXIII was moved to speak out for rapprochment with the Soviet world in the early 1960s it became easier for many Italian Catholics to vote Communist. The party reached its high point in the mid-seventies with the 'historic compromise' of its leader, Enrico Berlinguer, which called on the party to collaborate with all progressive elements. In the 1975 regional and municipal elections the Communists became the largest party in 7 of the 15 regions they contested and, in alliance with the Socialist party, became dominant in most large cities.

Many Greens in Italy believe that this careful conciliatory behaviour of the two big political formations did much to stifle concern about environmental problems, since neither the Catholic culture nor Italian Marxism, even when critically re-examined by the young, contained any ecological awareness. The only major environmental organisation until the 1970s was the World Wildlife Fund, and industrial development was able to take place with little or no concern for its environmental impact. The predominantly rural and considerably poorer south of Italy is scattered with derelict or inefficient heavy industrial plants, and the northern cities are choked with the pollution generated by intense industrial and human activity. Much of the cultural heritage of Europe is black and eroding.

Although problems like the eutrophication of the Adriatic and factory emissions were making themselves felt by the 1970s, political dissent turned round civil liberties, with the tiny, dynamic and anarchical Radical party gaining support for its stand on divorce, abortion, prison conditions and the power of magistrates. Professor Enrico Falqui, regional counsellor for the Liste Verdi in Toscana, reckons that about 70% of the early influence on Italians about ecological problems came from outside the country.[2]

The key starting date for the Green movement in Italy was 1975, when the government published a national energy plan. Italy was one of the first countries in Europe to place an order for a nuclear power plant back in 1956, but the ambitious proposal to build 20 nuclear reactors by 1985 and a further 22 to 42 by 1990 startled several people, including some members of the Radical party. An 'Anti-Nuclear League' was formed specifically to challenge Italy's nuclear energy plans, and this group evolved by 1977 into Amici della Terra (Friends of the Earth) who organised an international anti-nuclear conference in May of that year in Rome. It was chaired by

Aurelio Peccei, founder of the Club of Rome.

From the earliest days, one of the key features of the Italian Green movement has been its ability to attract and harness the talents of experts and intellectuals. In the summer of 1977 a petition against expansion of the nuclear programme was organised among scientists and technicians. A board of lawyers was established to deal with legal opposition to plant construction, and when a debate on the energy plan took place in parliament in the autumn of that year large demonstrations provided the final incentive to the government to reduce the initial number of stations from 20 to 12.

For several years Amici della Terra concentrated on its anti-nuclear campaign, focussing its campaigning on the proposed sites, organising conferences on Soft Energy for Europe at Rome university and commissioning scientific work on the design safety of the reactor vessels proposed for earthquake-prone Italy. Important links with other parts of the developing environmental movement were made in 1979 when Amici della Terra collaborated with the anti-hunting movement to collect signatures for referenda on blood sports and nuclear power, although, in the event, the constitutional court ruled the referenda inadmissible. Nowadays the Italian Friends of the Earth have loosened their ties with the Radical party (which provided their finance), while developing their local organisation and strengthening their links with the broader Green movement.

Also distressed by the national energy plan in the 1970s were some members of the Italian Communist party, which maintained an official pro-nuclear policy until the mid-1980s. The anti-nuclear members formed a Committee for Control of Energy Strategy which provoked a big argument in the party and, according to Professor Falqui, resulted in a serious haemorrhage of intellectuals. Many of today's prominent Greens, including Enrico Falqui and well-known Green MPs like Rosa Filippini, Massimo Scalia and Gianni Mattioli, left the Communist party at this time. In 1980 the Lega per l'Ambiente (Environmental League) was formed by such Communist dissidents, but the Communist party continued to provide funding through its cultural organisation ARCI until 1985, when the serious participation of Greens in local elections led to this being cut off. However, Communist party activists remain involved with Lega per l'Ambiente's magazine, *La Nuova Ecologia*, which, since a facelift in 1984, has increased its circulation to about 35,000.[3]

Federazione delle Liste Verdi

It was in the northern region of Trentino-Alto Adige that the first stirring of Green politics began. In the municipal elections of 1978 two 'new left' lists, Nuova Sinistra in Trento and Neue Linke in Alto Adige, each had one councillor elected, with 4.3% and 4.5% of the poll respectively. In the culturally and politically tense Alto Adige, that councillor was Alexander Langer. Both new political groups evolved over the next few years, with the Nuova Sinistra becoming the Lista Verde and the Neue Linke list becoming the Lista Alternativa.

A little later, in Lugo di Romagna in the region of Emilia Romagna, an 'alternative list' using the Danish anti-nuclear movement's symbol of the smiling sun put up a list for the 1980 municipal elections. On the list, which included two of the present Green MPs, Anna Donati and Michele Boata, were ecologists, dissident Catholics and leftists. No seats were obtained. Boata and Donati were also founders, in Mestre in 1982, of an important initiative for the development of the Green movement – the Federazione Università Verdi Italia.

The idea of providing a series of theoretical and practical courses on a wide range of ecological subjects was quickly taken up and now the Green University has around 40 member groups offering many different courses. All are self-financing and most are organised on a part-time basis in cooperation with local schools and colleges. Local experts and researchers provide the lectures and practical experience. The Green University is now recognised by the ministry of education, although it has yet to affect official education policy and the centrally designed curriculum. A survey of students, 50,000 of whom have registered since the courses were started, reveals that they are attended by students, teachers, technicians, clerks, peasants, factory workers and housewives in roughly that order, although there are variations depending on the type of course being offered.[4]

Although it is organised separately from the Liste Verdi, the political Greens acknowledge the importance of the Green University to their movement. Its president is Gianfranco Amendole, a popular Green guru who is also a Rome magistrate and a long-time defender of the environment through the courts. He has pointed out: 'We must seek to use all the legal instruments that we have – but with discretion, because ecology should not be a matter of legal repression. As with all culture, it should slowly penetrate people's consciousnesses and inspire a new state of mind.'[5]

Both Donati and Boato were members of an informal coordination called Arcipelago Verde, which was formed in 1981 in an attempt to coordinate local activities. In 1983 a collection of essays by members, also called *Arcipelago Verde*, was published by Panorama, Milan. Over this period local Green lists had begun to organise and after the June 1983 national elections, which saw a drop in the vote for both the major parties (particularly the Christian-Democrats) and a rise in support for the centre parties, the first meeting about the development of a national Green political movement was held in Trento in October 1983. Also present were members of the German and Austrian Greens, and the Italian Radical party was represented by its leader, Marco Panella.[6] In elections held later that year, Alexander Langer was elected to the Trentino-Aldo Adige regional council with 4.6% and a further three seats were obtained on the provincial councils of the region. Elsewhere Greens acknowledge four seats won by lists in Lombardia and one seat in Marche.

On 8 November 1984 the first national assembly of the different Green groups was held in Florence to consider future activity. Alexander Langer opened the meeting as the only official speaker. In 1985 two further meetings were held – in the north in February, again in Florence, and in the south in April, in Bari. The objective of these meetings was to coordinate lists for the May local elections. Enrico Falqui remembers that the decision to contest these elections in as coordinated a fashion as possible was influenced by two main considerations – a total mistrust of the other parties over environmental issues, especially the national energy plan, and the success of the Greens in Germany.[7]

Green lists were presented in 11 of the 13 regions where elections to the regional councils were due, and over 100 Green lists in 15 of the 20 regions sought seats on municipal councils, athough most activity was concentrated in the north and centre of Italy. The efforts to coordinate the lists were on the whole successful and *La Nuova Ecologia* published a supplement in May 1985 called *Pagine Verdi*, detailing most of the lists and their multiple logos. The

impact on the press and the public was big and the Greens
received considerable media coverage. 'We were the only
new event,' points out Falqui. The results were encouraging – 10 regional councillors, 16 provincial councillors and
115 municipal councillors. The average vote for the Green
Lists was 2% in the regional elections, 2.6% for the elections
to provincial councils and 3.5% in the municipal elections.
High spots in these last elections were 8% and 8.4% for lists
in Trento and Bolzano (in Trentino-Alto Adige) respectively,
while in Dronero in the region of Piedmont, scene of
objection to a nuclear plant, Liste Verdi polled 10.8%. In
other cities, the Greens polled 4.4% in Venice, 4.2% in
Mantua, 3.1% in Florence, 2.6% in Milan and 1.6% in Turin,
while a list in Rome headed by Rosa Filippini, the charismatic and energetic president of Amici della Terra, polled
2.7%.[8]

Although the results of Liste Verdi in the 1985 elections
were modest in relative terms, the nature of the Italian
system meant they were able to have considerable impact on
public opinion and on the local councils to which they were
elected. From the beginning the Greens have declared that
they will make their alliances, politically and practically,
with whoever supports their position, either on the council or
among the local campaigning groups. For example, in the
muncipal elections in Florence, a city gravely congested with
traffic, the Greens allied themselves with the Amici della
Bicicletta. Afterwards, the two Green city councillors were
able to play a major role in persuading the council (40%
Communist and 11% Socialist) to close half the historic
centre to all but resident and two-wheeled traffic. According
to one of the Green councillors, Tommaso Franci, the Greens
have been able to accomplish a significant philosophical
turnabout of the council. Thus a big polluting incinerator
has been closed down, debate is taking place over how to
proceed with a waste recycling programme, and Florence is
the first city to accept the principle of a consultative
referendum. One on traffic and one on hunting are due in
October 1988. Franci is gratified by the speed at which Green
proposals are adopted by the council, but disappointed that
putting the proposal into action seems to go rather more
slowly.[9]

La Nuova Ecologia of March 1988 lists one region, 2
provinces and 11 municipalities where Green List councillors have opted for supporting the majority on the council.

Usually the main majority party is the Communist party, but in Cologno Monzese near Milan the majority is formed by the Communists, the Christian-Democrat party and the Greens. In Palermo, Sicily, the Green List decided to join a coalition between the Christian-Democrats, the Social-Democrats, local Catholics and the independent left in order to support the Christian-Democrat mayor's attempts to change the way of running a town where the Mafia is very influential.

Meanwhile, more meetings were being held to improve the coordination of Liste Verdi, so that a federation could be registered in time for the national elections due before 1987. In September 1985 a convention was held in Pescara and in May of the following year, after many intervening meetings and working groups, a set of statutes was informally approved by a meeting in Senigallia, near Ancona. Following a successful international congress in September 1986, also in Pescara, the statutes were officially agreed at a delegate congress on 16 November 1986 at Fina le Ligure, near Genoa. Seventy-six of the local lists represented approved the statutes immediately and the remaining groups approved them later. Since this congress, only lists that adhere to the statutes are officially able to join the federation, after approval by the coordinating group and a delegate convention.[10] At present 134 lists are official members of the federation and 59 more are seeking membership, but the reality is more muddled than this, especially at election time.

Most Greens in Italy take great pains to point out that they are not a party, but a federation of lists put together for electoral purposes. Michaela Buonfrate, technical secretary to the Federazione, points out that the national organisation exists simply for administrative purposes such as handling the monies due to parties contesting elections and for coordinating the activities of the local lists, which are completely autonomous in their activities, as are any parliamentarians or councillors elected from them to public office.[11] Rosa Filippini, now elected to parliament on the Liste Verdi, is passionate in her defence of the 'intuition' that inspired those early organisers of the Federazione:

> The idea from the beginning was one of *tolerance* between a number of very different groups. Everyone recognised that everyone came from different points of view – from different points of

the political spectrum – and this coming together
was only possible because the groups were already
very politicised... The lists were made with the
conviction of openness and that the organisation
should be maintained this way. The difference
between the Italian and the German or Austrian
Greens for example is that they made compromises
to come together as one unit. In Italy everyone can
stay with their own characteristics. The problem
now is to maintain this organisation because it
will take a lot of work to keep it going.[12]

With the practical hurdle of establishing their Federazione
cleared, the Greens were able to prepare politically for the
expected June 1987 elections to the national parliament. At
an assembly in Mantua at the end of April, the delegates
voted unanimously to contest the elections together and
against a proposed pan-Italy alliance with the Socialist,
Radical and Social-Democrat parties for elections to both the
lower house and the senate. In the end, some members of
these parties formed an alliance for the elections to the
senate in five regions. The Greens joined them only in the
constituency of Trento-Bolzano, as part of their strategy of
cutting across the considerable tensions that exist between
the Italian- and German-speaking communities in that
region.

Liste Verdi were present in all but two of the 32 constituencies, although in the south of the country they sometimes
managed little more than a paper presence. The power of a
small party to stir up the political waters in Italy was
demonstrated by the reaction of the other parties to the
newcomer. They promptly studded their own lists with
ambientalisti (environmentalists). The June 1987 edition of
La Nuova Ecologia identifies and provides a brief pedigree for
over 70 such *ambientalisti*, from all but the Social-Democrat
and the extreme-right MSI lists. All parties made efforts to
establish their Green credentials during the campaign, and
the Communist party made much of a visit to Italy by the
American Barry Commoner just prior to the elections, when
he announced that if he was Italian he would vote for the
Communists and not for the Greens.

In the event Liste Verdi polled an average 2.5%
nationwide, enough to give them 13 seats in the chamber.
Again the north/south disparity of support for the Greens

was evident, with the high scores being in the north, particularly in the regions where the Greens had been active for longest: for example, Trentino-Alto Adige (4.6%) and Veneto (3.7%). For the elections to the senate, one seat was obtained in Lombardia by Piergiorgio Sirtori for the Liste Verdi, and one in Trentino-Alto Adige by Marco Boato, as a Green on the PSI-PSDI-PR coalition list. These lists obtained 2.6% and 11.7% respectively. Now Sirtori sits with the *misto* (mixed) group in the senate and Boato with the 9-member European Federalist and Ecologist group, which includes Radicals, Socialists and the one ecologist. The name of this last group, and indeed the coalition list that provided senators for it, may be viewed as part of the Radical party's preparations for the 1989 elections to the European Parliament. As for the *ambientalisti* from the other parties: twenty were elected and Liste Verdi view them as a bonus rather than a threat to their work in parliament.

The entry of the Greens into the Italian parliament made news around the world, albeit sandwiched between the serious commentary on the increased support for the Christian-Democrats and Socialists at the expense of the Communists and amazement that 'porno queen' Ilona Staller, known professionally as Cicciolina, should have won a parliamentary seat on the list of the ever-inventive Radical party. The *Observer* of 21 June 1988 noted:

> The Greens have a remarkable, idealistic backing of smart young scientists and economists giving early warning of environmental risks which their 15 MPs can expose in parliament... 'We are not romantic idealists {say the Greens} we are on an absolutely practical crusade to preserve world resources, our collective health and an economy which relies so heavily on tourism and foreign trade. We have to find a new social model, and whichever party supports our respect for the environment will ultimately be the winner.'

Immediately the Greens ploughed about 40% of the reimbursement they received for their 971,728 votes into a campaign to hold the referendum on nuclear power that had been aborted by (and was partly responsible for precipitating) the general election. Despite some very confusingly phrased questions and a turnout of only 65% the result had to be interpreted as a clear 'no' to nuclear power. 80.6% of the voters wanted the construction of any nuclear power station to be a *local* decision not a national one and 71.8% were against Italy's continued support for the Super-Phénix project. The Italian government is now obliged to change its legislation appropriately and is due to publish in autumn 1988 a new national energy plan – without nuclear power.

Even with the 'Chernobyl effect' taken into account, the Greens feel that the results of this referendum are the culmination of a long and hard fought anti-nuclear campaign in Italy and they are proud of the boost it gives to the Europe-wide anti-nuclear movement. Long-time activist Massimo Scalia, professor of physics at Rome university and now a Green MP, notes that a poll in 1980 showed around 30% of Italian people opposed to nuclear power. Since then he and other expert activists have worked hard on a campaign based on sound scientific reasoning. Local people were given the knowledge and therefore the power to debate the issue and mount their own campaigns, connections were made in many state institutions, including the energy companies and public health, and meetings and talks were held with members of workers' organisations. Thus when the accident at Chernobyl occurred Scalia and his friends were well placed to help the by now 'well-informed doves' in those institutions to influence their colleagues. The final push that Chernobyl gave to Italian opinion so that a majority voted against nuclear power in the referendum must be viewed against this well prepared background, says Scalia.[13]

Also in November 1987 the Liste Verdi held an assembly at Aricca near Rome and decided to support the World Wildlife Fund's campaign for non-chemical agriculture in Italy. True to their federal nature, they then returned to their regions to take up local campaigns. According to Sergio Andreis, a Green MP from Milan with responsibility for foreign affairs in the Green parliamentary group, he and his colleagues will also be concentrating on trying to close down some of the worst of the polluting chemical plants. In Milan itself, for example, the Alfa Lancia car plant puts about 15 tons of highly toxic products into the air daily. Although the Lombardia regional council has formally given the company four months to come up with a plan for reducing toxic emissions, the company's response has been to protest through the regional courts and demand a 36-month delay for producing this plan.[14]

May 1988 brought the next electoral test for the Greens, and both they and the papers agree that it was a test satisfactorily passed. Although only present in some 20% of the 413 *comuni* involved in the elections, the Green Lists polled an average of 3.7% and won a total of 61 more seats on municipal councils. In the three elections to provincial councils, Liste Verdi won 2 more seats, one in Pavia in Lombardia and one in Ravenna in Emilia Romagna, with 4% and 4.4% of the vote respectively. *Il Tempo* summed up the election results in the following headline: 'PCI falls, PSI grows, DC recuperates – lay parties are stable, the MSI is changeable, the Greens hold firm.'[15] In June, Greens won 3 regional, 3 provincial and 10 municipal councillors in Friuli-Venezia-Giulia as well as their first seat on the Valle d'Aosta regional council, and hold high hopes for further gains in the November elections in Trentino-Aldo Adige.

Future Prospects

With their ability to make considerable impact on local and national politics despite their modest numbers on councils and in parliaments, the Italian Greens are understandably satisfied with their progress so far.

In the national parliament the Gruppo Verde have some legislative proposals in the pipeline, including one on national parks and one on soil conservation – both important proposals, especially for the south of Italy where quarrying and tree loss causes extensive erosion and even land slippage. They admit their failure to influence the 10-year plan for road building but give pride of place to the success of their amendments to the Italian budget, which shifted the equivalent of about £1,000 million from environmentally damaging projects to environmentally friendly ones, such as conservation of energy and resources, organic agriculture and fish farming and national parks.[16]

The Gruppo Verde are also anticipating the new national energy plan and are carefully preparing their response and amendments. The Greens favour new regional energy authorities set up by a temporary central agency, with significant commitments to alternative energy and energy conservation, and are particularly keen on the *efficient* use of energy, which means no increased use of oil and coal. As

Massimo Scalia points out, the very powerful Italian state-owned energy and oil companies have turnovers that are larger than the Fiat car company, so it is doubtful whether they could be trusted to administer the sort of energy plan of which the Greens would approve.[17]

However, despite the enviable open support that the Federazione delle Liste Verdi receives from Italy's environmental groups, including the World Wildlife Fund, most Greens are aware that, in the words of Sergio Andreas, 'The first phase for Green politics is at an end. We are now an institutional presence and no longer a new thing. The environmental groups are going through a change too, and the challenge for us all is to go beyond the slogans and develop working alternatives and to build social majorities for them.' There is little doubt that awareness that environment and health will have to be given the same consideration as employment and capital is pervading many parts of Italian society, and at a recent conference the unions involved with the Italian chemical industry agreed to stay in permanent consultation with environmentalists.[18]

Although Gianfranco Amendole accuses the Federazione of becoming like the other political parties with its symbols, money, statutes and a coordinating secretariat,[19] Tomasso Franci of the Florence Greens is not worried. He believes that Liste Verdi will be able to use the apparently chaotic nature of Italian politics that confuses and even alarms many incomprehending observers in order to remain an genuine 'anti-party party'. 'Italians are used to *sfumato* in politics,' he says. *Sfumato*, according to another Florentine, Leonardo da Vinci, is a painting technique by which different tones are blended into one another 'without lines or borders, in the manner of smoke'. The Italian Greens plan to employ plenty of *sfumato* in their own organisation as well as in their relationships with other groups and political parties.

Certainly the Italian Greens' strategy of making alliances locally and nationally with whoever supports their issues means that the other political parties with their fragile coalitions have to react. Bettino Craxi, Socialist party leader, is open about his own strategy of making his party stronger than the Communists and then ending the reign of the Christian-Democrats in government. He sees this as being possible by the 1990s and is naturally interested in eliciting support from the Greens. Massimo Scalia believes that the Greens' strategy must be against such alliances.

'Only tackling the big environmental problems really matters. The health of the environment must be central to any alliances contemplated by the Greens.' Rosa Filippini makes the same point like this:

> The practical results of the Green movement's strategy so far has been to make the nuclear issue a national one and to win the battle. I tell people that the Greens are a unique guarantee – if you want the other parties to be Green *after* the elections, you need us in the institutions.[20]

Notes

1 Quoted in R. R. Palmer and Joel Colton, *A History of the Modern World Since 1815*, Knopf, New York, 1971.
2 Interview with Enrico Falqui, 25 May 1988.
3 Interview with Silvia Zamboni, editorial board of *La Nuova Ecologia*, 30 May 1987.
4 Interview with Anna Donati, 31 May 1988.
5 From interview reported in *Emois*, September 1987.
6 Interview with Gianluca Felicetti, press officer of Gruppo Parlamentare Verde, 30 May 1988.
7 As note 2.
8 *La Nuova Ecologia*, June 1985.
9 Interview with Tommaso Franci, 25 May 1988.
10 Interview with Gianluca Felicetti, press officer, Gruppo Parlamentare Verde, 30 May 1988.
11 Interview with Michaele Buonfrate, 30 May 1988.
12 Interview with Rosa Fillipini, 31 May 1988.
13 Interview with Massimo Scalia, 1 June 1988.
14 Interview with Sergio Andreis, 31 May 1988.
15 *Il Tempo*, 31 May 1988.
16 *Raggi* 4, 1-15 February 1988.
17 As note 13.
18 As note 14.
19 *La Nuova Ecologia*, Janaury 1988.
20 As note 12.

Main Party Publications

Arcipelago Verde, Panorama, Milan, 1983.

Verdi is the federation's newsletter.
Raggi is the parliamentary group's newsletter.

Studies of Federazione delle Liste Verdi

SILVESTRINI Gianni, *La Cultura dei Verdi*, Angeli, Milan, 1986.
DIANI Mario, *Isole nell'arcipelago*, Il Molino, Bologne, 1988.
LODE & BIORCHIO, *La Sfeda Verde*, Liviana, Padua, 1988.

Addresses

Federazione delle Liste Verdi
via Panisperna 237
00184 Rome

tel: (39) 6 4820852/3/4

Gruppo Parlamentare Verde
via Uffici del Vicario 21
00186 Rome

tel: (39) 6 67179837/6717507

Organogram:
Federazione delle Liste Verdi

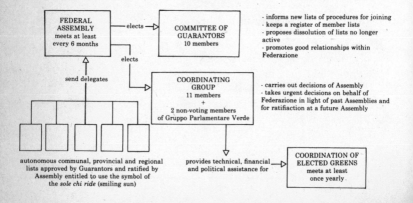

Green Vote in Regions

	National[1]		Regional[1]		Provincial[1]			Municipal[1]		
	1987	1988	1985	1983	1988	1985	1983	1988	1985	1983
Piedmont	**1** *3.5*		**1** *1.7*			**3** *2.2*		**6** *6.4*	**14** *7.6*	
Lombardia	**4**[2] *3.3*		**2** *2.4*		**1** *4.0*	**5** *2.7*		**17** *4.7*	**18** *4.2*	**4**[3] *?*
Trentino-Alto-Adige	**1**[24]*** *4.6*			**1**[4] *4.6*			**3**[5] *4.3*		**22**[6] *5.9*	
Veneto	**2** *3.7*		**1** *2.6*			**3** *3.1*		**8** *6.5*	**14** *4.3*	
Friuli-Venezia-Giulia	- *3.5*	**3**[10] *?*			**3**[10] *?*			**10**[10] *?*	**2** *3.3*	
Liguria	**1** *4.0*		**1** *3.2*			**1** *3.3*		**5** *4.8*	**3** *2.6*	
Emilia-Romagna	**2** *2.5*		**1** *2.3*		**1** *4.4*			**6** *3.9*	**9** *2.9*	
Toscana	- *2.7*		**1** *1.6*			**1** *2.5*		**3** *2.8*	**15**[7] *3.5*	
Umbria	- *1.9*							- *1.8*		
Marche	- *2.6*		**1** *2.2*			**1** *2.9*		**5** *3.3*	**7** *4.0*	**1** *3.0*
Lazio	**2** *2.9*		**1** *2.3*		- *2.8*	**1** *2.9*		**2** *2.9*	**2** *2.7*	
Abruzzo	- *1.9*		- *1.2*					- *2.3*	**2** *2.7*	
Campania	- *0.9*		**1**[8] *1.0*					**4** *3.0*	**1** *2.4*	
Puglia	- *1.6*		- *1.1*			**1** *1.4*		**2** *3.4*	**3**[9] *3.2*	
Basilicata	- *1.0*							**1** *5.6*		
Calabria	- *0.8*							**2** *3.0*		
Sicilia	- *1.2*		(1986) *0.6*					- *1.0*	**3** *?*	
Molise	- *1.1*									
Valle d'Aosta		**1** *2.5*								

Sardegna has no Green List.

Seats in bold, *Percentages* in italics – see note 1.

References
La Nuova Ecologia, June 1985 and July 1987.
Information Services, Camera dei Deputati, Rome.
Il Tempo, 31 May 1988.
Il Voto Verde, Gruppo Consiliare Verde Regione Liguria.
Documents from Liste Verdi.

Notes

1 The percentage for National and Regional lists is of total vote cast in the region. For the Provincial and Municipal elections, where lists are not always presented over the entire region, the percentage is the average number of votes obtained by the Green lists.

2 One senator was elected from both Lombardia (Lista Verdi 2.6%) and Trentino-Alto Adige (coalition list with PSI, PSDI and PR 11.7%).

3 Two seats in Viadana, one seat in Milan for 'Lista per Monza' and one seat for 'Lista Civica' which is now in the Liste Verdi.

4 Lista Alternativa.

5 One from Lista Verde, two from Lista Alternativa. In this region the two provinces, Trente and Bolzano, have similar status to the regions.

6 13 Lista Alternativa in Bolzano and 9 Lista Verde in Trente.

7 Two seats in Florence obtained by Lista Verde and Amici della Bicicletta in coalition.

8 Seat won by Marco Pannella who led a coalition list of Liste Verdi and Lista Civica. He stepped down immediately and the seat was taken by Liste Verdi.

9 Two seats won by list called Cattolici e Laici per il Cambiamento.

10 In the elections in Fruili Venezia Giulia on 26 June 1988, one regional seat, one seat in Trieste province and two seats in Trieste commune were taken by a concurrent local green list, I Verdi. These seats are included in the table.

* Regional elections in Trentino-Alto Adige are in November 1988.

Election Results: National

	NATIONAL (Camera dei Deputati)				EURO-PEAN	
	1987 Jun	1983 Jun	1979 Jun	1976 Jun	1984 Jun	1979 Jun
8 Social Movement (MSI/DN)	**35**	**42**	**30**	**35**	**5**	**4**
	5.9	*6.8*	*5.3*	*6.1*	*6.5*	*5.4*
6 Christian-Democrat Party (DC)	**234**	**225**	**262**	**262**	**26**	**29**
	34.3	*32.9*	*38.3*	*38.7*	*33.0*	*36.4*
5 Liberal Party (PLI)	**11**	**16**	**9**	**5**	[1]	**3**
	2.1	*2.9*	*1.9*	*1.3*		*3.5*
4 Republican Party (PRI)	**21**	**29**	**16**	**14**	**5**	**2**
	3.7	*5.1*	*3.0*	*3.1*	*6.1*	*2.6*
4/10 Radical Party (PR)	**13**	**11**	**18**	**4**	**3**	**3**
	2.6	*2.2*	*3.4*	*1.1*	*3.4*	*3.7*
3 Social-Democrat Party (PSDI)	**17**	**23**	**20**	**15**	**3**	**4**
	2.9	*4.1*	*3.8*	*3.4*	*3.5*	*4.3*
3 Socialist Party (PSI)	**94**	**73**	**62**	**57**	**9**	**9**
	14.3	*11.4*	*9.8*	*9.6*	*11.2*	*11.0*
1 Communist Party (PCI)	**177**	**198**	**201**	**228**	**27**	**24**
	26.6	*29.9*	*30.4*	*34.4*	*33.3*	*29.6*
1 Proletarian Democracy (DP)	**8**	**7**	**6**[2]	**6**[4]	**1**	**1**
	1.7	*1.5*	*1.4*	*1.5*	*1.4*	*0.7*
10 Greens (Liste Verdi)	**13**[3]					
	2.5					
11 Miscellaneous/Regionalist	**7**	**6**	**6**		**2**	**2**[2]
	3.3	*3.0*	*2.6*		*1.6*	*2.7*

Key: **Seats** in bold, *Percentages* in italics.

References
The Times Guide to the European Parliament, Times Books, 1984.
Information Services, Camera dei Deputati, Rome.
Italian Embassy, London.

Notes
1 The Liberal and Republican parties formed a single list for the 1984 elections to the European Parliament.
2 The six seats in 1979 went to Partito d'Unità Proletaria (PdUP), as did one seat in the 1979 elections to the European Parliament. Subsequently the PdUP stood on the PCI list and the Democrazia Proletaria took over as the independent Communist list.
3 The Greens also have two seats in the Italian Senate. One senator, from Milan, was elected from a Lista Verdi. The other, from Trento, contested his seat on a coalition list with the PSI, PSDI and PR. In official results therefore he is recorded as one of the 9 senators won by this list.
4 For these elections the DP was in a cartel with Lotta Continua and Partito d'Unità Proletaria.

9: LUXEMBOURG

Déi Gréng Alternativ

Area: 2,586 sq. km.
Population: 367,200 (1986)
Density: 142 per sq. km.

founded: 23 June 1983
members: about 125

Member: UN, European Communities, OECD, NATO,
    WEU
Language: Luxemburgish
GNP per capita: US $12,990 (1985)

Background and Electoral System

Luxembourg became a grand duchy in 1815 then finally
obtained independence in 1839. Although Luxembourg maintains cultural ties with France, it has its main economic ties
with Belgium with which it has long formed a customs union.
It was when Luxembourg joined the Benelux economic union
after the Second World War that the country abandoned the
'perpetual neutrality' which it had maintained since 1868.

Luxembourg was a founder member of the European
Communities (the Common Market, the European Coal and
Steel Community and the European Atomic Energy Com-
munity) and plays host to several of its institutions. Conse-
quently Luxembourg has been able to sustain a profile in
European politics despite being a small country.

The Grand Duchy of Luxembourg is a hereditary
monarchy, with the grand duke playing a largely representative role. Legislative and executive power lies mainly with
the one-chamber parliament. All legislation must pass
through parliament twice within a three-month time period
before it may be enacted. A 21-member council of state is
selected (for life) by the grand duke. The council may pass

opinions on proposed laws and amendments and other matters passed to it, and make administrative decisions. For administrative purposes the country is divided into four regions – South, East, Centre and North.

Elections to the European Parliament, Chamber of Deputies and municipal councils in districts with a population over 3,000 are conducted under a system of proportional representation which permits electors to distribute among the various party lists and the candidates on those lists the same number of votes as there are seats available. In the 1984 elections to the European Parliament, for example, there were six seats available so each voter had six votes. In the elections to the Chamber of Deputies, voters in the Centre district each had 23 votes; in the North, 9 votes; in the South, 25 votes; and in the East, 7 votes. The larger the number of seats available, the lower the percentage of the vote a candidate requires to obtain a seat. Councils in the smaller local districts are elected by a simple majority system. There are no financial barriers to contesting any election and voting is obligatory in Luxembourg.

Factors Influencing the Development of Green Politics

In the 1970s approximately 15,000 people belonged to traditional environmental groups like the Organisation for the Protection of Birds and Nature, and Natura, which acted as an umbrella organisation for local groups. The anti-nuclear movement was also quite small although Jean Huss, one of Déi Gréng Alternativ's first members of parliament who was president of the Young Socialists at the time, recalls that a campaign coordinated by a local group Biergerinitiàtiv Müselldall successfully ended government plans to build a nuclear power station at Remerschen in 1975. Since then the anti-nuclear movement has concentrated on the reactor site of Cattenom just over the border in France.

Towards the end of the 1970s a new non-party Mouvement Ecologique grew out of an association called Jeunes et Environnement (Youth and Environment) and published a monthly journal called *De Késeiker* (*The Hedgehog*, present circulation about 3,000). The end of the 1970s also saw increasing disillusionment among supporters of the Socialist

party. Until 1974, the Christian-Social party had been the
senior partner in every government since 1919, with the
Democratic party and the Socialist party taking turns to
provide the junior partner. Briefly, between 1974 and 1979,
the Democratic party and the Socialist party managed to
form a government before the Christian-Social party
resumed its traditional role. With the small Communist party
in Luxembourg adhering to a pretty orthodox line, many
left-wing sympathisers found themselves without a political
home at this time.

In 1979, a small Alternative Lëscht : Wiert lech! (Alternative List : Resist) contested the national elections in all four
districts, polling an average of 0.9% of the vote but disband-
ing immediately afterwards. A little later a new magazine
Perspektiv was founded with the intention of rethinking the
orientation of left-wing politics in Luxembourg. Jean Huss,
who had already left the Socialist party, was one of the
editoral board of *Perspektiv* (now defunct). He remembers
becoming more aware of the importance of environmental
politics in the early 1980s as the extent of the pollution
damage to trees became understood and tiny Luxembourg
seemed in danger of disappearing under a cross-hatching of
motorways. It is out of this rethinking process that Huss
considers the Green party in Luxembourg to have emerged.[1]

Déi Gréng Alternativ

About a year before the elections to the Chamber of Deputies
and the European Parliament which were due to be held
simultaneously in June 1984, several people began to meet to
consider forming a party and putting up candidates for both
elections. Although inspired by the example of Die Grünen's
success in Germany, many people were reluctant to become
involved in electoral politics. However they did agree to form
a party and, on 23 June 1983, as required by Luxembourg law,
the declaration of principles and the statutes of Déi Gréng
Alternativ were published and the party legally registered.
At the first meeting of the new party about 80 people decided,
by a tiny majority, not to participate in the forthcoming
elections. However, in April 1984 the party experienced a
change of heart which prompted a unanimous decision in
favour of contesting both elections. Jean Huss and Jup

Weber, a publicist for a bank, stood in the more favourable South and Centre electoral districts respectively. Huss also headed a national list for the European Parliament even though the party did not expect to win one of the six seats. Despite the newness of the party and the hastily put together campaign, Huss was elected to the Chamber of Deputies with 5.7% of the vote and Weber with 6%. In the European election Huss polled 6.1% of the vote, which was, as anticipated, somewhat short of the approximately 16% required to win a seat.

Almost immediately Déi Gréng Alternativ ran into internal difficulties. All the candidates for the elections had agreed in advance that, depending on their domestic circumstances, one-third or one-quarter of their parliamentary salaries would go to the movement and they would rotate at mid-term. Jup Weber prevaricated over both these points, refusing to hand over any of his salary and showing reluctance to cooperate with his parliamentary colleague and the party at large. A crisis meeting was held in February 1985 and Jup Weber asked to return his mandate to the party. Weber's counter-motion to cancel this demand was unanimously voted down. However a motion to forbid Weber from acting in the name of the party (in effect, excluding him from the party) was won with a majority of three votes. After the meeting, Jup Weber made a press statement announcing that henceforth he would be sitting in parliament as an independent.

This meeting prompted about twenty people to leave the party, the total membership of which was between 60 and 70 at the time. They were distressed not only at the dubious democratic status of this vote, as the party statutes demanded a majority of three-fifths for such a major decision, but also by the uncompromising attitude of some other members, particularly those who came from the group around the *Perspektiv* journal. While denying any support for what they saw as 'arrogant and provocative' behaviour on the part of Weber, the group felt that their idea of how a Green-Alternative party should be run was irreconcilable with that of those members who were more used to the political expediency and robust language of traditional left-wing political activity. In their declaration the group vowed to continue to pursue their beliefs in other ways.[2] Several of these people have subsequently rejoined the party.

In the October 1987 district elections Déi Gréng Alternativ presented lists in four large industrial towns in the South, and one list in Luxembourg city which is in the Centre. In the South they polled between 8.5% and 10.5% of the vote and obtained one seat in each town. For lists presented in three smaller towns Déi Gréng Alternativ polled between 12% and 21% but, under the Luxembourg electoral system, failed to win seats. In Luxembourg city, Déi Gréng Alternativ won a seat with 4.9% of the vote. However a list headed by Jup Weber also won a seat, polling 5.6% of the vote.[3] It is widely thought that a single list in Luxembourg city could have obtained three seats.

Future Prospects

The split between the only two members of parliament of a small party in a small country has caused considerable confusion among Luxembourg voters. It has probably also set back the development of a significant environmental movement in Luxembourg, as Weber and Huss each have radically different styles and political priorities. Because at least five signatures from deputies are required on proposals for or amendments to laws in parliament, the lack of cooperation between the two men elected on 'green-alternative' tickets has killed any hopes there might have been of forming parliamentary alliances around issues rather than along party lines.

However, the 1989 elections to the national and the European parliaments loom and, if nothing else, the problems of the Greens have helped to ensure that most people in Luxembourg not only know of their existence but also understand at least some of the issues at stake. François Bausch, a member of Déi Gréng Alternativ's coordinating committee, feels that the people of Luxembourg expect there to be a united list for these next elections, which his party wants to try and negotiate with Jup Weber. But Bausch also feels there is little chance that Weber will enter into discussions with Déi Gréng Alternativ. Although Weber has a small group of supporters around him, he is a flamboyant and well-known personality in Luxembourg and should easily keep his seat in the Centre district. Déi Gréng Alternativ feel confident that they too will win seats in the South district. However, they may not have the territory to themselves. Weber has said in an interview that it is good to have two or more Green lists so that people may choose between them.[4]

It will be unfortunate if the individualistic behaviour of one man ends up by damaging what election results have shown to be an important and growing amount of sympathy for Green ideas among the people of Luxembourg.

Notes

1 Interview with author, 9 April 1988.
2 Declaration by six members of the party coordination and thirteen ordinary members, February 1985.
3 Report to the European Greens, October 1987.
4 Interview with François Bausch, 18 June 1988.

Main Party Publications

Declaration of Principles, 1983.
Virschléi fir eng ökologesch Politik, 1988 (policies and strategy).

Address

Déi Gréng Alternativ
Boîte Postale 2711
1027 Luxembourg

tel: (352) 490049

Organogram: Dé Gréng Alternative

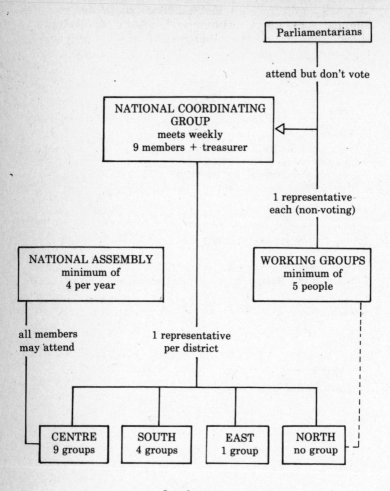

Parliamentarians

attend but don't vote

NATIONAL COORDINATING
GROUP
meets weekly
9 members + treasurer

1 representative
each (non-voting)

NATIONAL ASSEMBLY
minimum of
4 per year

WORKING GROUPS
minimum of
5 people

all members
may attend

1 representative
per district

CENTRE	SOUTH	EAST	NORTH
9 groups	4 groups	1 group	no group

Local groups
125 members pay monthly subscriptions
proportionate to salary and have voting rights
120 members pay flat rate annual subscription
and have no voting rights

Election Results

	NATIONAL (Chambre des Députés)			EURO-PEAN	
	1984 Jun	1979 Jun	1974 May	1984 Jun	1979 Jun
6 Christian-Social Party	**25** *39.0*	**24** *36.4*	**18** *28.0*	**3** *34.9*	**3** *36.2*
5 Democratic Party	**14** *22.8*	**15** *21.9*	**14** *22.1*	**1** *22.1*	**2** *28.1*
3 Social-Democrat Party		**2** *6.4*	**5** *9.1*		
3 Socialist Party	**21** *29.3*	**14** *22.5*	**17** *29.0*	**2** *29.9*	**1** *21.6*
1 Communist Party	**2** *2.5*	**2** *4.9*	**5** *10.4*	*4.1*	*5.0*
10 Greens (Déi Gréng Alternativ)	**2** *2.9*[1]			*6.1*	
11 Miscellaneous	**2** *1.7*	**2**[2] *8.3*	*1.4*		*9.1*

Key: **Seats** in bold, *Percentages* in italics.

References
The Times Guide to the European Parliament, Times Books, 1984.
Green Party papers.
Annuaire Statistique du Grande-Duché, 1987/88.

Notes
1 Percentage given is nationwide. One seat was gained in each of the two constituencies where Déi Gréng Alternative presented a list. The average vote for the two lists was 5.9%.
2 Includes 0.9% for Alternative Lëscht-Wiert lech.

10: NETHERLANDS *De Groenen*

Area: 33,943 sq. km.   *founded: December 1983*
Population: 14.53 million (1986)   *members: not known*
Density: 428 per sq. km.

Member: UN, NATO, OECD, European Communities, WEA
Language: Dutch
GNP: US $8,500 per capita (1984)

Background and Electoral System

Before the separation of north and south Netherlands after the Belgian revolt in 1830, the country was made up of seven very autonomous provinces held together by a weak central government. The 1848 constitution altered the relationship between parliament and government by providing for direct elections to the new lower house and giving it power to amend government proposals, initiate enquiries and question ministers.

Dutch society is traditionally considered to be arranged around three main *zuilen* or pillars – Calvinist, Catholic and lay (the *verzuiling* theory of social organisation is explained more fully in Chapter 2 on Belgium). In the Netherlands, the two religions sided against liberal attempts to reform education before World War I, but the rise of socialism brought the liberals and the religious groups into collusion. More recently the political parties have cut across religious divisions when forming coalitions and the religious parties are in decline. In fact the main conservative party today, the Christian-Democrats (CDA), is the result of a merger between a Catholic and two Protestant parties.

The Netherlands is a constitutional monarchy. The reigning monarch exercises executive power through a cabinet of the governing party/ies, and legislative power is shared through the two-chamber Staten-General (parliament). Members of the 75-seat First Chamber (senate) are elected by the 12 provincial councils and the 150-seat Second Chamber (lower house) is directly elected by the entire population. Both chambers are elected for a four-year term. Members of the government may not sit in parliament, to which they are answerable.

The 12 provinces are further subdivided into around 720 municipalities and each province has its own elected body, known as the Provincial States. Its size depends on the size of the province, and it is responsible for electing the members of the First Chamber of the Staten-Generaal. The Staten-General and the provincial council each elect an executive of six members which is known as the Deputy States. Both Provincial and Deputy States are presided over by a commissioner of the queen who is also the chief magistrate of the province.

The municipalities directly elect a council for a four-year term, which in turn elects several *wethouder* (lawholders) – the number depends on the size of the municipality – to deal with the day-to-day business of the council. The *wethouder* are also responsible for the enforcement of the law and are presided over by a *burgmeester* appointed by the Crown.

The Netherlands employs an electoral system based on absolute proportionality for all elections. All legal votes are added up and divided by the number of seats being contested. This gives the *kiesdeler* (quota) which is required to obtain one seat. For elections to the Lower House, the *kiesdeler* is 0.7%. To allow for provincial differences in nomination of candidates the country is divided into 19 electoral constituencies for national elections. However the country is treated as one constituency when the votes are counted and the local votes for a particular party may be aggregated.

Any party not already represented in the Lower House must pay a deposit of 1,000 guilders per constituency (250 guilders for elections to the provincial and municipal councils). This deposit is returned if the party obtains at least three-quarters of the *kiesdeler*. All parties that have a candidate registered (by 25 signatures) and have paid their deposit in every constituency, are given a state allowance of 10,000 guilders to make two television programmes and two radio programmes of twenty minutes each which are then broadcast during the national election campaign.

Factors Influencing the Development
of Green Politics

The fact that there is not a strong Green party in the Netherlands is somewhat bewildering to outside observers because, unlike Belgium, the *zuilen* do not seem to have prevented a broad-based ecological movement from developing.

The Netherlands has a long history of environmental concern which paradoxically may have combined with the traditional conservatism of the Dutch and the considerable wealth of the country to make life tolerable for most people in one of the world's most densely populated nations. However this wealth, boosted by resources of natural gas, also fuelled considerable industrial and agricultural development. Now the consequences of polluting industries and intensive agriculture and stock-rearing are becoming acutely felt. The Dutch too have been much affected by their situation at the mouth of the Rhine, which acts as the industrial sewer for Europe. One campaign ended successfully in 1981 when Greenpeace succeeded in obtaining a legal injunction against the dumping of low-level nuclear waste in the sea.

Indeed the anti-nuclear movement in the Netherlands is viewed as being one of the strongest. Although two reactors were commissioned in the 1960s, strong protests were mounted over the proposal of the Labour government in 1974 to build three 1,000 MW fast-breeder reactors. The project was successfully delayed until 1985 when it was dusted off by the Conservative/Liberal coalition. Their proposal to build two new reactors was certainly influenced by the rapid depletion of the country's natural gas resources and was made counter to the recommendations of an official commission into the future of energy supplies in the Netherlands. The Brede Maatschappelijke Discussie, which had reported the previous year, also revealed that 77% of the people they had interviewed wanted no more nuclear plants and 52% wanted the two existing plants closed down. In the event, the accident at Chernobyl put the Dutch nuclear plant back on the shelf.[1]

Even though they were less lucky in influencing government defence policy, the Dutch people also put up a strong opposition to the stationing of cruise missiles on their soil. The campaign included presenting to the government in

November 1985 a petition signed by three million people.

The Dutch peace and environmental movement is respected not only for its militant activity but also for its technical expertise and its intellectual contribution to the development of the Green movement. Deserving particular mention is the study carried out by the Centre for Energy-Saving (CE) to develop a 'conserver economy' for the Netherlands. Influenced by the anti-nuclear debate of the 1970s, the Dutch government funded the development of three scenarios for the Dutch economy for the period 1980-2000, one of which was the CE study. The results provided very important evidence that a viable human-scale economic system can be based on environmental conservation and energy saving.[2] In September of the same year the Landelijk Milieu Overleg, a study group of nine environmental organisations, produced a programme (backed by a further 11 provincial environmental federations), which incorporated the ideas of the CE-scenario.[3]

Why then, hasn't a strong Green party emerged in the context of the long-standing and relatively influential Dutch environmental and anti-nuclear movement – not to mention the easy access to the electoral system? Paradoxically the reasons for failure are to be found in those seemingly perfect circumstances. Firstly, the need for political parties to practise pragmatism in order to survive means that the established parties do absorb certain environmental issues into their programmes. So well in some cases that Joop den Uyl, the Labour leader who defended the 'atoms for peace' campaign for nuclear power in the early 1970s, was able to come over in the 1986 elections to the national parliament as one of the greenest politicians around. Similarly the small left-wing political parties with antiquated ideologies and seriously declining electoral fortunes set about trying to claim the Green label with the vigour of dogs fighting over a bone. All parties, large and small, were inspired by an opinion poll published the year before the 1984 elections to the European Parliament. In it one-third of the people canvassed felt a need for the creation of a Green political party.[4]

The second reason for the non-emergence of a successful independent Green party is that the attempts which have been made fail to reflect either the high level of debate among intellectual circles or the level of awareness and understanding among the general population about ecological matters.

The best example of this is the election manifesto produced by De Groenen for the same 1986 general election. It was generally ignored by the press and other political commentators for its lack of substance, and its sloganeering failed to inspire confidence in the voters. Like their counterparts in Denmark, De Groenen learned the hard way that the slogans of the 1970s no longer work for the 1980s.

De Groenen

One of the earliest attemps to incorporate Green ideas into a political programme was made by the Politieke Partij Radikalen (PPR) who are usually described as 'progressive Catholic'. Even though the coalition manoeuvrings of the small Dutch left-wing parties have done much to devalue political labels such as 'progressive', 'innovative', 'new' or 'radical', the PPR does embrace some Green policies. Indeed, after the 1979 elections to the European Parliament the PPR took part in the original coordination of Green and Radical parties that was set up. However it should be noted that it was the differences between the Green parties and the two Radical parties that promoted the eventual split in that coordination. (See Chapter 15.)

Conscious of their declining popularity at the polls, some members of the PPR began to discuss options for the impending 1984 elections to the European Parliament. For this at least 4% of the vote had to be polled to obtain a seat. They saw three options for future strategy:

> 1) to be an independent radical party that wants to work together with all other progressive parties;
> 2) to be a Green party, with the objective of being an ecological party as part of a wider cooperation;
> 3) to be a radical party as part of a small leftist cooperation (working closer with the Pacifist Socialist Party (PSP) and the Dutch Communist Party (CPN)).[5]

While these discussions were taking place, two prominent members of the PPR — Bas de Gaay Fortman and Wouter van Dieren – registered the name Groene Partij Nederland (GPN — Green Party of the Netherlands) giving two reasons for doing so; they wanted to prevent any extreme right party from co-opting the name and they also wanted to avoid the creation of an independent ecology party.[6] Part of the PPR's debate about its future strategy involved discussions within a forum known as the Groen Platform (Green Platform) which brought together members from the broader Green movement. However, there were irreconcilable conflicts that the PPR could not solve. The party was determined to make it over the 4% hurdle in the European elections, and there was strong political (not to mention mathematical) pressure to do so in coalition with the PSP and the CPN. Neither of these parties, particularly the CPN, were overjoyed at the thought of taking on overtly Green policies. On the other hand many of the independents taking part in the Groen Platform were very keen on the idea of a distinctly Green party and not at all keen on close association with, particularly, the CPN.

Time began to press and, encouraged by the announcement that the German Greens wished to go into the European elections in an international coordination of the alternative left parties (*Volkskrant*, 6 May 1983), Wim de Boer, president of the PPR and chair of the negotiations, put forward a take-it-or-leave-it proposal to the parties and the Groen Platform discussion group:

> 1) The list would be called the Groen Progressief Akkord (GPA — Green Progressive Accord) and would involve the PPR, PSP, CPN, the Groen Platform and the EVP (a small evangelical party that had become involved in the discussion);
> 2) The candidates would be ranked as follows: 1-PSP, 2-PPR or Groen Platform, 3-CPN, 4-EVP, 5-PPR or Groen Platform;
> 3) A rotation system for elected MPs would assure everyone got a chance to sit in the parliament;
> 4) No collaboration with parties from other countries would be decided until after the elections.

The PPR accepted this proposal on 19 November 1983. The PSP did so on the 27th but criticised the participation of the Groen Platform and the effect it would have on the programme. The CPN also agreed on the same day but the EVP withdrew on 10 December, not wishing to be associated with the PSP or the CPN. The EVP decided not to contest the elections at all. The Groen Platform were due to decide at a meeting in Utrecht on 17 December but as the time approached it became obvious that they would vote against the proposition. Despite a last attempt by some members of the PPR who had been involved with the Groen Platform to save the day by holding a parallel meeting which voted for the proposal, the Utrecht meeting voted against it. Their statement said that the proposal was 'the last alternative of the PPR and, because of the behaviour of numerous members of the PPR but mainly because of our unanimous opinion that ecological politics must be detached from the politics of the left, the extreme left, the people present at Utrecht on 17 December 1983 have decided to create the party De Groenen'.

Bas de Gaay Fortman and van Dieren responded by taking De Groenen to court to try to prevent them from using the new party's name on the ballot paper. The court ruled in their favour but the Greens had carefully lodged the fail-safe name De Europese Groenen which the court accepted. The judge then turned on the newly created Groen Progressief Akkord and disallowed their own name! In the end they had to appear on the ballot paper as the PPR, PSP, CPN and the GPN. The GPN, the Green Party of the Netherlands, was the paper party registered at the end of 1982.

Despite the support (more moral than practical) of the European Greens, the tiny new party polled a very disappointing 1.3% in the elections six months later. But if they had failed to rally the potential Green voter to the polls then so had the Groen Progressief Akkord. Even with Die Grünen as their active champion they only polled 5.6%. This was not even the total of their individual results in the 1982 national elections. Despite their dirty dealings at home (in taking De Groenen to court) and abroad (see Chapter 15) they had not attracted the magical Green vote either.

In the event the GPA did obtain two seats in the European Parliament, but the relationship between the member parties remained purely electoral. They contested the 1986 elections to the Dutch national parliament separately and all experienced a decline in their respective votes. The PPR managed to hang on to its two seats but the PSP lost two of its three seats with its support cut nearly in half. The Communist party lost all its three seats and disappeared from the Dutch parliament for the first time since the Second World War.

After the European elections De Groenen were rather optimistic about the future, confident that their modest vote would be enough to get them into parliament in May 1986. However, deciding not to participate in the municipal elections of March 1986, because 'they were a lot of work for little reward,' may well have been a serious tactical mistake, since, when the peace and environmental movements published a critique of the party manifestos prior to national elections a couple of months later, they did not bother with De Groenen's. Its lack of substance and a rather fragmented campaign caused the party to poll only 0.2% and lose a lot of election deposits.

Future Prospects

After the disappointment of the national elections many of the people who set up De Groenen left: exhausted or disillusioned or both. The very federalised organisation of the party and large post-election debts have contributed to its disintegration. A federal council does still meet every two months but its business is dominated by arguments over money. Much of the dynamic has been taken up by Roel van Duijn who was once a strong protagonist of the GPA and topped the list for the Groen Platform in the 1984 elections to the European Parliament. An individualist, he founded his own party – the Amsterdam Greens – and scraped a seat on Amsterdam city council in March 1986. Although many people find it difficult to work with him and he is variously described as 'having subscribed to every avantgarde group since the hippies' or as 'good on paper but disastrous in practice', he is now considered to be a loyal and constructive participant in efforts to form an independent Green party. On 27 February 1988 Green Amsterdam and De Groenen fused.

Other enthusiasts for an effective Green party are at work and Hein van Meeteren is one of them. He has just organised a meeting at Amsterdam zoo which brought together 450 people around the theme of The Green Spirit and is a moving spirit in another group, the Green Table network, which regularly attracts about 200 people to its meetings. Recently van Meeteren and about 30 friends staged a takeover of the Groen Platform, which was sleeping quietly under the careful negligence of president Bas de Gay Fortman and president-elect Wouter van Dieren. The objective of van Meeteren and his friends is to end the farce of Green organisations that exist only on paper, and to bring into an organised network all people who are genuinely interested in Green ideas and Green politics. Out of this an efficient goal-directed Green political party will be established, they say. Working with van Meeteren are members of De Groenen and Green Amsterdam and everyone stresses that Green politics in the Netherlands are in a state of extreme flux at the moment.

The Groen Platform takeover bid coincides with the moment when the thoughts of the PPR must be turning towards the 1989 elections to the European Parliament. For these they will no doubt be seeking to uncrumple their discarded Green paper credentials. The party, with getting on for 10,000 members, is divided about its future strategy and it will be interesting to see if it eventually decides to continue with its attempt to resuscitate the corpse of the 'small Dutch left' or whether it has the vision and the courage to transform into a Green party – that is, take up the second of the options it discussed back in 1983.

Notes

1   Andrew Holmes, *A Changing Climate, Environmentalism and its impact on the European energy industries*, Financial Times Business Information, London, 1987.
2   Theo Potma et al, *Het CE-scenario*, Centrum voor Energiebesparing, Delft, 1982.
3   *Environment and Economy in the Eighties*, LMO, Donkerstraat 17, 3511 KB Utrecht.
4   *Volkskrant*, 2 May 1983.
5   Undated PPR discussion paper (written between November 1982 and June 1983).
6   *Radikalenkrant* 15, journal of the PPR, 25 November 1982.

Main Party Publications

Hoopvol Naar 2000 (Hope for 2000): *Eeen sociaal/ecologisch perspectief*, 1986.
Liever Leven, 1986 election programme.

Gras, six-weekly newsletter.

Main Studies of Green Politics

RUDIG Wolfgang, *The Dutch and French Greens in the 1984 European Elections*, case study, Manchester University, 1985.
'Groenen op weg het parlement', *De Ronde Tafel*, December 1985.
'Is Groen Alleen Als er Groen op Staat?', *Vuurland*, May 1987.

Four main actors in Dutch Green politics have written books (in Dutch):
BIERMAN Martin, *Groene Politiek, de weg terug naar vooruitgang*, De Horstink, Amersfoort, 1983.
VAN DUIJN Roel, (ed.), *Groene Politiek*, De Horstink, Amersfoort, 1984.
FORTMAN Bas de Gaay & VAN DIEREN Wouter, *De Politieke pendule, Pleidooi voor een nieuwe toekomst*, Zomer en Keuning, Antwerpen, 1987.
VAN MEETEREN Westerouen, *Leven in de politiek, een groene kijk op mens en samenleving*, Markant, Nijmegen, 1986.

Addresses

De Groenen
Postbus 3244
1001 AA Amsterdam

tel: (31) 20 996418

(co-ordinating secretary of Green Table, De Groenen, Green Amsterdam:)
Aga Veltman
Henri Dunant Straat 31
1066 HV Amsterdam

tel: (31) 20 179543

Election Results

	NATIONAL (Staten-General)[1]				EUROPEAN	
	1986 May	1982 Sep	1981 May	1977 May	1984 Jun	1979 Jun
8 Centre Party (Centrumspartei)		**1**				
	0.4	*0.8*	*0.1*		*2.6*	
7 Liberals (VVD)	**27**	**36**	**26**	**28**	**5**	**4**
	17.4	*23.1*	*17.3*	*17.9*	*18.9*	*16.2*
6 Christian-Democrats (CDA)	**54**	**45**	**48**	**49**	**8**	**10**
	34.6	*29.4*	*30.8*	*31.9*	*30.0*	*35.6*
6 State Reform (SGP)	**3**	**3**	**3**	**3**		
	1.8	*1.9*	*2.0*	*2.1*		
6 Reformed Political Assn (GVP)	**1**	**1**	**1**	**1**		
	1.0	*0.8*	*0.8*	*1.0*		
6 Evangelical Political Federation (RPF)	**1**	**2**	**2**			
	0.9	*1.5*	*1.2*			
6 Protestant Coalition (Calvinist)					**1**	
					5.2	
6 Evangelical People's Party (EVP)		**1**	**2**			
	0.2	*0.7*	*0.5*			
4 Radical Political Party (PPR)	**2**	**2**	**3**	**3**	**2**[2]	
	1.3	*1.7*	*2.0*	*1.7*	*5.6*	
4 Democrats 66 (D66)	**9**	**6**	**17**	**8**		**2**
	6.1	*4.3*	*11.0*	*5.4*	*2.3*	*9.5*
3 Labour (PvdA)	**52**	**47**	**44**	**53**	**9**	**9**
	33.3	*30.4*	*28.2*	*33.8*	*33.7*	*30.4*
2 Pacifist Socialist Party (PSP)	**1**	**3**	**3**	**1**	[2]	
	1.2	*2.3*	*2.1*	*0.9*		
1 Communist Party (CPN)	**3**	**3**	**2**	[2]		
	0.6	*1.8*	*2.1*	*1.7*		
10 Greens (de Groenen)	*0.2*				*1.3*	
11 Miscellaneous (includes various parties over the years)		*1.6*	*1.0*	*1.9*	*0.4*	*8.3*

Key: **Seats** in bold, *Percentages* in italics.

References
SMITH Gordon, *Politics in Western Europe*, Heinemann, 1984.
The Times Guide to the European Parliament, Times Books, 1984.
The Statesman's Year Book (ed. John Paxton), Macmillan.
Green Party documents. Royal Netherlands Embassy, London.

Notes
1 The Second Chamber of the Staten-Generaal. The First Chamber is indirectly elected.
2 For the 1984 European elections, the PPR, PSP, CPN formed an electoral coalition called the Green Progressive Accord (GPA); they polled 5.6% and won 2 seats.

11: SWEDEN *Miljöpartiet de Gröna*

Area: 449,964 sq. km.   *founded: 20 September 1981*
Population: 8.4 million (1985)   *members: 6,500*
Density: 19 per sq. km.

Member: UN, OECD and EFTA
Language: Swedish
GNP per capita: US $11,510 (1984)

Background and Electoral System

Sweden's military exploits were abandoned to a policy of neutrality in 1814, since when the country pursued a transformation into the 'model democracy'. In the twentieth century rapid generation of great national wealth and a comprehensive social welfare system have been combined with democratic representation and a decentralised administration. The concept of civilised mediation and defence of the underdog enshrined in the office of Ombudsman, and the prestige of the Nobel Prize awards, all added to modern Sweden's international reputation as an example to be followed. It has been said that while Sweden may have failed to dominate the world militarily, it has succeeded in doing so morally.

But cracks have developed in Sweden's apparent perfection. Political scandals surrounding the murder of the popular Olof Palme and the illegal export of arms from the Bofors factory, for example, have dented Sweden's moral authority internationally and embarrassed its citizens. The effects of radiation from the Chernobyl accident on the Sami people in the north and of acid rain in the south have prompted the health-conscious Swedes to put the environment at the top of their list of most important political

questions.[1] A growing number of people on welfare[2] and an
uneasiness about Sweden's vulnerability in an increasingly
unstable world market (Sweden's economy is heavily dependent on the export of manufactured goods, including arms
and technology for civil nuclear reactors) have unsettled
many people, especially the young, who are also concerned
about the intrusiveness of the benevolent state into every
part of their lives.

Between 1809 when the constitution put the first curbs on
the absolute power of the king, and 1975 when the monarch
became solely representative, successive reforms have been
made to the Swedish parliamentary system. However as late
as the 1950s it was still possible to describe the Riksdag
(national parliament) as the government's 'transport company'; implying that the elected representatives of the people
merely 'transported' the government's policy through the
decision process.[3] Subsequent reforms were intended to
ensure that 'all public power in Sweden proceeds from the
people' and that the one-chamber parliament would become
an 'interesting political arena' as well as the central decision-
making body. However the new formula for democracy did
not remove from the Riksdag the concept of majority rule.
The Constitutional Commission had hoped that bills could be
debated, amended, passed or defeated independent of 'bloc'
political allegiances, and that theoretically governments
could be defeated on a particular issue without falling.
Instead polarisation actually increased. The deadlock that
occurred between the two political blocs in 1973 was dealt
with by the unsubtle expediency of reducing the number of
seats in the Riksdag from 350 to 349.

National, county and municipal elections are held on the
same day every three years. All elections are conducted on a
proportional basis. For elections to the Riksdag the country
is divided into 28 constituencies returning 310 members, and
the remaining 39 seats are allocated to all parties obtaining
at least 4% of the vote nationally or 12% in any constituency.
The 24 *län* (counties) are each administered by a board with a
government-appointed chair and 14 members elected by the
county council. The *län* are further subdivided into 284
kommunfullmäktige (municipal councils). All levels of local
government have considerable and wide-ranging powers.

Finance for elections is linked to representation and to
past electoral results. Past results of over 1% (2.5% up to
1982) ensure financial assistance for delivery of ballot papers;

each voter requires a party-specific ballot paper to be able to vote for that party.

Factors Influencing the Development of Green Politics

In 1976 a conservative coalition ended an unbroken 44-year period of Social-Democrat government. Four conservative coalitions preceded a return to power of the Social-Democrats in 1982, this time in coalition with the Communists. The famous Swedish 'Social-Democrat consensus' was being displaced by the power-brokerage associated with coalition building.

During this unsettled political time the Swedes held a referendum on the future of their nuclear power programme. Inspired by the accident at Three Mile Island and a long national debate over future power sources, the poll took place in March 1980 when Sweden had six stations in use, four more ready to go and two under construction. Three choices were offered:

1) to go on with the programme (18.9% voted for this);
2) to dismantle the programme over 30 years (39.1% voted for this);
3) to dismantle the programme over 10 years (39.7% voted for this).[4]

The ambiguity of the result was fully exploited. It was viewed as a defeat for the anti-nuclear vote (option 3) with the anti-nuclear implications of option 2 neatly reinterpreted as a '30-year stay of execution' for the industry. Since the referendum four more stations have been brought into use and nuclear production of electricity has increased to 30%. As Sweden has a fairly strong environmental movement whose membership is spread across the political parties the result of this referendum made a lot of people 'politically homeless'. The Social-Democrats supported nuclear power and the Centre party, traditionally viewed as a defender of the environment, at least from the farmers' point of view (it changed its name from Farmer's Alliance to Centre party in 1958), had played a dominant role in three of the four non-socialist coalitions, so blotting more than its anti-nuclear copybook.

Meanwhile, during 1979, a Liberal member of parliament, Per Gahrton, was becoming increasingly disillusioned not only with his party and its pro-nuclear policy but also with the whole parliamentary system. After resigning from parliament and from his party he wrote a doctoral thesis on the functioning of a political group within the Riksdag which caused quite a stir when it was published in 1983. Among other things, it provided hard data demonstrating political patronage at work, and mischievously portrayed the extensive facilities (ranging from meeting rooms to shops, chapels and saunas) provided to meet the needs of parliamentarians working in the Riksdag as a 'total institution' not dissimilar to a prison or a madhouse. He wrote: 'According to a rich literature, long-term stays in total institutions carry with them mental defects such as a breakdown of self-consciousness.'[5]

Gahrton also joined the anti-nuclear movement, wrote articles about the need for a new political force and made contacts. After the referendum on nuclear power he sent his 'personal manifesto' to about 22 people, and some small parties with representatives on about 10 different local councils (some of them already using Miljöpartiet { = Environment party} in their title). A committee was established, and on 20 September 1981 Miljöpartiet was founded as a national political party in the city of Örebro.

Early Days

The new party set off to a brisk start and grew rapidly, drawing new members from the 'politically homeless' but also from the other parties. In 1984 Gahrton estimated that about 25-30% of Miljöpartiet's members were former Centre party supporters, a similar percentage came from the Social-Democrat camp or were 'non-voters' and the rest were former Liberal or Communist supporters.[6] Two dominant features of Miljöpartiet at this time (and indeed subsequently) have been its desire to remain outside the tangle of the two political blocs and to develop a new style of doing politics.

In the build-up to the elections of 19 September 1982 the hopes of the new party were high. Opinion polls indicated that it might obtain the necessary 4%. However the fight between the two principal blocs was close and Miljöpartiet's national vote was squeezed to 1.7%. Nor were its candidates successful in the elections for the county councils either, though they did gain 124 seats on 96 of the 284 municipal councils, averaging 2.7% where they stood.

In the following three years Miljöpartiet devoted itself to creating an efficient decentralised organisation and to getting its finances back into shape. In May 1982 it also established a weekly newspaper, *Alternativet*, benefitting from a state subsidy for small newspapers. One condition of the subsidy is that the newspaper must contain general reporting as well as party-specific material, but the relationship between paper and party is somewhat unclear.[7] Legally the newspaper is a *stiftelse* (foundation), and the committee set up by the party only controls the leader page and the 'dandelion pages' of announcements of meetings etc. around the country. However funding of the paper remains precarious. At the end of 1987 it reported a subscription circulation of 4,854.[8]

At its January 1985 congress the party voted to add 'de Gröna' (the Greens) to its name and went into the elections of 15 September with high hopes of echoing the electoral successes of Green parties in other countries – events in Finland and West Germany being extensively reported in the Swedish press. Thanks to the 1982 law on electoral financing the party could also anticipate having its ballot slips for the elections to parliament and to some of the local councils paid for by the state this time round. But once again the 'bloc squeeze' affected Miljöpartiet's result which was a disappointing 1.5% nationally. However its candidates improved their results locally, obtaining a 3% average where they stood and gaining 260 seats on 160 councils. On several councils, notably the cities of Göteborg and Uppsala, they held the balance of power, and Miljöpartiet eventually formed governing coalitions with the left-wing and right-wing blocs respectively.

Success

Miljöpartiet particularly blamed its poor results on the media, which either ignored or misrepresented it, and on the refusal of the major opinion poll organisation SIFO to give the party a separate listing.[9] What seemed at the time to be sour grapes after a lacklustre campaign later acknowledged to be full of mistakes (Per Gahrton, *Alternativet*, 19 September 1986) proved to be the key to reversing Miljöpartiet's fortunes.

In December 1986 Radionämnden (a semi-official body in charge of assuring the political impartiality of radio and television) ruled that Miljöpartiet had indeed been discriminated against during the 1985 election campaign. Subsequent coverage improved not only for Green events but also for routine statements and comments on current political events emanating from the party. Also at the end of 1986 the head of the SIFO poll agency, during a tv interview about his move to the editorship of the rather conservative daily newspaper *Svenska Dagbladet*, disingenuously admitted that it was unfair for Miljöpartiet to be excluded from the polls and recommended that it should be included before the next election.[10] Miljöpartiet pressed the new SIFO chief to honour his predecessor's promise and the party entered the polls at 3% in January 1987. In February its standing improved to between 3.9% and 5.5%. By June support for Miljöpartiet was running at about 8% and in October the IMU (another polling organisation) recorded 10% support for the Greens, ahead of the Centre party at 8% and the Communists at 4.5%.

Future Prospects

Being in the public eye means that Miljöpartiet has benefitted from public concern about the environment; concern that increased considerably after the disasters at Chernobyl and on the Rhine. An opinion poll carried out by the Research Group for Social and Information Studies showed that 53% of Swedes believed good environmental policies to be more important than which bloc got into power (*Alternativet*, April 1988) The party was also able to exploit public indignation over the growing number of mistakes being made by the Social-Democrat government. Miljöpartiet member Ingvar Bratt, an engineer who left Bofors to become the peace group Svenska Freds' so-called 'Bofors leak' when they reported the arms company to the police for smuggling in 1984, attracted considerable attention when the company eventually admitted liability in March 1987.

The growth of support for Miljöpartiet in the polls both seemed to assure it of seats in the national parliament at the coming election (September 1988) and also suggested that it could hold the balance of power. A spirited debate within the party about how they should prepare for this eventuality was extensively reported in *Alternativet*. Per Gahrton initiated the debate in the issue of 25 July 1986 after analysing the results for Die Grünen in the 15 June elections in the West German state of Lower Saxony. The 'Chernobyl factor' had failed to work and the German Greens had only improved their vote by 0.6%. Gahrton believed this was because of lack of clarity over how they would act if they held the balance of power after the election. In Sweden, Miljöpartiet had tried two 'models' already. In 1982 they had left the question open, in 1985 they had put '20 questions' to the other parties to help them decide. Most parties had, of course, replied ambiguously or not at all. For 1988, Gahrton thought Miljöpartiet should make it clear that a vote for the Greens was a vote against a right-wing government and for a Social-Democrat government. The party met this statement with considerable exasperation.

Eleven months later at their congress in Karlskoga, the party voted to leave the decision until *after* the 1988 election when a thorough appraisal of the other blocs would be made. They also decided that all their MPs would vote according to the party's decision. The same congress, rather quixotically, decided to allow local party members to belong to more than one political party.[11]

Gahrton unequivocally supported the Karlskoga decision, seeing that any attempt by the party to brand one political bloc as 'less bad' than the other would tarnish the ideological and strategic independence of Miljöpartiet. The slump in the Social-Democrats' credibility over the past year had also helped him to change his mind. Now, 'The question of which government to support could be transformed from a Green problem into a Green trump card!' (*Alternativet*, 19 June 1987). Miljöpartiet could play an important historical role by helping the Riksdag to fulfil the intention of the Constitutional Commission: to make the Swedish parliament into an interesting political arena, an important centre of political decision-making.

As the September 1988 elections drew nearer, however, the

attacks of the other political parties on Miljöpartiet grew fiercer. The Social-Democratic party particularly tried to wrap itself in an 'environmental' mantle, although an analysis of its parliamentary activity in the form of questions tabled and legislation proposed does not reveal any actions in support of their claims.[12] The prime minister, Ingvar Carlsson, even suggested that Miljöpartiet's entry into parliament would be a threat to democracy. Miljöpartiet felt that the media and other big institutions were closing ranks with the major political parties. 'They want everything to be as it was, they want to scratch each other's backs in peace and quiet, share a sauna, and then act out the farce of an election campaign. The Green movement is a threat both to the comfortable "ombudsmanocracy" and to the equally comfortable capitalist circus. They are, therefore, prepared to use any means they can to stop the Greens.' That is how Miljöpartiet spokesman Birger Schlaug put it in a controversial statement in July 1987.

Towards the end of the campaign, when opinion poll ratings of up to 10% raised the possibility that Miljöpartiet might even hold the balance of power, those means included publishing the (supposedly secret) tax returns of some Miljöpartiet candidates, and when Birger Schlaug drove his wife's inadequately insured car down a remote country lane, not only were the police waiting for him, but the event received banner headlines in the national press the following day.

In the end, Miljöpartiet polled 5.6% and won 20 seats to become the first new party to enter the Swedish parliament for 70 years. In the simultaneously held local elections Miljöpartiet also did very well, now being represented in all of the *län* and holding the balance of power on 40 of the 284 local councils. As the Social-Democrats won more seats than the three 'bourgeois' parties (Conservative, Centre and Liberal) put together and the Communists won 21 seats, the Greens (rather to their relief) do not hold the balance in the Riksdag. Nevertheless it does look as though Miljöpartiet will alter a few parliamentary habits. The party has not only reaffirmed its intention to decide on how its MPs will vote issue by issue, but it is also possible that an influential 83-seat 'Green bloc' may develop in the Riksdag which cuts across traditional left-right party lines – both the 'bourgeois' Centre party and the Communists like to pride themselves on their environmental awareness.

Notes

1 *Alternativet*, 13 March 1986.
2 7% in 1985 (*Economist*, 7 June 1986).
3 Per Gahrton, 'Not Chaos, but Democracy', in *Alternativet*, 19 June 1987.
4 *Alternativet*, 20 February 1987.
5 Per Gahrton, *Riksdagen Inifræn – En studie av parlamentarisk handfallenhet inför ett samhälle i kris*, Prisma, Stockholm, 1983.
6 'Some Facts About Miljöpartiet and the Political Situation in Sweden', paper to the European Greens, 1984.
7 *Alternativet*, 11 April 1987.
8 Susan Miles, 'Note on *Alternativet*', unpublished, 1986, updated in personal communication, February 1988.
9 Per Gahrton, 'The Green Situation in Sweden', Report to the European Greens, November 1985.
10 *Alternativet*, 12 December 1986.
11 *Alternativet*, 5 June 1987.
12 *Alternativet*, 16 and 23 October 1987.

Main Party Publications

Nu Kommer Miljöpartiet, 1982 (essays from party personalities and party programme).
Grön Grund, 1985 (guide for study groups on ideology of Miljöpartiet).
Guld ella Gröna skogar, by Per Gahrton.
Miljöpartiet's Gilla Gröna, 1987 (long manifesto for election workers).

Alternativet (weekly paper), Erstagatan 9, 116 36 Stockholm.

Study of Miljöpartiet

BRATT Peter, 'What is Miljöpartiet?', *Dagens Nyheter*, 29 November 1987.

Address

Miljöpartiet de Gröna
Box 15264 (letters)
Urvädersgränd 11 (visits)
104 65 Stockholm

tel: (46) 8 4111351

Organogram: Miljöpartiet De Gröna

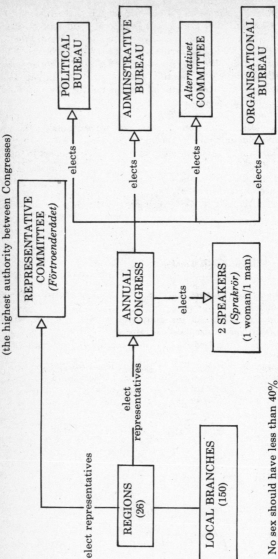

(the highest authority between Congresses)

REPRESENTATIVE COMMITTEE (*Förtroenderådet*)

POLITICAL BUREAU — elects

ADMINSTRATIVE BUREAU — elects

Alternativet COMMITTEE — elects

ORGANISATIONAL BUREAU — elects

ANNUAL CONGRESS — elects → 2 SPEAKERS (*Språkrör*) (1 woman/1 man)

elect representatives

REGIONS (26)

LOCAL BRANCHES (150)

elect representatives

No sex should have less than 40% representation on any elected body or electoral list.

Election Results

NATIONAL (Riksdag)

	1988 Sep	1985 Sep	1982 Sep	1979 Sep	1976 Sep
7 Conservative (Moderaterna)	**66**	**76**	**86**	**73**	**55**
	18.4	*21.3*	*23.6*	*20.3*	*15.6*
6 Christian-Democrats (Kds)					
	3.0		*1.9*	*1.4*	*1.4*
6 Centre Party	**42**	**44**	**56**	**64**	**86**
(formerly Agrarian)	*11.4*	*12.4*	*15.5*	*18.1*	*24.1*
5 Liberal (Folkpartiet)	**44**	**51**	**21**	**38**	**39**
	12.3	*14.2*	*5.9*	*10.6*	*11.1*
3 Social-Democrats	**156**	**159**	**166**	**154**	**152**
	43.5	*44.7*	*45.6*	*43.2*	*42.7*
1 Communists (Vpk)	**21**	**19**	**20**	**20**	**17**
	5.9	*5.4*	*5.6*	*5.6*	*4.8*
10 Greens (Miljöpariet de Gröna)	**20**				
	5.6	*1.5*	*1.7*		
11 Miscellaneous					
		0.5	*0.3*	*0.8*	*0.3*

Key: **Seats** in bold, *Percentages* in italics.

References
SMITH Gordon, *Politics in Western Europe*, Heinemann, 1984.
The Statesman's Year Book (ed. John Paxton), Macmillan.
Green Party documents. the Swedish Institute, Stockholm.

12: SWITZERLAND
Le Parti Ecologiste/Die Grüne Partei

Area: 41,293 sq. km.
Population: 6.5 million (1985)
Density: 157 per sq. km.

founded: 28 May 1983
members: about 4,000

Member: OECD, EFTA
(In March 1986 the Swiss voted against joining the UN)
Official languages: German, French, Italian, Romansch
GNP per capita: US $14,300 (1984)

Background and Electoral System

The origins of the Swiss Confederation date back to the end of the thirteenth century. People from the neighbouring areas of Schwyz, Uri and Unterwalden did not like it when laws and administrative systems were imposed on their independent communities by the zealous Habsburgs. These three cantons formed a 'defensive league' on 1 August 1291. More cantons were added, first by other struggles against the Habsburgs, then through various military adventures and an entanglement with France. A treaty guaranteeing eternal Swiss neutrality was signed in Vienna in 1815 but internal religious conflicts persisted. The 1848 and 1874 Constitutions established the present federal and cantonal administrative system for the then 22 cantons. Jura, the 23rd canton, was established on 1 January 1979 after a national referendum.

Swiss appreciation of the benefits of neutrality developed during the wars of religion and the Thirty Years War. More recently it survived both world wars. Switzerland has developed a reputation for humanitarianism through the International Red Cross and its tradition of welcoming political refugees. But for most people Switzerland remains a rather fairy-tale country of chocolate, cuckoo-clocks, mountains and secret bank accounts.

Switzerland is a republic and the highest authority is the electorate who are all citizens over 20. There are three administrative levels, federal, cantonal and communal.

The federal assembly consists of the 200-seat Nationalrat (national council) and the 46-member Ständerat (estates council). Members are elected directly to the Nationalrat every four years from the cantons according to their population. At present the numbers of seats are allocated as follows:

Zürich	35	Graubünden	5
Bern	29	Neuchâtel	5
Vaud	16	Schwyz	3
Aargau	14	Zug	2
St Gallen	12	Schaffhausen	2
Genève	11	Appenzell Rhoden	
Luzern	9	(outer)[2*]	2
Ticino	8	(inner)[2*]	1
Valais	7	Uri	1
Solothurn	7	Unterwalden	
Basel		(Upper)[2*]	1
(country)[2*]	7	(Lower)[2*]	1
(town)[2*]	7	Glarus	1
Thurgau	6		
Fribourg	6		

The Ständerat has 46 members, elected from the cantons by mostly majority vote. Each canton sends two councillors, each half-canton sends one. The half-cantons are starred in the above list.

The federal assembly (246 electors) elect 7 members to the Bundesrat (federal council). These are elected for a four-year term to run the government departments. One of their number is elected to be president of both the Bundesrat and the whole Confederation. This post is renewable every year.

The cantons are not merely the next administrative level. Each one is a small sovereign state. The larger ones elect a parliament, often called a Grosser Rat or a Kantonsrat. In some smaller cantons the Landsgemeinde still exists. This is an open-air gathering of citizens held annually in order to deal with the business of the community. Some cantons collaborate via jointly established and elected regional councils to deal with common matters.

The 3,022 communes have very varied ways of organising, but generally speaking they tend to follow the model of the canton. Some communes come together as districts to deal with common interests.

The Nationalrat is elected by the d'Hondt system of proportional representation. Each voter chooses the party they prefer but may vote for as many individual candidates as they like up to the quotient for their canton, mixing names from other party lists and even recording a candidate's name twice if they wish. For the Ständerat most cantons use a two-round majority voting system similar to the French one. Jura uses a proportional system, Geneva a one-round majority system.

Most cantons employ proportionality for elections to the Kantonsrat although some of the smaller cantons still use a simple majority system. In the communes the general rule is that larger ones use a proportional system and the smaller ones a simple majority.

It is relatively easy to put up a list for an election in Switzerland. For the Nationalrat 50 signatures from the appropriate canton are required, for the Ständerat it varies but is generally very small – frequently only three signatures. Equally modest requirements exist for elections in the cantons and communes. Financial assistance for parties is very limited. Voting papers are provided free for federal elections and the cantons often refund up to half the cost of printing voting papers for any party obtaining more than 5%. Exceptionally Geneva pays for official posters and gives 10,000 Swiss francs to parties obtaining over 5% in a federal or cantonal election.

Access to political debates on tv and radio is given to parties represented in more than five cantons during a federal election, but cantonal elections are generally covered by just one debate broadcast at an awkward time. Communal elections are not usually covered at all except perhaps for results in the bigger towns.

Apart from the Bundesrat, members of the federal parliament are part-time politicians. They receive a small sum of money for attendance but are expected to keep up their usual employment 75% of the time.

The Swiss democratic system involves regular consultation of citizens by the parliament. No new law or amendment to the Constitution can be passed unless it is approved by the cantons and the citizens through referenda. Similar rules apply at cantonal and communal level. The Swiss people also have the right to put forward ideas in the form of constitutional amendments (popular initiatives) or demand a referendum on any new or revised federal law. Popular initiatives must be backed by 100,000 signatures collected within 18 months and a referendum requires 50,000 signatures obtained within 3 months. All in all, Swiss democracy demands that its citizens go to the polls about four times a year.

Factors Influencing the Development of Green Politics

Swiss democracy has been much admired for the example it offers of harmonious coexistence between potentially very conflicting interests. Differences of language and religion that have shattered other countries have not destabilised Switzerland.

Switzerland's ability to deal with conflict lies of course with the great autonomy enjoyed by the cantons and communes, but of equal importance is the machinery that makes it possible to contantly amend and adapt the Constitution to changing circumstances.[1] Thus, for example, the desire of Jura to become an independent canton could be achieved relatively smoothly, or Romansch added to the Constitution as an official language.

However, all is not perfect. In some of the cantons and communes, especially the smaller ones, the voting system is still by simple majority and the autonomy of the cantons means that the smaller ones can block change for all fairly easily. For example, women did not obtain the vote until 1971, and are still denied this right in two cantons where the Landsgemeinde remains the main decision-making method.

There are also some crucial areas of federal legislation that are out of reach of popular initiative. The law approving the nuclear power programme came into force in 1960 for example, but authorising the building of a new plant can be done under that law as a purely administrative matter, not one requiring consultation and approval of the people. An important criticism of the system is that the time lapse between taking a decision and its implementation can be very long. For example, a 1971 referendum to pass a law on environmental protection was not enforced until the beginning of 1986.

But perhaps the biggest problem with Swiss democracy is that the majority of the population don't participate. Of the total electorate entitled to vote in the October 1987 elections to the federal parliament only 44% did so. The majority of those who do go the polls are middle-aged, well-to-do men. Consequently, Switzerland's authorities have been guided by a minority of the population for decades and it is the conservative parties that consistently obtain the positions of power.

The early popularity of the Swiss Green parties can partly be attributed to the ease with which new parties can contest elections, but it is also due to the refreshing splash the Greens made on the jaded Swiss democratic palate. Reasons for not voting are often complex but in Switzerland's case they include feelings of complacency ('Everything's fine as it is') and impotence ('It doesn't matter how I vote, that lot in Bern will get their own way in the end').[2]

During the 1970s the issues that jolted the stolid burghers and the small rural communities as well as broader bands of society like women and young people were principally nuclear power, motorway building and air pollution. Later on, concern about the increasing reluctance of Switzerland to accept refugees, and embarrassment at the arms trading of their supposedly neutral country (not to mention the service that secret Swiss bank accounts offer to other arms traders), were added to growing alarm about the pollution from acid rain and industrial catastrophes such as Chernobyl and the fire at the Sandoz chemical factory in Basel.

The role that the Swiss environmental groups have begun to play in electoral politics is also worth noting. After a trial run for the 1983 cantonal elections, which they judged to be effective, the larger organisations like the World Wildlife Fund, Schweiz Naturischist Bund, Verkehrclub der Schweiz (Swiss Automobile Club), Schweizer Gesellschaft für Umweltschutz (Swiss Society for Environment Protection) and Rheinanbund (Rhine League) got together and put demands for environmental protection, wild-life protection, traffic regulation and so on, to the political parties contesting the 1987 elections to the Nationalrat. Only the Greens replied. The groups then assembled a list of 35 candidates from the different parties who had a good track record of working for environmental causes. These names were sent round to their own memberships (which total about 300,000) and published in the newspapers. Again the environmental groups feel that this campaign has given them more MPs favourable to their causes than might otherwise have been the case. The Green party agrees.

Early Days

The first Green parties to stand for election in Switzerland were in the cantons of Neuchâtel and Vaud. The Mouvement Populaire pour l'Environnement (MPE) was founded in Neuchâtel in December 1972 with the particular objective of preventing the N5 motorway from being built along the shore of Lake Neuchâtel. The MPE was an eclectic political mix of socialists, liberals and conservatives who were united by their desire to prevent the banks of their lake from disappearing under four lanes of concrete. On 7 May 1972 they obtained 17.8% of the vote and 8 of the 41 seats. This made them the third largest political group on the Neuchâtel town council. By 1975 the council decided that, after all, the road could go underground. The MPE had succeeded against some very powerful vested interests. Although it had intended to dissolve once its objective was achieved the MPE decided to remain a distinct political party. In 1976 they lost one seat on the council but their president was elected to the executive of the city.

Eventually the strains of the different traditional political tendencies trying to practise ecological politics together began to show and the MPE experienced some tough years which included a split and re-fusion of two factions. The party won only 5 seats in the May 1984 local elections.

However the success of the MPE in Neuchâtel had not gone unnoticed. In Vaud a certain Jean-Jacques Hédiguer decided to set up an MPE-Vaud – by correspondence. On 11 November 1973 the postal members won 5.6% of the vote in Lausanne, gaining 5 seats on the 100-seat town council and 15 further seats in suburban communes. The inevitable perils of employing such a method to establish a party then became apparent. One member, an elderly doctor who was fond of prescribing 'liquidation of foreigners' as a solution for environmental ills, saved everyone a lot of embarrassment by expiring before he could read out his prescription in the council chamber.[3] Further quaint activities by Monsieur Hédiguer provoked a split and a new party was formed around the elected councillors called Groupement pour la Protection de l'Environnement (GPE). The MPE-Vaud fizzled out and GPE went on to win 8.2% in November 1977, thereby increasing its seats on the town council to 8.

Those 8 seats gave the ecologists the balance of power, with the left parties holding 44 seats and the right 48. The potentially powerful position this gave them was compounded by the fact that in Lausanne, it is the council members who elect the 7 seats on the executive. The ecologists tried to resist the ensuing bargaining by proposing that they would join a majority to support an executive with 3 seats for each of the left and right blocs and 1 seat for the ecologists. The socialists refused but the right accepted. The fallout from this decision may have affected the vote in the March 1978 cantonal elections, when the GPE obtained only 7.1% and 4 seats. However, it did not seem to prevent the citizens of Lausanne from making Daniel Brélaz the first Green in the world to be elected to a national parliament on 21 October 1979. He polled 6.5% of the vote.

Indeed, after its strange beginnings the GPE went from strength to strength. In the 1982 canton elections it had already increased its representation to 6 seats and in October 1985 it won a total of 74 seats in the local communes.

Meanwhile in other parts of Switzerland, local Green parties were being established and most have a different story to tell. In Zurich, for example, Hans Beat Schaffner, who had been toying with the idea for some time, was finally jolted into action in 1978 by a speech from the Swiss president which urged citizens to take up their democratic rights and responsibilities. After a slow start the Grüne Partei Zürich won seats wherever they stood, from the February 1982 communal elections until April 1987 when they obtained 22 of the 180 seats in the cantonal parliament.

The Bern Freie Liste was founded only one month before the October 1983 elections to the federal parliament round the charismatic and energetic Leni Robert, who had experienced a turbulent split with her party, the Radical Democrats. Her new party's programme highlighted environmental protection and the quality of life, and to her delight won Leni Robert a seat in the new Nationalrat at the expense of her old party. Until she was elected to the executive of Bern in the May 1986 elections (the Freie Liste had won 11 seats in the canton elections a month earlier) Leni Robert sat and worked with the other Greens in the national parliament.

Föderation der Grünen Parteien der Schweiz/ Fédération des Partis Ecologistes de Suisse (GPS/FPE)

The coming together of the various Green groups engaged in electoral politics in Switzerland was not easy. With the approach of the 1983 federal elections it was, naturally, in the front of many people's minds. In 1982 a group tentatively called Association pour la Création du Parti Ecologiste were thinking towards 1983 and at the end of January the Parti Ecologiste Genévoise (PEG) was founded.

However the first initiative to establish a federation came from a group called Demokratische Alternative – Bern (DA-Bern). They sent out an invitation to 'all Green groups and alternative parties' to come and 'discuss the idea of a national Green alliance' on 15 January 1983. Laurent Rebeaud describes the meetings that were held between January and May in painful detail – the anarchy of the organisation, where the agreed principle of one group, one vote was ignored and everyone voted; how new groups were able to arrive and upend agreements made during the previous meeting. Rebeaud admits that deep down there were many shared objectives, but feels there was a serious incompatibility of style, language and approach.[4] The ecologists felt unable to endure the chaos and the struggle of working with people who continually opened up conflicts and divisions and then went on to set them in concrete. The last straw came when a compromise programme which had been agreed by one meeting was then rejected by the next. The ecologists abandoned hope of a joint federation and announced to the press that they would be forming their own federation.

This they did at two meetings held on 14 and 28 May 1983 in Fribourg. Statutes making it possible for more than one party per canton to join were agreed, and the programme ultimately rejected by the 'alternatives' was adopted with a few amendments and the addition of five criteria the Geneva party had developed as key notions to guide ecological thinking – long-term, quality, humanism, anti-technocracy, decentralisation. Founder members were:

– Groupement pour la Protection de l'Environnement (GPE), Vaud
– Mouvement pour la Protection de l'Environnement (MPE), Neuchâtel (later called Ecologie et Liberté)
– Parti Ecologiste Genévoise (PEG), Geneva
– Grüne Partei des Kantons Zürich
– Grüne Partei Nordwest Schweiz (GPN), Basel, Solothurn, Aargau

Subsequently the following groups joined the federation, which changed its name to Grüne Partei der Schweiz/Le Parti Ecologiste Suisse (GPS/PES) in May 1986:

– Grüne Partei des Kantons Thurgau
– Freie Liste, Bern
– Movimento Ecologista Ticinese, Ticino
– Demokratische Alternative, Bern
– Parti Ecologiste Fribourgeois
– Glarner Umweltgruppe   }
– Parti Ecologiste Valaisan   } observers
– Grüne Mitte Basel   }

The 'alternatives' also formed a national group, Alternative Verte de Suisse, but failed to win any seats in the October 1983 elections to the federal parliament. The ecologists, however, obtained three seats and Daniel Brélaz was accompanied by Laurent Rebeaud from Geneva and Arnold Müller from Zurich. They were also joined initially by Leni Robert from the Freie Liste, Bern who was replaced by Lukas Fierz when Robert was elected to the executive of Bern canton in 1986. Arnold Müller eventually left the Green group to sit as an independent after repeated conflicts with his colleagues over policy and his refusal to pay 10% of his parliamentary salary to the federation.[5]

Whereas in 1979 the other parliamentarians had been able to view the solitary Brélaz as a quirk of the electoral system, things were very changed in 1983. Greens were being elected to other national parliaments and in Switzerland they had been making electoral gains in several cantons. Thus the arrival of three more in the federal parliament had to be taken as evidence of a trend rather than just a flash in the pan. A notice eventually marked where they sat in the parliament, and even the defection of Müller did not diminish the general acceptance that the Greens were a political group in their own right. However, to be a group technically (and so gain the right to sit on certain committees and take part in certain debates) required the group to have at least 5 members. Perhaps learning from past experience the Greens resisted the request from several other small groups to form a technical group and decided to stay independent.

They feel this tactic paid off. During the next four years they say they were able to expand the parliament's and (helped by a generally sympathetic media) the public's understanding about the breadth and depth of Green politics. The proposals they put forward in parliament were generally voted down, but some popped up later as governmental proposals, like the allocation of a percentage of the tax on petrol to improving public transport.[6]

Future Prospects

Indeed the people of Switzerland seem to like the Greens, who by summer 1988 sat in the cantonal parliaments of Vaud (5 seats), Zürich (22), Thurgau (6), Genève (8), Bern (14), Ticino (2), Fribourg (1), Basel city (3) and Basel country (1), as well as on many communal bodies. Eleven of the 80 city councillors in Geneva are Greens. And on 18 October 1987, the Greens at last got their own group in the federal parliament when they gained between 7% and 11.6% to win 9 seats. A tenth seat was missed by 300 votes.[7] Although the opinion polls were anticipating up to 13% for the Greens in these elections – which prompted the newspaper headlines to report a 'disappointing' result for them – they themselves had expected to double their seats but very little more.[8]

However, the Greens are still far from implanted in all the cantons. Although the majority of their seats in the federal parliament come from Bern and Zürich, Die Grüne Partei der Schweiz/Le Parti Ecologiste Suisse is predominant in the French-speaking area. An Alliance Verte of left and alternative groups was re-established for the 1987 elections but gained only 1 seat from the canton of Aargau. Elsewhere it achieved mixed results and wherever there was a direct confrontation with the Swiss Green party the latter achieved significantly better results.[9] However the Greens anticipate that some members of the Alliance will integrate with them soon, while the rest seem to remain committed to an extreme-left political tradition.

The apparent perfection of Swiss democracy actually hides what many feel is a serious democratic crisis as voter 'absenteeism' increases. Despite the official 'sovereignty' of the cantons, there is a progessive centralisation of power and resources. It is still possible to build a nuclear power station against the wishes of the local people, for example, and even local agricultural practice may be influenced through 'aid' given by central government to small farmers. Therefore, despite the seemingly enviable democratic climate in which they live, the Swiss Greens have as tough a task ahead of them as Greens anywhere. However, the passive majority who do not participate in elections might prove an important constituency to mobilise around Green ideas and policies.

Notes

1 Oswald Sigg, *Switzerland's Political Institutions*, Pro Helvetia, Zurich, 1987.
2 ibid.
3 Laurent Rebeaud, *La Suisse Verte*, l'Age d'Homme, Lausanne, 1987, p. 31.
4 op. cit., p. 75.
5 ibid., p. 109.
6 ibid., p. 113.
7 Daniel Brélaz, Report to the European Greens, October 1987.
8 Hans Beat Schaffner, Report to the European Greens, 8 March 1987.
9 Daniel Brélaz, op. cit.

Main Party Publications

Programme of the GPE-Vaud, 1979.
Grüne Partei Schweiz Info Broschüre, 1986 (programme and criteria).
Ecologie d'abord 1986 (programme and criteria).

Studies of Le Parti Ecologiste/Der Grüne Partei

REBEAUD Laurent, *La Suisse Verte*, L'Age d'Homme, Lausanne, 1987.
REBEAUD Laurent, *Die Grünen in der Schweiz*, Sytglogge, Bern, 1987.
BLUM & ZIEGLER, *Hoffnungswahl*, Pendo, Zürich, 1987.

Address

Der Grüne Partei/Parti Ecologiste Suisse
Postfach 1441
3001 Bern

tel: (41) 31 619959

Organogram:
Le Parti Ecologiste/Die Grüne Partei

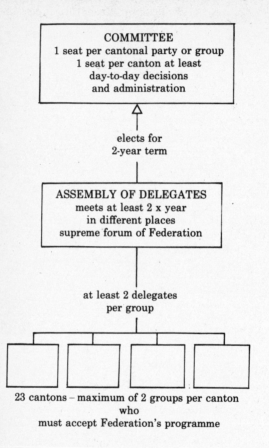

COMMITTEE
1 seat per cantonal party or group
1 seat per canton at least
day-to-day decisions
and administration

elects for
2-year term

ASSEMBLY OF DELEGATES
meets at least 2 x year
in different places
supreme forum of Federation

at least 2 delegates
per group

23 cantons – maximum of 2 groups per canton
who
must accept Federation's programme

1. Total delegates calculated by most
favourable of following:
- 1 delegate per 1,500 electors in best election
over last 4 years;
- for every 2% at most recent cantonal
election;
- for every 150 paid-up members.

2. Decisions affecting Federation require
double majority, of delegates and of local
groups represented.

Election Results

NATIONAL
(Nationalrat)

	1987 Oct	1983 Oct	1979 Oct
8 National Action (NA)	**3**	**5**	**2**
	3.2	*3.5*	*1.3*
7 Republican Movement			**1**
			0.6
5 Christian-Democrats (CVP)	**42**	**42**	**44**
	20.0	*20.6*	*21.1*
4 Liberal-Democrats (LPS)	**9**	**8**	**8**
	2.7	*2.8*	*2.8*
4 Radical-Democrats (FDP)	**51**	**54**	**51**
	22.9	*23.3*	*24.0*
6 Evangelical People's Party (EVP)	**3**	**3**	**3**
	1.9	*2.1*	*2.2*
6 Swiss People's Party (SVP)	**25**	**23**	**23**
	11.0	*11.1*	*11.6*
3 Social-Democrats (SP)	**41**	**47**	**51**
	18.4	*22.8*	*24.9*
2 Progressive Alliance (POCH)	**4**	**3**	**3**
	4.0	*3.7*	*2.1*
1 Party of Labour	**1**	**1**	**3**
	0.8	*0.9*	*2.1*
10 Greens (PE/GP)	**9**	**4**	**1**
	5.1	*2.6*	[1]
11 Landesring ('Independents') (LDU)	**8**	**8**	**8**
	4.2	*4.0*	*4.2*
11 Automobile Party	**2**		
	2.6		
11 Miscell./Independent	**4**	**2**	**2**
	5.9	*2.3*	*3.5*

Key: **Seats** in bold, *Percentages* in italics.

References
The Statesman's Year Book (ed. John Paxton), Macmillan.
The Swiss Embassy, London.
Bundesamt für Statistik, Bern.

Note
1 In 1979 the percentage vote for the Greens was calculated under Miscell./Independent.

13: UNITED KINGDOM

Green Party

founded as PEOPLE in February, 1973

Area: 243,362 sq. km.   *members: 8,000*
Population: 55.78 million (1981)
Density: 229 per sq. km.
(325 in England and Wales, 66 in Scotland, 113 in Northern Ireland)
Member: UN, OECD, The Commonwealth, NATO, WEA, European Communities, Colombo Plan
Languages: English (Welsh and Gaelic)
GNP per capita: US $7,640 (1984)

Background and Electoral System

The history of the United Kingdom shows how its geography, climate and resources have influenced its internal politics as well as its relations with the rest of the world. A thriving agriculture and plentiful energy supplies fuelled the industrialisation process, while a defence policy oriented to a sea-going navy rather than a costly land army encouraged the exploration that was to further bolster Britain's economy through trade with and exploitation of its colonies. Despite the unprecedented social upheavals that industrialisation caused, the country managed at the same time, not only to maintain constitutional and political stability, but also to move towards democracy and the development of an advanced system of social welfare. It seems possible to at least partly explain this by the way the British have managed to resolve each political and social problem separately as it came along. Certainly the practice of 'absorbing' potential divisive conflicts has, until recently, made it possible for the two main opposing political parties to ensure a smooth change of government.

But British trading patterns (importing cheap food and raw materials while exporting manufactured goods), once the essential grist to the mill of the industrialisation process, began to falter in the 20th century. The shift from domination of to dependence on the world economy, particularly for needs so fundamental as food and raw materials, has had repercussions on every facet of British life and activity – at home and abroad. Only the discovery of considerable reserves of oil and gas in the North Sea appears to have cushioned the country from major economic collapse.

The United Kingdom of Great Britain {England, Scotland and Wales} and Northern Ireland is a constitutional monarchy. Legislative power lies with the 'Crown in Parliament', comprising the House of Commons and the largely advisory House of Lords. Members of the 650-seat House of Commons are elected from single-member constituencies. Members of the (in 1986) 1,172-seat House of Lords are either hereditary peers/peeresses (by appointment or descent) or else they are life peers/peeresses or archbishops and bishops of the Church of England by political appointment. Average attendance in the House of Lords is about 320.

The arrangement of local government differs from country to country. In England and Wales there are 53 counties, 368 district councils, and approximately 10,000 English parish and 1,000 Welsh community councils. In Scotland there are 9 mainland regions and 3 island areas subdivided into a total of 53 district councils. In Northern Ireland there is a single tier of 26 district councils.

Local elections and elections to the UK and European Parliaments are conducted by a simple majority (first-past-the-post) system in England, Wales and Scotland. Northern Ireland uses a Single Transferable Vote system of proportional representation for all elections.

Candidates for election to the European Parliament require 30 signatures of electors registered in the constituency in which they are standing and a deposit of £750, returnable to those obtaining more than 5% of the vote. For national elections the equivalent requirements are 10 signatures and a £500 deposit.   A cross-party committee of (outgoing) members of the House of Commons and the two broadcasting authorities – the British Broadcasting Corporation and the Independent Broadcasting Authority – decree the amount of television and radio time to be allocated to each party for election broadcasts. This was traditionally calculated in proportion to the number of seats each party held in the House of Commons, with special 'home' broadcasts for the national parties of Wales, Scotland and Northern Ireland. However, tradition was 'adjusted' to accommodate the emergence of the Social Democratic party and its subsequent alliance with the Liberal party.

All parties not represented in the outgoing Parliament are allocated time for one 5-minute radio and television election broadcast if they contest 50 or more of the 650 national constituencies. For the European elections at least 20 of the 81 constituencies must be contested for the same access to the media.

Factors Affecting the Development of Green Politics

The Green party (originally called PEOPLE and then the Ecology party) was founded at a time when there was much debate over the incompatibility of increased consumption of resources and a rising population in the context of a finite planet. One of the most important books discussing the 'limits to growth' was *A Blueprint for Survival*.[1] It also contained proposals for action, including the establishment of a Movement for Survival which would be a coalition of environmental groups, starting with those who had already expressed support for the Blueprint – the Conservation Society, Friends of the Earth, the Henry Doubleday Research Association, the Soil Association and Survival International.

When they were invited to address members of the House of Commons, the authors of the *Blueprint* told the press that they had no intention of setting up a new political party. They felt that they had managed to make their point to sitting MPs.[2] The Movement would keep up an influence on government. However, at a meeting in June 1972 the environmental groups proved less keen about participating in the Movement than the *Blueprint* authors had anticipated. They may have been put off by a statement in the *Blueprint* which said that 'if need be {the movement should} assume political status and contest the next general election'.[3] However, subsequent commentators have suggested that *Blueprint* and other writings of one of the editors of the *Ecologist*, Edward Goldsmith, were 'too reactionary'.[4]

What is certain is that the new party was founded by people who did not believe that pressure-group activity on its own was sufficient to affect change. In this the British party differs little from Green parties in other countries. However, unlike the majority of other Green parties operating in industrialised nations, the UK Green party has had to survive in an electoral system extremely hostile to new parties. As one Belgian Green put it in 1984: 'It is a matter of astonishment that a Green party exists in Britain at all.'

Given the constraints of the British political system it is not surprising that environmental groups have felt pressure could be exerted most effectively on different levels of government through 'respectable and responsible' discussion. It was to safeguard what was seen as a privileged access to the policy-making process of both the Labour and Conservative parties that most environmental groups have proved reluctant to associate closely with a separate Green party. However, successive governments became adept at exploiting this 'special relationship' with the environmental groups, so that even when attempts to shift government policy failed, protest was successfully dissipated in the convoluted corridors of 'consultation procedures' or the 'public enquiry'. Anti-nuclear protest in particular has been defused by this process.

Even though it has had to survive some very low points, the fact that a Green party endures in the British political climate does require some explanation. As Jonathon Porritt has pointed out:

> The role of the Ecology Party is obviously of considerable importance to the development of green ideas in this country. It's my contention that party political activity will always remain an essential part of that development; for better or worse, the Ecology Party is the only organisation prepared to take on that role to its fullest extent... It just so happens that elections are an extremely practical way of getting one's message across. Our primary concern is at the local level, and our primary goal is to start winning seats on local councils. Such is the power of our centralised media and political power structure that we

>cannot possibly achieve this without a simulta-
>neous and equally strong commitment to politics
>at the national level...[5]

It is also worth noting that the Green party, despite its
marginality, is in fact part of that 'respectable and responsible' tradition of handling protest in Britain. After all what
could be more respectable than taking part in a democratic
process (however flawed) that has inspired much of the
world? One Labour MP has even suggested that if the Green
party didn't exist, it would have to be invented. Guy
Woodford, one of the party's seven district councillors,
believes the party's resilience to repeated setbacks in the
national elections and the ebb and flow of disarray at the
party's centre is entirely due to the strength of the local
parties – 'the life blood of the party'.[6]

Philip Lowe and Jane Goyder estimate that nearly three
million people belong to an environmental group, a larger
number than the membership of any political party or trade
union. They also note that, as defined by column inches
devoted to environmental issues in *The Times*, there has been
a huge increase in interest in environmental matters over the
last two decades.[7] A survey conducted in 1984 noted that 80%
of Green party members belonged to some environmental
organisation, with Campaign for Nuclear Disarmament
(44%), Friends of the Earth (21%) and Greenpeace (12%)
topping the list.[8]

It seems therefore that belonging to and being active in
different parts of a growing movement in a climate of
increasing public awareness about environmental issues has
been able to compensate for the inevitable lack of satisfaction that can occur through long-term engagement in minority party politics in Britain. Further inspiration has no
doubt been gained from the successes of their counterparts
on the continent.

More evidence of latent support for the Greens came from a
MORI poll conducted just before the 1983 general election. It
suggested that 12% of the electorate would vote for the
Ecology party if they could (i.e. if there was a Green
candidate in their constituency). However, just how many
people would vote Green if the UK electoral system was
different will have to remain a matter of speculation.

Since the formation of the British Green party there have
been some other serious attempts to channel protest via the

ballot-box. These have involved voting for the nationalist parties or for the Liberals. All other direct political protest has taken the form of trying to influence the two main parties, Conservative and Labour, either from within or through 'ginger groups' established for the purpose. Apart from Northern Ireland, support for nationalist parties, at its height in 1974, proved to be ephemeral, and internal Labour party strife ultimately led four prominent members of its right wing to split away and form the Social Democratic party (SDP) in 1981.

High hopes that 'the mould' of the stultifying two-party system would be broken by this move were held by many people beyond the immediate supporters of the new party. However, ferocious battles over electoral alliances and then a bitter merger negotiation between the SDP and the Liberal party have destroyed any prospect of the new political formation offering a realistic alternative to the Labour party as the main party of opposition. There is little doubt that the attention of political commentators and the general public has focussed on this upheaval among the political parties to the detriment of the Green party. Jeremy Seabrook described the abortive attempt to realign British politics as a tragic diversion from the truly radical changes the Green party was proposing.[9]

Early Days

In the summer of 1972 solicitors Tony and Lesley Whittaker (who were later to become smallholders in Devon) began to discuss the growing ecological crisis with a group of colleagues and friends in the Napton Bridge pub at Napton, Warwickshire. Tony Whittaker had read an article in *Playboy* magazine[10] and been 'profoundly affected' to find his worries about the future expressed in print at last.

That autumn, two meetings were held, one in the boardroom and the other in the canteen of the Herbert-Ingersoll machine tool company in Daventry. The meetings were organised by Bob Richley, personnel officer of the company (and denizen of the Napton Bridge pub) and were attended, among others, by the receiver's men. With uncanny symbolism, the phoenix of Europe's first ecological political party rose out of the ashes of a bankrupt company in the heart of industrial Britain.

These meetings led to the brief existence of the Thirteen Club (after the number of attenders at the first meeting) who spent the rest of the year meeting and reading about the ecological crisis. In particular they were influenced by the *Blueprint for Survival*, the Report of the Club of Rome[11] and other writings of Paul Ehrlich.[12]

By Christmas a split had developed in the Club between those who wanted to simply read and learn and others who felt more had to be done. The Whittakers, along with estate agent Mike Benfield and his assistant Freda Sanders, decided that political action was necessary in view of the urgent and extensive changes that would have to be made to avoid ecological catastrophe. After an attempt to correspond with the existing political parties brought uncomprehending replies (an interesting contrast to the apparently understanding hearing the *Ecologist* team felt they had received) the four decided that the only option that remained was to form their own party. Although an advertisement in the name of PEOPLE asking for candidates for the elections was placed at the end of January,[13] the founding of the party was considered to have taken place at a meeting held in Mike Benfield's office some time in February 1973. Over 50 people were present.[14]

Called PEOPLE, the new party took the colours of coral and turquoise, and based its programme on the four principles that the *Blueprint for Survival* offered as the 'principal conditions of a stable society – one that to all intents and purposes can be sustained indefinitely while giving optimum satisfaction to its members...'[15]

  i) minimum disruption of ecological processes;
  ii) maximum conservation of materials and energy;
  iii) a population in which recruitment equals loss;
  iv) a social system in which individuals can enjoy, rather than feel restricted by, the first three conditions.

The editor of the *Ecologist* was an early member of the new party and contributed the mailing list of the Movement for Survival.

But because of the 'communist' overtones the press presisted in giving the party by calling it the 'People's party', and because coral and turquoise often came out as red and blue in low-cost printing processes, a change of name and colour was made in 1975. After hesitating over the choice between Ecology and Values (the name of the New Zealand ecology party founded in 1972) the former was chosen and the colour green adopted. The name of the party newsletter edited by Mike Benfield was changed too, from *PEOPLE* to *Alliance*, but a small monthly magazine, *Towards Survival*, whose 29 issues had been edited by Keith Hudson and also sent out to members, finally failed in March 1975 through lack of funds.[16]

Just as the promoters of the Movement for Survival imagined that the groups devoted to environmental issues would rally round, so did PEOPLE/Ecology party. The front page of *Alliance* listed 44 organisations that the editor saw as like-minded, and many party members were also members of these groups. But the environmental and peace groups kept their distance. They felt that their influence on government and opposition parties would be hampered by direct involvement with a minor political party.

Undaunted, the early members, based mostly in Coventry, Leeds and Cornwall (where the *Ecologist* was published) set about developing a programme, which was published as the *Manifesto for a Sustainable Society*. This document, regularly amended and expanded, remains the party's detailed statement of policy from which shorter documents and leaflets are drawn. The party also contested its first national election on 28 February 1974, standing in five constituencies, Coventry North-East, Coventry North-West, Eye, Leeds North-East, Liverpool West-Derby and Reigate. Lesley Whittaker obtained the best result with 3.9% of the vote in Coventry North-West and the average over all five seats was 1.8%. The four candidates who stood in the 10 October 1974 election, in Birmingham Northfield, Coventry North-West, Leeds East and Reigate fared less well, with the average vote down to 0.7% and the top vote, still in Coventry North-West, being 0.8%. In both elections the party affiliated with other candidates, in February with an Independent and a People & Agrarian candidate, and in October only with the latter.[17]

The coolness of the pressure groups, disappointing results and strong differences over the development of the *Manifesto* affected the first national conferences of the party in 1974 and in 1975. Several active members who wished ecological politics to be expressed in a more explicitly socialist programme left at this point. Some of them joined the Socialist Environment and Resources Association (SERA) which had been founded in 1973 with a view to influencing the Labour party. As Labour had regained power in the 1974 elections, first through an uncomfortable alliance with the Liberal party and then with a slim 5-seat majority, they no doubt felt SERA to be a more direct route to political influence than the tiny new party.

But while the next three years represented a period of low activity for the Ecology party, environmental concern among the public had begun to shift away from the difficult to absorb, often apocalyptic global warnings of the last decade and come closer to their everyday experience. This concern was reflected in the rapid increase in membership of environmental organisations during the 1970s. Many new groups were formed and issues such as motorway development, wildlife protection, the cutting back of public transport and pollution were widely debated. Not all of these new groups were sure that extra-parliamentary pressure would be sufficient to effect change. Friends of the Earth, perhaps tempted by the early successes of Amis de la Terre in French elections, flirted with taking up party politics and a group called the Green Alliance, including members from the House of Lords, was formed in July 1978 to sound out support for a new political party. However, in the end both groups stuck to extra-parliamentary activity. In 1977 the Liberal Ecology Group was founded, with the objective of influencing the Liberal party.

Also stirring during the late 1970s were the campaigns against nuclear power and against the military deployment of nuclear devices, with the civil/military links becoming better understood. SCRAM (the Scottish Campaign to Resist the Atomic Menace) was formed in 1975 and played a major role in trying to prevent the building of a nuclear power station at Torness. A public inquiry over the placing of a nuclear fuel reprocessing plant at Windscale was held in 1977. Anti-nuclear groups and campaigns proliferated and some attempts were made to form umbrella organisations, such as Energy 2000 in 1977.[18] Later on, in 1979, the Anti-Nuclear Campaign was formed in which members of the Ecology party were closely involved. However, although public opinion was undoubtedly influenced, the practical results of these efforts were effectively nil.

Although party membership was low before 1979, new

members were joining and the party worked on its programme and passed a constitution at its 1977 Birmingham
conference. At the same conference the authors of the
constitution, Jonathan Tyler and Sally Willington, were
elected chairman and national secretary. So the scene was
set, outside and inside the party, for the 1978 conference, also
held in Birmingham and generally viewed as the historic
turning point in the fortunes of the party.

1979 – 1987

When Lesley and Tony Whittaker were considering the
formation of a new party, they 'came up with the surprising
fact that to form a political party one merely had to perform
and act like one'.[19] Tony also reported to the 1978 party
conference as it considered the impending general election
that in order to obtain a 5-minute election broadcast on both
radio and television a party had to stand candidates in at
least 50 parliamentary constituencies. This seemed an impossible task to the party which had, at the time, only about 550
members. The 60 or so who were at the conference were
counselled by Jonathan Tyler to concentrate effort and
resources on, say, 10 carefully selected constituencies, but in
the end they were swayed by an impassioned speech by Keith
Rushworth of Leeds to go for the 50 and obtain the badly
needed publicity for the party and its policies.

The enthusiasm with which this decision was embraced
carried through from the conference to May 1979 when 53
candidates were fielded in the general election. The results
averaged 1.5% over the 53 seats, with 12 candidates obtaining over 2% of the vote. The election manifesto *The Real
Alternative* and the professionally produced broadcasts made
an impact that went beyond the purely electoral. Jonathon
Porritt, the vice-chairman who, with David Fleming, had
been the main coordinator of the election campaign, reported
in *Econews* 2, May-June 1979, that even hard-bitten political
commentators were viewing the Ecology party as providing a
'breath of fresh air' and a 'note of reality'. There were a few
signs that the other parties were rattled, particularly from
David Steel, leader of the Liberal party, who unblushingly
co-opted the slogan 'The Real Alternative' for his own
electioneering.

Membership of the party soared to over 5,000 as an immediate result of the election campaign, revealing the frailties of the Ecology party's organisation and slim resources. Enquiries lay unanswered and requests for membership remained unprocessed for many months. A big effort to stand three candidates in the June elections to the European Parliament finally emptied the party's coffers as well as the pockets of many members. Jonathon Porritt in London Central, Mike Benfield in Midlands Central and Teddy Goldsmith in Cornwall and Plymouth scored 4.1%, 3.9% and 3.0% respectively in the massive Euro-constituencies.

The period between the 1979 and 1983 general elections was mixed for the Ecology party. New and inspiring links were forged with developing Green parties on the continent, particularly in Germany, France, Belgium, the Netherlands and Italy, but back at home the party struggled with a series of difficulties only partly attributable to disorganisation but certainly exacerbated by it. In 1978 regional groupings of branches were established, somewhat arbitrarily based on where the membership was at the time – almost entirely south of Leeds. But the shambles after the 1979 election increased the demand for a central office to service enquirers as well as the party as a whole. A furious debate ensued which was billed as being between 'centralists' and 'decentralists' but was in fact more complex than that. Mixed up in it was confusion about the actual role of the party – should it be contesting elections at all, or concentrating on campaigns and actions? Was party political activity an ecological activity in the first place? Did the party represent 'socialism with a green face' or not? How should it relate to other parts of the movement? For example, it was hard for the party to pretend that, like the German Green party, it could offer the best political vehicle for the aims of the peace movement. The Campaign for Nuclear Disarmament (CND) certainly remained firmly convinced that the Labour party offered the best vehicle for its aims.

But despite the lack of a clear strategy and a significant fall-off in membership, the London office was established, the more anarchist tendencies in the party organised events and published magazines to their liking, Green CND was founded to try to make inroads into the thinking and the not-so-democratic processes of national CND, members took part in many actions and campaigns organised by the party or by other like-minded organisations and local elections were contested each year.

In the 1980 elections to the district councils results were 5.8% on average. Several individual results were over 10%, one as high as 40.75% and a few candidates polled better than the Liberals and occasionally Labour. One seat was gained unopposed in Caistor, Lincolnshire.[20]

For the 1981 county council elections the party made a massive effort and contested over 250 seats but obtained patchy results. Poor results from Leeds and London brought the overall percentage down, but elsewhere about 30 candidates topped the 10% mark. Most important of these was Jeremy Faull in Bodmin who retained the party's one county seat by 1 vote (50.1%), beating the costly and elaborate campaign of ex-Liberal MP Paul Tyler.[21] Parliamentary by-elections fought during this period brought miserable results.

The 'Falklands factor' and the new centre Alliance between the Liberal party and the recently formed Social Democratic party had a significant effect on the 1982 local elections. Percentages were down for most of the candidates with only odd pockets of inspiration.

By the end of 1982, past difficulties were brushed aside in a frenzy of preparation for the 1983 Parliamentary elections. 109 candidates stood, including 2 affiliated candidates from Women for Life on Earth. Despite the arrival on the scene of the Alliance, the party's hopes were high. Greens had been elected to parliaments in Switzerland, Belgium, Germany and Finland and a MORI poll conducted at the end of May revealed that 12% of people would vote Ecology if they could. A General Election Coordination Committee was formed, again convened by Jonathon Porritt, and an attractive *Manifesto* prepared. Not so impressive election broadcasts were compensated for by Porritt's excellent performance on BBC-TV's *Election Call*. The UK response to the World Conservation Strategy,[22] published two days prior to the election, effectively endorsed a significant number of the party's policies and even the three major quality daily newspapers, the *Daily Telegraph*, *Guardian* and *Times*, began to wonder if the Ecology party might not gain a lot of votes. Just in case, all three contemplated the possibility in editorials during the last few days of the campaign.

Despite the excitement, the party suspected that its vote would be 'squeezed' in these elections. Nevertheless the actual result came as a bitter blow. Only four candidates topped 2% and the average vote was 1.0% – less than in 1979. Some solace was to hand in the results of the simultaneously held local elections when 28 candidates polled over 10% of the vote and several seats were won on town and parish councils.

Again the party displayed the resilience that often astonished outside observers. Despite winning the dubious accolade for losing the most election deposits in 1983, the Ecology party prepared for the elections to the European Parliament to be held in June 1984. This time only two of the 17 candidates failed to obtain at least 2% of the vote and Felicity Norman in Hereford and Worcestershire polled a record 4.7%.

Between the 1983 and 1987 general elections the Ecology party managed to sustain a sufficient level of funding to expand into a larger national office and employ an office manager, a press officer and a part-time UK election coordinator. Several local parties also opened offices. A major campaign (for which the party employed another part-time worker) was mounted in reaction to the huge majority of seats gained by the Conservatives in the House of Commons, despite the fact that most of the voters had voted against them. (The Conservatives obtained an overall majority of 144 seats after polling only 42% of the vote.) The Campaign for Real Democracy (CaRD) proposed a system of proportional representation for UK elections, a Freedom of Information Act and a Bill of Rights, as well as a devolution of powers to local government enshrined in a Charter. In particular, the campaign focussed on a bill going through Parliament which proposed, among other things, to raise the electoral deposit for candidates from £150 to £1,000. The Ecology party's evidence was taken and debated, and was instrumental in lowering the finally agreed deposit to £500 with a return threshold of 5%.

The party also contributed evidence on uranium mining to the enquiry into the construction of Sizewell B nuclear power station and supported the peace camps at Greenham and particularly Molesworth – evicted by police and army in a heavy-handed dawn raid. At its September 1985 conference, after extensive and heated debate, the party changed its name from Ecology to Green. By this time the word Green was becoming widely used for environmental and ecological groups as well as by political parties. However other political traditions were also beginning to use the word while diligently trying to place their own interpretation on the ideas that lay behind it. By taking Green into its formal title, the Ecology party felt it could remain the yardstick by which others had to measure their green-ness.

But perhaps the most important initiative taken by the party was the setting up of The Other Economic Summit (TOES). Since the days of the *Manifesto for a Sustainable Society* which talked of a 'stock' economy replacing a consumption-based economy, the party had been acutely conscious of the need for new economic theories and practices to provide a consistent framework for its environmental, social and peace policies. Learning the lesson of the cold shoulder given the party by pressure groups and other organisations in the past, members of the Green party set up TOES as an independent organisation, donating money and the full-time services of Paul Ekins, one-time general secretary and chairman of the party.

Through a series of meetings which coincided with the annual 'official' economic summits and solicited contributions from pioneers in 'new economic thinking' from many countries, TOES began to develop the economic theories and tools that the Green party badly needed. The TOES papers were edited by Ekins into a book[23] and helped the Green party produce a more coherent economic policy framework for its 1987 general election manifesto. TOES has now transformed into The New Economics Foundation and continues its pioneering work in the field of new economics.[24]

Although the party's one county councillor, Jeremy Faull, stood down for the 1985 county elections, over 248 candidates managed to average 4.4%. In the 1986 local elections 269 candidates polled an average vote of only slightly less – 4.3%. In Woodspring, near Bristol, Dr Richard Lawson beat a Conservative and an Independent candidate for a seat on the district council and in Stroud, John Marjoram won his seat with 38% of the vote, beating Conservative and Labour candidates. In 1987, Guy Woodford beat Labour and Conservative with 44% to become the party's third district councillor. Two more members were elected to district councils on Independent tickets in Devon where party labels are often shunned and further gains brought the total number of locally elected councillors to 55. In the 1987 local elections the Green party's 260 candidates polled a record 5.9%.[25]

However the 1987 general election results dealt the party

another blow when 133 candidates polled an average of 1.4% – up on 1983, but still not as high as 1979. Only 10 candidates managed to top the 2% mark.

Despite the positive activities and improving local results, the 1983-87 period was also marked by an underlying and deepening malaise in the Green party. At the end of June 1984 a delegate strategy conference at Spode revealed a lack of innovative thinking and placed an over-optimistic emphasis on a system of proportional representation being in place for the 1989 elections to the European Parliament. The same year saw Jonathon Porritt step down from active national involvement with the party when he joined Friends of the Earth as their new director. Although he was one of three co-chairs, the party had failed to appreciate the importance of the focus he had provided for the media as well as for the party itself through his writing and his personality. By late 1985 when three women were elected to the co-chair posts and indeed women held the majority on party council, the party had lost a lot of momentum that even the name change was unable to check.

This setback was not due to the new gender balance of the council but rather to the relative inexperience of many of its members as well as the cumulative problems of chronic disorganisation. Like many voluntary organisations the Green party had tended to attach tasks to people rather than to posts. So when people moved on, as many in the Green party did during this period, some tasks remained either inexpertly done or not done at all. It became clear that national coordination had for some time depended more on the relationship between council members than on any formal organisational framework.

Aware for some time that its organisation was not what it should be, the party had set up a Party Organisation Working Group (POWG), convened by Jonathan Tyler and Paul Ekins. They brought their conclusions in the form of complicated constitutional amendments to the February 1986 conference and experienced a defeat, more at the hands of their own extremely complicated procedural motion than because the majority of members present were against the proposals. These were certainly not perfect. Although they had been developed from the first principle of absolute representation for party members, they did not have the flexibility and resilience the party would require should it become large and successful. For example, there were no feedback checks to deal with any members of the proposed executive who might abuse their potentially powerful positions, and no mechanism to frame the crucial relationship between the local and national party and any members who were elected to local councils or to parliament. On the other hand, the POWG proposals had the distinct advantage of being easier to amend in order to iron out such faults than the existing constitution. In the end though, this skirmish with organisation put even the 'decentralists' off their stroke and party organisation swiftly became a taboo subject.

Tyler and Ekins took their defeat very hard, feeling it symbolised all that was wrong with the party. In their despondency they prepared and called a meeting in May 1986 of people whom they felt would contribute to a discussion on the role and relevance of the Green party to furthering Green ideas in the present political climate of the UK. In the papers prepared to trigger the debate Ekins provocatively pre-empted the discussion by outlining a parallel organisation, called Maingreen, that would, among other things, put up a slate for election to the party council. On the invitation list were most of the past chairs of the party as well as some Green party council members and office bearers, including Jo Robins, one of the then co-chairs. What happened next confirmed Tyler and Ekins' worst fears.

Robins consulted the two other co-chairs (but not the authors of the papers) and they together decided that the Maingreen proposals constituted an attempt to 'subvert' the party which merited the calling of an emergency meeting of the party council. This meeting was called for the same day as the Maingreen meeting and effectively decreed that party council had the right to proscribe any meetings and circulation of papers between members of which they (council) did not approve. Seemingly unaware that this was already an infringement of the basic human rights of freedom of expression and association, the meeting then went on to condemn the 'secrecy' of the Maingreen meeting. The peak of ludicrousness was reached when some more vocal party officers insisted that all meetings between party members on matters concerning the party must be 'open'. As one disgusted party member put it: 'Does this mean that when I discuss Green politics in bed with my husband (also a member) I have to invite party council along?'

The affair sickened a great many members. Without asking permission from the authors, the co-chairs circulated the

papers around the entire party and the following conference
was very uneasy. Many people agreed with much of the
analysis the papers made of the party's problems even though
they were not attracted by Ekins' suggestion for a solution,
but conference was reluctant to undertake the unpleasant
task of condemning party council. However, council's loose
grip on priorities, if not democracy, was highlighted when it
was pointed out that it had been Maingreen and not
Chernobyl that had prompted them to call an emergency
meeting.

The Maingreen episode led to many previously active
people retiring from national involvement and both Ekins
and Tyler resigned from the party after the 1987 election.
Council remained deeply divided and the 'siege' mentality
developed by several members carried over into a badly
planned and lacklustre election campaign, despite the
availability of more resources than ever before.

Future Prospects

Another change of party council members took place at the
end of 1987. Although again many of the new council still
lacked experience, they did not demonstrate the same bunker
approach to protecting the party from outside criticism and
attack as their predecessors. Attempts are being made to sort
out the worst of the party organisation's discontinuity
problems and a more outward-looking approach is being
taken to policy development and campaigning. The May 1988
local election results proved very satisfactory for the Green
party. 395 candidates contested the elections and a third of
them polled over 5%. In the 325 seats contested by at least
four candidates the Green party averaged 4.1%. Two more
district council seats were won in Stroud, with polls of 58%
and 34%, and a near miss was recorded in the Highland
district of Scotland.   In June 1988, it was reported that two
sitting Liberal councillors (one in Salisbury and one in the
county of Suffolk) had defected to the Green party, and for
the first time the party figured in a major political opinion
poll.[26] A Harris poll conducted for the *Observer* newspaper
recorded support for the Green party running at 1%
nationwide (26 June 1988).

However the party is a very long way away from facing up

to the realities of politics in Britain today, and the habits acquired after fifteen years in the political twilight have left it ill prepared to handle any rapid growth that might come its way.

After the 1983 general election, in which Mrs Thatcher led the Conservative party to its second landslide victory, many people (not least one member of her then Cabinet, Francis Pym) were moved to express concern about the health of British democracy. Oddly this concern for the democratic process was not expressed to the same extent after the 1987 general election when the Conservative party won another overall majority, this time of 101 seats for only 42% of the vote. Doubly odd when the main opposition party shows even fewer signs of being able to mount the strong oppositional challenge – in the House of Commons or at the polls – on which the British political system depends for its democratic health.

As nothing short of a political cataclysm appears to stand between the Conservative party and a fourth victory in the early 1990s, it would seem that Britain, once held up as a model for parliamentary democracy, is in the grips of a constitutional crisis. All the more so when it is noted that, while talking of decentralisation of responsibility to ordinary people in their communities, the present government is actually centralising the powers and the means that people require to be able to take up such responsibilities. The growing gap between what the government apparently thinks is happening and what is actually happening is potentially explosive, especially if at the same time the channels of satisfactory protest are reduced.

Under such circumstances, therefore, it would seem very important for the Green party to carefully consider its strategy not only up to, but beyond, the next general election. Much more could be at stake than a few more percentage points and seats in elections to ever weakening local councils, or trying to minimise the defeat at the national polls. After all it is not by chance that Green parties should first appear and develop in countries which have a more or less advanced system of democracy.

Obviously it would be going too far to imply that the Green party holds the key to safeguarding democracy in the United Kingdom. However, it is part of a rapidly expanding world movement, one that is perceived as a trustworthy guardian of an extremely powerful diplomatic tool – the urgent need to

replace environmental devastation with environmental conservation. It is quite possible that by intelligent manipulation of this diplomatic tool Greens could play a major role,
in the not too distant future, in the conservation of one
particular threatened species – British democracy. However,
this can only happen if the Green party is prepared for it, and
at present it is not.

Notes

1 The *Ecologist, A Blueprint for Survival*, Penguin, 1972.
2 Sally Willington, 'Being There', unpublished article, n.d.
3 *A Blueprint for Survival*, loc. cit., p. 9.
4 Wolfgang Rudig and Philip Lowe, 'The Withered "Greening" of British Politics: A Study of the Ecology Party', in *Political Studies* XXXIV, 1986.
5 Jonathon Porritt, *Seeing Green*, Basil Blackwell, Oxford, 1984, p. 9.
6 Guy Woodford, personal communication, 23 January 1988.
7 Philip Lowe and Jane Goyder, *Environmental Groups in Politics*, Allen & Unwin, 1983, pp. 9 & 37.
8 Chris Studman, 'Who Are the Ecologists?', unpublished paper, 1984.
9 Jeremy Seabrook, 'The Mould Breakers Who Stole the Green Light', *The Times*, 21 April 1987.
10 Paul Ehrlich, 'A Playboy Interview' in *Project Survival*, The Playboy Press, Chicago, 1971.
11 Meadows et al, *The Limits to Growth*, Earth Island, 1972.
12 *The Population Bomb*, Ballantine, New York, 1968, and with Ann Ehrlich, *Population, Resources, Environment*, W. H. Freeman, San Francisco, 1972.
13 *Coventry Evening Telegraph*, 31 January 1973, copy kindly supplied by Mike Benfield.
14 Tony Whittaker, 'Now we are Ten!', *Econews* 17, April 1983.
15 *A Blueprint for Survival*, loc. cit., p 30.
16 Sally Willington, op. cit.
17 Alistair McCulloch, 'The Ecology Party and Constituency Politics: The Anatomy of a Grassroots Party', paper for PSA Annual Conference, University of Newcastle, April 1983, and Wolfgang Rudig & Philip Lowe, op. cit.
18 Philip Lowe and Jane Goyder, op. cit., p. 34.
19 Tony Whittaker, op. cit.
20 *Econews* 8, June 1980, and *Econews* 10, April 1981.
21 Report of Party Election Agent, May 1981, and *Ecobulletin* 6, July 1981.
22 *A Resourceful Britain*, Kogan Page, 1983.
23 *The Living Economy*, Routledge & Kegan Paul, 1986.
24 Details and quarterly newsletter available from The New Economics Foundation, 27 Thames House, South Bank Business Centre, 140 Battersea Park Road, London SW11 4NB, UK.

25 Chris Rose, 'Green Party Election Countdown', May 1986, and Chris Rose, 'UK Green Party, Past Election Results', February 1988 (party documents). From 1984 onwards Rose has calculated the average percentage polled by Green party candidates in local elections for only those electoral districts where one seat was being contested. This removes the distortion of the often much higher percentages polled by candidates in multi-seat contests. Rose has further calculated the average percentage in contests where the Green party candidate was one of at least four. The average results for these candidates were 3.1% in 1984, 3.4% in 1985, 3.4% in 1986 and 3.6% in 1987.
26 *Econews* 40, September 1985.

Main Party Publications

Manifesto for a Sustainable Society (continuing).
Politics for Life.
1987 General Election Manifesto.
Will They Thank Us for This? (nuclear power).
Our Borrowed Land (agriculture).
Peace broadsheet.

Studies of the Green Party

STUDMAN C. J., 'The Ecology Party, A Survey of Members', July 1984, Hatfield Polytechnic, unpublished.
McCULLOCH Alistair, 'The Ecology Party and Constituency Politics: The Anatomy of a Grassroots Party', paper for Political Science Association Annual Conference, April 1983, University of Newcastle.
RUDIG Wolfgang & LOWE Philip, 'The Withered "Greening" of British Politics: A Study of the Ecology Party', *Political Studies* XXXIV, 1986.

Address

The Green Party
10 Station Parade
Balham High Road
London SW12 9AZ

tel: (44) 1 6730045/6/7

Organogram: Green Party

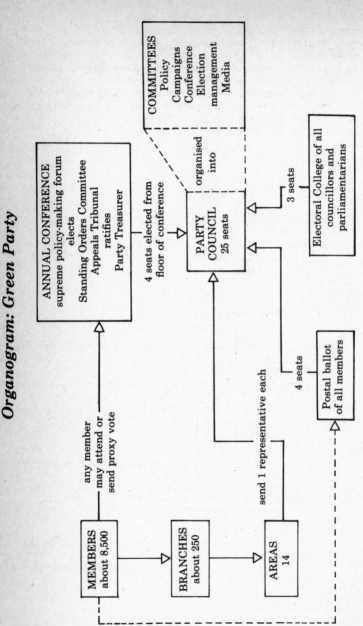

Election Results

	NATIONAL (House of Commons)				EUROPEAN	
	1987 Jun	1983 May	1979 May	1974 Oct	1984 Jun	1979 Jun
7 Conservative Party	**375**	**397**	**339**	**276**	**4 5**	**60**
	42.3	*42.4*	*43.9*	*35.8*	*40.8*	*50.6*
5 Social Democratic Party (SDP)	**5**	**6**				
	22.6[1]	*25.4[1]*			*19.5[1]*	
4 Liberal Party	**17**	**17**	**11**	**13**		
			13.8	*18.3*		*13.1*
3 Labour Party	**229**	**209**	**269**	**319**	**32**	**17**
	30.8	*27.6*	*36.9*	*39.3*	*36.5*	*33.0*
9 Scottish Nationalists (SNP)[2]	**3**	**2**	**2**	**11**	**1**	**1**
	1.3	*1.1*	*1.6*	*2.7*	*1.7*	*1.9*
9 Welsh Nationalists (Plaid Cymru)[2]	**3**	**2**	**2**	**3**		
	0.4	*0.4*	*0.4*	*0.6*	*0.8*	*0.6*
9 Ulster Unionists United [23]	**9**	**11**	**1**	**10**	**1**	
9 Democratic Unionists	**3**	**3**	**3**			
9 Ulster Unionists	**1**		**5**		**1**	
9 SDLP	**3**	**1**	**1**	**1**	**1**	
9 Sinn Fein	**1**	**2**				
11 Independendents			**2**	**1**		
10 Greens (Green Party)	*1.4*	*1.0*	*1.5*	*0.7*	*2.5*	*3.7*
average over	134 seats	108 seats	53 seats	4 seats	17 seats	3 seats

Key: **Seats** in bold, *Percentages* in italics.

References
The Statesman's Year Book (ed. John Paxton), Macmillan.
SMITH Gordon, *Politics in Western Europe*, Heinemann, 1984.
The Times Guide to the European Parliament, Times Books, 1984.
The Official Handbook, House of Commons Information Ofice, 1988 edition.
Green Party publications and documents.

Notes
1 The percentage is for the Alliance, an electoral coalition of Liberal and SDP.
2 The nationalist parties contest seats only in Scotland, Wales or Northern Ireland.
3 In Northern Ireland the elections to the House of Commons are conducted with a STV system of proportional representation.

14: GREECE/ICELAND/ NORWAY/PORTUGAL/SPAIN

The previous chapters have told the story of the member parties of the European Greens, and of Finland and Italy where Greens have been elected to national parliaments. No less interesting is the story of Green political development in the remaining five countries of 'western' Europe – Greece, Iceland, Norway, Portugal and Spain.

Greece

The last skirmish in a very long history of political turmoil in Greece took place when Lt-Gen. Phaedon Ghizikis ousted President Papadopoulos by a coup in November 1973. Ghizikis' regime, short on ideas and public support, fell apart when Turkey and Greece clashed over Cyprus in 1974 and power was handed back to civilians. Constantine Karamanlis returned from exile to become prime minister again and oversee the restoration of democracy. His New Democracy party gained an absolute majority in November 1974 and a referendum confirmed that 69.2% of the Greek people preferred to belong to an 'uncrowned democracy'.

In 1977, increased support for the Pan-Hellenic Socialist Movement (PASOK) also saw the Communist party (re-legalised since 1974) split between its Eurocommunist and Moscow-linked factions. In 1981 PASOK gained an overall majority with a electoral system which favours the leading parties. However, stability in Greek politics is not to be taken for granted and prime minister Andreas Papandreou has to tread a careful line between the Communists who took a considerable number of votes from PASOK at local elections in October 1986 and the New Democracy party which is gaining ground again in the national parliament. Apart from problems with his domestic policies, Papandreou has trouble keeping up his anti-American rhetoric (bases out when current agreement expires on 31 December 1988) while the Greek economy needs the considerable sums of money from the Americans, who threaten to move to Turkey if they are thrown out of Greece.

With massive air pollution due to the high concentration of industry around major cities, proposals to remove 'forest status' from 5.2 million hectares of land (42% of the total) and extensive damage done to the general environment by the tourist industry, there would seem to be plenty of scope for a Green party in Greece. Although tentative efforts have been made nothing much has come of them. Activities centre around local groups, in particular the *Ecological Initiative*, a newspaper produced in Athens, a new Ecological Club and a group in Thessalonika, but so far no attempt has been made to contest elections on a Green platform.

Iceland

> As I pick out
> the worms from the cod
> I egg you on to greater things...
> As I wring out nappies
> throw the dirty dishes into the sink
> my mind salutes you.
> I clean up quickly
> the mess around me
> trying to harness the force
> that is meant for you.
> Remember
> you are fighting our fight
> that of hundreds of mothers
> in hundreds of kitchens
> a thousand years of daily labour
> in a barren hostile country...

> Elisabet Thorgeirdóttir[1]

This poem was written by a single mother living in a fishing village in the western fjords of Iceland. It was sent to Vigdis Finnabogadóttir who became the first woman president of Iceland in 1980. Although the presidency is largely a ceremonial position in Iceland, the incumbent is not appointed but elected on a political platform. Vigdis' platform was a commitment to national independence, pacifism and feminism. Her election (and subsequent re-elections in 1984 and 1988) had a profound effect on Icelandic women.

It was, in fact, one of the major inspirations that led to the founding of the Kvennalistinn (Women's Alliance) in 1983. Iceland is the only country in the world where a women's party has succeeded in gaining representation in a national parliament. In 1983 they gained 3 seats with 5.5% of the vote and on 25 April 1987 they doubled their seats with 10.1% of the vote. Although the word 'green' is not used once, their programme reads as Green as Green can be. Some extracts:

> The Women's Alliance aims for a society where respect for life and shared responsibility are of primary importance. We give priority to women's freedom of choice focussing on the right of women to be judged on their own merits equal to men. We put aside ideas about equal rights which imply the right of women to be the same as men. Women are moulded by their role of bearing and raising children, we do different kinds of work and consequently we have a different experience in life from men. Women's experiences lead to a different set of values, other than those dominant in the male world. Accordingly women have a different outlook on the world.

> Women have much to offer which can help to turn us from the road of danger and destruction to a road of peace and freedom.

> Throughout the centuries the aim of each generation has been to secure the future of their children and guarantee a better life for them. Now it would appear that the part of mankind that lives in the Northern hemisphere has lost sight of that aim. The world community, future generations and the environment are threatened by the arms

race, over-exploitation of natural resources, land
waste, industrial pollution, mismanagement and
greediness. Poverty and injustice is on the
increase in the world in spite of technical progress.
Weapons have the final word and power is used
without constraint to oppress individuals and
nations... Women have been outside the power
structure...have been treated unjustly, both
overtly and covertly... We cannot allow this to
continue. Women must therefore become active
participants in the decision-making process of
society. We must fight our own fight for our rights
and for a better world, nobody else is going to do it
for us...

We therefore want to cooperate with all those men
and women who consider that the insane arms
race and the irresponsible treatment of nature and
natural resources are the greatest threats facing
humanity today. Both are the work of humanity
and both can be stopped. This is what we want to
work for.[2]

The birth of the women's movement in Iceland can be dated
precisely. The year 1974 – United Nations International
Women's Year – the day 24 October. On that day most of the
women of Iceland downed tools, pots, pans, typewriters and
(so history relates) babies. They went on strike and held
outdoor meetings to demonstrate the importance of their
contribution to the economy and social structure of their
country.

In 1982 groups of women in the cities of Akureyri and
Reykjavik decided to put up lists of women candidates. They
were concerned about the lack of women in local government
and wanted to see women's values and experience used for
the benefit of women and children. They also wanted to see
women's work re-evaluated on the job market. 'As it is often a
continuation of work done in the home, why not acknowledge at least four years experience at home when hiring in
the waged labour market?' says Guòrún Agnarsdóttir, a
doctor with three children.

Two   women   were   elected   to   each   city
council – immediately doubling the proportion of female

councillors from 6% to 12%. This encouraged the founding of
Kvennalistinn in March 1983, in time for the national
elections in May. 'No one wanted to run,' recalls Guòrún.
'Everyone wanted to support someone else in running. I had
the thumbscrews put on me, though my self-confidence was
very fragile. It's been important for us to nurture confidence
amongst all the women.'[3]

The campaign for the national elections was short and
'brazen'. Twenty women took a bus around the country
speaking to and listening to women in towns and villages.
Guòrún remembers: 'The bus was decorated with all sorts of
things...bras, and so on. Some people were shocked, the media
ignored us, but on the whole we were tremendously successful.' Successful enough for three women, one of them Guòrún,
to be elected to parliament.

Since then, of course, things have moved very fast for the
Kvennalistinn. The women MPs and their assistants have
learnt to survive in politics and are working (with other
women MPs and different groups as well as the broader
women's movement) towards getting women's issues
accepted. 'We will continue to work towards our goal, which
is a different and better society where there is equality,
where both sexes have the same status and where children
will live their youth in the security of a future that will bring
peace and justice.'[4]

To many women in many countries the story of the
Kvennalistin will sound like a fairy-tale come true. But in the
same way that the Green movement in other countries stirs
up powerful opposition, so the opposition in Iceland is
growing. The establishment is beginning to understand, not
only the radicalism, but also the power of what the Kvennalistinn is saying. Guòrún recognises that although the
Kvennalistinn doubled its number of MPs the hard part is
only beginning. 'They have a thousand ways to neutralise
you,' she says. 'You must be constantly aware in order not to
be neutralised by this system. It's a man's system. We must
act to be here.'

Perhaps inspired by the interest shown in the Kvennalistinn, the International Green Congress held in Stockholm at
the end of August 1987 was told that an independent
Icelandic Green party had just been formed. The
announcement was made by a man.

However, in Iceland people seem to recognise that Green-
ness goes deeper than the name of your party. They like the

fact that the Kvennalistinn refused to compromise its principles in order to form a coalition government in 1987. 'We were ready to take part in the government,' explained Kristín Hallaórsdóttir, 'but only if it would really matter. We didn't want to be flowers to make the government look good to the world.' People also like it that spokeswomen for the party take their knitting and their children into the tv studios. So much so that opinion polls in June and July put the Kvennalistin ahead of all the other political parties with a support of around 30%.[5]

Norway

Although it might be premature to say that a Green party already exists in Norway, there are definitely moves to try to establish one. Several Green lists contested the September 1987 local elections, some scoring up to 8% of the vote. Altogether 14 seats on local and county councils went to candidates claiming to be Green.[6] In Oslo and the nearby county of Akershus local groups plan meetings from spring 1988 to try to establish a nationwide party. The motivation is the national elections of 1989 and the 3,000 signatures which are needed to register a new political party. As the electoral laws are under review at the moment, the embryonic Greens are worried that the Norwegian electoral system of absolute proportionality will be changed and a 4% threshold installed.

Also posing a problem for any new Green political party is the Future In Our Hands movement. Although they have a long and honourable reputation for promoting Green ideals they are very sceptical about these being taken into the political arena. Founded in 1974, after the publication of the book of the same name by Erik Dammann,[7] the movement now has about 25,000 members as well as sister organisations in Sweden, Denmark, Britain, Ireland and the USA. It organises an Information Centre, a monthly magazine called *Folkevett* (Common Sense) and sponsors projects in several countries. It also supports the Project for an Alternative Future, which was set up in 1981. This project now receives the greater part of its US $600,000 annual budget from the government, and funds research into 'value-based alternatives to current policies and societal arrangements'.[8]

The impulse to form a Green party has come from people

who are no longer confident that other political parties are taking Green issues seriously enough. Norway is pursuing an industrial programme no less aggressive than other European countries, and the feeling is growing that there is more talk about environmental protection than there is action.

Portugal

After 13 years of political instability (6 presidents, 40 prime ministers, 2,000 cabinet ministers and 24 coups d'état; all changes took place through military action), Dr Antonio de Oliviera Salazar took power in 1926, also through an army coup. Until 1932 he was finance minister and then dictator of the Estado Novo (New State) which was given a constitution the following year. The legislature had an upper and a lower house but all power rested with the prime minister. The sole political organisation was União Nacional (National Unity), which won all elections in multi-member constituencies by organising 'block votes'. Opposition parties were allowed to be active only during the election campaign. The president was a leading member of the army.

In 1968 Dr Marcello Caetano replaced Salazar and tried some cautious liberalisation, for example increasing press freedom and tolerating religious activities. However, the cost of running an African empire increasingly disturbed by nationalist movements, and the frustrations caused at home by 'moderate dictatorship', led to Caetano being overthrown by an army coup of mainly junior officers on 25 April 1974. As in Spain, the people most active in the struggle to overcome fascism in Portugal belonged to left-wing political groups. They too found the legacy of debating and developing their political ideas in secrecy and isolation particularly hard to overcome. Their programme and style of operating were out of step with post-revolutionary Portugal because they were fashioned in and for the siege conditions of many years ago. The fall from favour of the Portuguese Communist party, once at the heart of the revolutionary process, and the present furious arguments going on within that party, suggest that they are beginning to understand the reasons for their failure.

In the meantime, the parties nearer the centre and on the

right were looking outward (not least towards the EC) instead of inward and they set about doing some very pragmatic politics. This resulted in a dramatic shift of electoral support from the Socialist party to the Social-Democrat party, with the ultra-pragmatic (and subsequently discredited) President Eanes' Social-Democratic Renewal party providing a convenient stepping stone.

But the Portuguese love of pragmatic politics only partly explains the huge success of Senhor Cavaco Silva's Social-Democrat party. Also important is the need of the Portuguese people for a leader who can promise stability. With popular Socialist party leader Mario Soares now president, only the Social-Democrat party could provide the charismatic, trust-engendering leader that the Portuguese people craved. Even supporters of the Communist party acknowledge the strength of this need in Portugal just now and bemoan the inability of their own leader, the aging Alvaro Cunhal, to provide it.

It cannot be said that the Green movement in Portugal is strong. Official figures say about 15,000 Portuguese belong to environmental groups and it is estimated that there might be around 300 of these, most locally based. There are four main national organisations – Amigos da Terra (Friends of the Earth), Liga Para a Portecção de Natureza (League for the Protection of Nature), Grupo de Estudos de Ordenamento Terratorio e Ambienta (Study Group for the Planning of Land and Environment), and Quercus – the Latin for oak. Spirited opposition is being mounted to Spain's desire to build a nuclear waste plant on its border with Portugal at Aldeadávilla, and to the extension of a military range at Alcochete as part of NATO's contribution to the American 'Star Wars' programme. However, there are at present *three* existing political parties that lay claim to the Green title in Portugal – Movimento Democrático Portugûes, Os Verdes, and Partido Popular Monarquico.

Partido Popular Monarquico (PPM — Popular Monarchist Party) was founded in May 1974 but traces its origins to 1961 when the Monarchists stood against Salazar. After the revolution, the PPM was invited by the Armed Forces Movement to take part in several of the provisional governments. This it did, asking for only one post – that of secretary of state for the environment. The modesty of the party's demands at this time it nowadays views as a tactical error. Then in 1980 the PPM negotiated a governmental

coalition with the Christian-Democrats and Social Democrats which put it beyond the pale as far as the rest of the left
was concerned. However, the PPM claims this coalition to
have been crucial in preventing certain things happening.
For example, the introduction of nuclear power, the building
of a large dam at Alqueva, the expansion of the motorway-
building programme and intensive eucalyptus afforestation
projects.

But the party does admit that it was 'infiltrated by
right-wing elements' in 1983, and a year-long struggle took
place to regain control of the party. As a result of this, the
PPM lost its parliamentary seats in 1983 but regained two
seats for independent candidates when it stood on the
Socialist party list in 1985. These seats it lost again in 1987 as
it put all its efforts into the European elections. In these the
PPM polled 2.5% nationwide with some high spots of 9% in
Lisbon and 7% in Oporto. However the party polled miserably in the country areas and missed winning a seat by about
200,000 votes. Today the PPM has about 5,500 members,
admits it is badly organised, and anticipates a split between
two factions: those who take seriously the idea of putting a
monarch back onto the Portuguese throne (they have a
pretender lined up) and those who accept the argument of
separating the pomp from the power of state but who are not
convinced that a monarch is essential to this process. This
latter group hope to rename themselves the Living Earth
party.[9]

Movimento Democrático Português (MDP — Portuguese
Democratic Movement) was founded in 1969 at a time of
arguments among the opposition to the dictatorship. In one
direction went the Communist party and its affiliated organisations, including the MDP. This group had the initials CDE
for Comissões Democráticas Eleitorais, which the MDP still
incorporates in its logo. In the other direction, using the
initials CEUD for Comissões Eleitorais Unitárias Democráticas, went the Socialists, the Monarchists and the Independents. All came back together again in October 1973 at a
Unified Opposition Congress held in Aveiro.

The MDP also participated in post-revolutionary government but only until 1976 when it joined the Aliança Povo
Unido (APU — Alliance for Unity), an electoral list put up by
the Communist party. In this way the MDP won one or two
seats in parliament but eventually it became unhappy about
the increasing domination of the Communists. A rebellion

occurred during what is now known as the 'rupture congress' in 1981. However, the break-away from the APU and the Communists was not finally accomplished until two months before the 1987 elections in which the MDP fared disastrously, losing its seats in the national parliament and scoring only 0.5% in the European elections.

Few people deny that the MDP has displayed great courage in liberating itself from the Communists. But it is also recognised as a party of intellectuals who could no doubt see the steady decline of the very rigid Communist party. Despite the intellectual reputation, the MDP displays the least knowledge about and understanding of Green ideas. Leaders admit to the party being in search of a new independent identity and in their quest for it some of them contacted Die Grünen just before the 1987 elections. To the MDP's surprise, the party received not only ideas but political patronage. However, behind the heavy-handed attempts and increasingly counter-productive efforts by certain members of the West German Green party to help MDP establish its Green credentials in a *technical* way, there does seem to be a genuine will on the part of the party to establish itself *intellectually* along Green lines. It remains to be seen if, exposed to various strands of ideas that are influencing the Green movement in other countries, the MDP can make its intellectual transformation. The party appears to have a strong grassroots organisation and it claims about 10,000 members.[10]

The third party, Os Verdes (The Greens), dates back to 1981, the same year that the relationship between the Communist party and MDP began to disintegrate. Antonio Gonzales was approached by a group of people claiming to be ecologists and he agreed to stand as an Independent on the APU list for the 1983 elections. His experience led him to doubt the genuineness of Os Verdes and he strongly suspected that they were a front organisation of the Communist party.[11] He was replaced for the 1983 elections by Maria Santoz, a vocal and charismatic woman who was, at that time, a local councillor, elected on the Communist ticket, for the town of Almada.

In 1987, with the APU coalition non-existent after the departure of the MDP, the Communist party formed the Coligação Democrática Uniária (CDU — United Democratic College). This time the electoral coalition included Os Verdes and Intervençion Democrática (ID — Democratic

Intervention), a dissident group who left the MDP in 1987. Os Verdes obtained two seats in the national parliament in this way but did not have a good enough position on the CDU list to win a seat in the European Parliament.

There is no doubt that Os Verdes have been the most assiduous of all three parties in developing a Green programme and courting Green parties in other countries. They claim a membership of about 1,000, but members of the executive are varyingly vague about how they are organised. Although they deny it and insist on their independence from the Communist party, the popular conception in Portugal is that they are one of that party's 'fronts'. Certainly the efforts of Os Verdes to obtain the blessing of Green parties in other countries are disproportionate to the domestic electoral threat posed by either the MDP or the PPM, and the party seems to be in the firm control of a small number of politically very experienced men. It is also entirely logical that the Portuguese Communist party should be chasing the Green vote for all it is worth. Not only does it need to go to the elections in a coalition with an anodyne name, but it would also like to annex an important growth area in politics as it struggles to survive.[12]

It seems obvious that the Portuguese people would prefer to learn about Green ideas in an atmosphere of stability and not revolution. But it is also clear that there is an urgent need for the intervention of those ideas as a poor and broken-down Portugal sets off unthinkingly on the 'Macdonaldisation' of its country and its culture. Many Portuguese people have small and insecure incomes and low quality housing, but the community support mechanisms and strong cultural traditions are not only still in place, but also reinforced after some very difficult years. The challenge of improving the condition of people without shattering those vital communities and traditions and the environment on which they depend is considerable. Bearing in mind the present political context, it would seem that all of the above parties offer a legitimate starting point for the growth and expression of Green ideas in Portugal. Although very different, each party has something that the others don't have. The rather anarchic PPM has the affection and the trust of many Portuguese people, the MDP has intellectual curiosity and a substantial local organisation, Os Verdes has the most developed programme and two young, attractive and dynamic members of parliament. When each has explored its own road a bit more they could eventually become a politically potent combination.

Spain

Although Spain is traditionally a monarchy there have been
two peacefully proclaimed republics. The last ended when
some generals mutinied against its left-wing government in
1936 and started the Spanish Civil War. Hitler and Mussolini
both sent support to General Franco, the rebel leader, and the
Russians coordinated support for the Spanish Popular Front.
Because of this, but not entirely accurately, the war in Spain
came to be seen as a left-right conflict in its purest form and
accustomed people to think of a Europe divided between two
ideological camps.

Franco eventually defeated the Republican forces after
three years of war in which perhaps a million Spaniards died,
and after which thousands more were executed and hundreds
of thousands emigrated. What was left was an enduring
legacy of fear, bitterness and division. The dictatorship
established by Franco, although authoritarian, cruel and
repressive, intensely nationalist and reactionary, actually
drew support from a wide range of people. Apart from the
out-and-out fascist Falange (the only legal political party
under Franco), monarchists, Catholic moderates and conservatives, the military and the less politically coloured interests of landowners and business also gave support to the
regime which ended not with rebellion but with Franco's
natural death. The true fascists in Spain were often discontented by concessions that Franco's regime made to the
existing social order.

Social conflicts in Spain are as complex as they are deep
and polarised, often criss-crossing the traditional divide
between the many rural poor and the few urban rich. Atheism
and agnosticism clash with religion; science, progress and
pragmatism shock those who prefer tradition and an established order. The spirit of egalitarianism and internationalism is incomprehensible to those committed to a narrow
nationalism or regionalism. Thirteen years after Franco's
death these divisions still exist, but the lobby for far-reaching
change has been swelled by young people who have developed their political awareness under a democracy. Older
people, on the other hand, talk of the 'total change' that has

already taken place.

The Spanish Communist party (PCE), driven underground and ruthlessly persecuted after its role in the Civil War, provided what is widely regarded as the strongest and most consistent opposition to Franco's regime. However, instead of the 30% vote anticipated by the party in the first post-Franco election in 1977, it polled only 8.9%. By 1982 the Communist vote had collapsed to 3.8% and the Socialist party (PSOE) gained an absolute majority. This collapse has been attributed to the failure of the long-time general secretary, Santiago Carillo, to match his Stalinist methods to his Eurocommunist words, also to the failure of the PCE to adapt to the evolution of Spanish society in the 1970s and 1980s.

In contrast, the PSOE did adapt and under the charismatic Felipe González swept to victory on a programme dominated by his promise to provide 800,000 jobs (a promise he did not keep, unemployment is up) and a pledge to bring Spain out of NATO (on which he did a remarkable U-turn). González's commitment to modernising Spain via membership of the European Community helps to explain the political risk he took in holding a referendum on NATO membership. As the results show, it was not certain that he would win the referendum as, following the Civil War, there is a deep-rooted desire for neutralism in Spain as well as anti-military and anti-Reagan sentiments, particularly amongst the young. It seems likely that González was encouraged to change his position on Spain's membership of NATO when, after his election, he became aware of the economic difficulties that entering the European Community would impose upon his country and it was explained to him how useful a cushion the 'economic advantages' of full participation in NATO would be.

The number of nature conservancy groups in Spain has risen from one in 1968 to about 300 in 1985. In an attempt to make sense of what it described as a 'heterogenous, heterodox and unfortunately uncontrollable big family', the nature magazine *Quercus* devoted an issue to their evolution and to their several attempts to form some sort of coordination.[13] One organisation, Asociación Española para la Ordenación del Territorio y el Medio Ambiente (AEORMA — Spanish Association for Planning of Land and Environment) was founded in 1970 and recognised as a pioneer group by the naturalists. AEORMA developed a 'global and profound analysis of the causes of environmental degradation' and concentrated on anti-nuclear and urban political ecology. Its demise as a result of internal dissension in 1976, one year after the death of Franco, is thought to have set back considerably the evolution of a political ecology movement in Spain.

In any event, the next important date was 1 May 1983. During an Ecological Film Festival in Tenerife the Manifiesto de Tenerife was signed. The German Green party had entered their national parliament a few weeks previously and Petra Kelly and Lukas Beckmann were guests at the festival. Inspired, several groups present at the festival agreed to create a provisional commission whose task it would be to form a Green party of Spain. An assembly of 50 groups and individuals from all over Spain gathered in Seville in December 1983. They agreed to hold the first conference of Los Verdes in June 1984. Meanwhile regional groups were to try to attract as many supporters as possible and prepare for the conference which would debate the political need for Los Verdes in Spain, methods of organising and participation, and a minimal programme of action. The June conference, held in Malaga, decided to register Los Verdes (The Greens) as a formal political party and established a *mesa confederal* (round table) of three representatives from each federated local party. The party Los Verdes was officially confirmed on 1 October 1984 and plans set in motion for its first congress to be held in Cardedeú near Barcelona on 1 February 1985.

The main purpose of this meeting was to approve the statutes and programme of the new party, and international observers were invited. It also witnessed demonstrations from about 50 members of other groups who were not in agreement with the direction Green politics was taking in Spain. The squabbling continued until the June 1986 general elections when three lists using the title Green – Los Verdes, Alternative Verde and VERDE — were presented. Their combined score of nearly 89,000 votes is not disgraceful when the fact that they stood in only five, seven and six out of the 52 constituencies respectively is taken into consideration.

VERDE is the heroically named Vértice Español de Reivindicación del Desarrollo Ecológico (Spanish Vertex for the Reclaiming of Ecological Development). Information about them is sparse but they are dismissed by everyone else as right-wing.

Alternative Verde was originally the name of the Catalan

group which belonged to Los Verdes but split away because
of personality problems and disagreement over the form any
national party should take. Residual members reformed
another group, Els Verds, which stayed with Los Verdes, but
the rest joined with a new group called Los Verdes Alternativos in Madrid. This latter group developed from La Assem-
blea Verde de Madrid which had been one of the dissenting
groups at the Cardedeú congress. Los Verdes Alternativos
has, since November 1986, reformed yet again into a Confederación de los Verdes. For the confused, all these
mutations are coordinated by one man, Manuel Valero. They
also confirm the enduring tendency for splits in Spanish
politics to owe more to personality conflicts than to serious
political differences. Also superimposed on the divisions
among the Greens in Spain is the considerable personality of
Santiago Vilanove I Tané, a journalist and an individualist
who moves from group to group. Valero accuses Los Verdes
of being a national party when any true ecological organisation would be based on the autonomous regions. However,
his own organisation is a collection of regional groups acting
as a national party at national election time, and the only
formal difference between this approach and that of Los
Verdes seems to be that the latter is a registered national
party. Apart from the legally obligatory national constitution and a minimal programme, Los Verdes is a confederation of autonomously federated local parties and bitterly
resents the constant name-changing of the others.

Only Los Verdes and Confederación de los Verdes presented a list for the first direct elections to the European
Parliament which were held in June 1987. Los Verdes polled
0.6% with 107,001 votes and the Confederación 0.3% with
64,847 votes. Although their combined vote would not have
been enough to gain them a seat, the presentation of two
Green lists (among a total of 35!) can have done nothing to
inspire confidence in the voter.

Organising in Spain is certainly difficult. It is a large
country and its regions defend their autonomy with passion.
In Catalonia and the Basque country in particular, the desire
of some for full independence has caused bitter divisions
among local people and spawned groups prepared to use
violence to achieve their goals. A sparsely spread population
means that any new political party wishing to make a
national impact has difficulty in establishing itself outside
the main centres of population. Los Verdes admit to having a

very small number of members, around 800-1,000 they estimate, spread between the 15 regional parties. In the local
elections of June 1987 Los Verdes gained two councillors, one
in Burgos, the other in Alicante. The number of members of
Confederación de Los Verdes is not known but they are
divided into zones rather than regions and contacts are given
only as a first name and a telephone number. They have no
councillors.

Despite considerable modernisation since the death of
Franco, Spain remains conservative in many of its traditions.
One young girl left the Cardedeú congress in disgust after
looking inside the meeting room. 'Paf! They are no different
from all the other parties,' she announced, 'the room is full of
middle-aged men.' At the 31st Congress of the Socialist party
in January 1988, Carmen Romero, the wife of prime minister
González, played an important role in swinging a vote in
favour of setting a minimum 25% quota of women on all party
executive bodies and on electoral lists. As only 57 of the 861
delegates at the conference were women, this should change
the Socialist party considerably.[14]

Los Verdes might take a hint from the Socialist party's
necessary reforms to the Spanish political scene as they
embark on the compromises which are implicit in their desire
to form a coalition list between the two main Green parties
and some regional lists in time for the 1989 elections to the
European Parliament. Although the conservation and anti-
nuclear movements remain uncoordinated in Spain, they still
represent an important potential constituency for a Green
party.

Notes

1 *Herizons* (Canada), March 1986.
2 'The Women's Alliance Policy Statement', 1983.
3 As note 1.
4 'Sweeping Skirts, the Emergence of the Women's Alliance', undated
paper from the Kvennalistinn.
5 *Dagblaolo* (daily paper), SKAIS opinion polls.
6 Report to European Greens, October 1987.
7 English edition Pergamon Press, Oxford, 1979. Erik Dammann's
subsequent book *Revolution in the Affluent Society* published in English
by Heretic Books, 1984.
8 Documents from Project for an Alternative Future, autumn 1987.

9 Interviews conducted by the author with members of the PPM, 23/24
February 1988.
10 Interviews with members of MDP, 23/24 January 1988, and MDP
documents circulated to the European Greens.
11 Interview with Antonio Gonzales, 22 January 1988.
12 Interviews conducted by the author 23/24 January 1988, and Os Verdes
documents circulated to the European Greens.
13 *Quercus* 20, autumn 1985.
14 *Financial Times*, 25 January 1988.

Greece

Panhellenic Centre for
Environmental Studies
(PAKOE) (independent
research)
7 Soufliuo Street
Ampelokipi
11527 Athens

tel: (30) 1 7770198/7752050

Ecological Club & FOE Greece
7 Anapafseos Street
11636 Athens

Ecological Movement of Salonika
19 Pavlou Mela Street
Thessalonika

Iceland

Kvennalistinn
(Women's Alliance)
Hótel Vík
Vallarstraeti 4
Reykavik

tel: (354) 1 651250

Men's Green Party
Skólavörôustigur 42
Reykjavik 101

Norway

De Grønne
(Oslo and Akershus Greens)
Rosenkrantzgate 18
0160 Oslo 1

tel: (47) 2 425512

Framtiden i vare hender
(Future In Our Hands)
PO Box 73 Ankertorget
0133 Oslo 1

tel: (47) 2 697650

Alternativ Framitid
(Alternative Future Project)
Hausmannsgt 27
0182 Oslo 1

Portugal

Movimento Democratico
Portugûes
R. Coelho da Rocha 27
1200 Lisbon

tel: (351) 1 662303

Os Verdes
Av. Torre de Belem 8-A
1400 Lisbon

tel: (351) 1 617046

Partido Popular Monarquico
Largo zu Picardeiro 9
1200 Lisbon

tel: (351) 1 366587

Spain

Los Verdes
c/ Pilar de Zarogoza 83,
28028 Madrid

tel: (34) 1 2567952

Confederación de los Verdes
c/o Los Verdes Alternativos
Apartado de Correos 52135
28080 Madrid

tel: (34) 1 4685147

Election Results: Greece

	NATIONAL				EURO-PEAN	
	1985 Jun	1981 Oct	1977 Nov	1974 Nov	1984 Jun	1981 Oct
8 National Campaign (EPEN)	*0.6*		**5** *6.8*	*2.3*	**1**	
7 New Democracy (ND)	**126** *40.9*	**115** *35.9*	**171** *41.9*	**220** *54.3*	**9** *38.1*	**8** *31.5*
6 Centre Union		*0.4*	**16** *12.0*	**60** *20.5*		
3 Socialists (PASOK)	**161** *45.8*	**172** *48.1*	**93** *25.3*	**12** *13.6*	**10** *41.6*	**10** *40.3*
1 Communists (Interior)	**1** *1.8*	*1.4*	**2** *2.7*	**8** *9.5*	**1** *3.4*	**1** *5.2*
1 Communists (KKE)	**12** *9.9*	**13** *10.9*	*9.4*		**3** *11.6*	**3** *12.7*
11 Miscellaneous	*1.0*	*3.3*	**2** *8.7*	*2.2*	*3.0*	**2** *10.3*

Key: **Seats** in bold, *Percentages* in italics.

References
The Times Guide to the European Parliament, Times Books, 1984.
The Statesman's Year Book (ed. John Paxton), Macmillan.
The Greek Embassy, London.

Election Results: Iceland

NATIONAL (Althingi)

	1987 Apr	1983 Apr	1979 Dec	1978 Jun
7 Independence Party	**18** *27.2*	**23** *38.7*	**21** *35.4*	**20** *32.7*
6 Progressive Party	**13** *18.9*	**14** *19.0*	**17** *24.9*	**12** *16.9*
3 Social-Democratic Party	**10** *15.2*	**6** *11.7*	**10** *17.4*	**14** *22.0*
2 New Social-Democratic Alliance/ Citizens Party	**7** *10.9*	**4** *7.3*		
1 People's Alliance	**8** *13.3*	**10** *17.3*	**11** *19.7*	**14** *22.9*
9 Regional Equality Platform	**1** *1.2*			
10 Women's Alliance (Kvennalistinn)	**6** *10.1*	**3** *5.5*		
11 Independent/Miscellaneous	**1** *1.2*	*1.0*		

Key: **Seats** in bold, *Percentages* in italics.

References
Women's Alliance documents.
Icelandic Embassy, London.

Election Results: Norway

NATIONAL (Storing)

	1985 Sep	1981 Sep	1977 Sep
8 Progress (Frp)	**2**	**4**	
	3.7	*4.5*	*1.9*
7 Conservative (Höyre)	**50**	**53**	**41**
	30.4	*31.7*	*24.5*
6 Christian People's Party (KrF)	**16**	**15**	**22**
	8.3	*8.9*	*9.8*
6 Centre (Agrarian) (Sp)	**12**	**11**	**12**
	6.6	*4.2*	*8.0*
5 Liberals (Venstre)		**2**	**2**
	3.1	*3.2*	*2.4*
3 Labour (A)	**71**	**66**	**76**
	40.8	*37.2*	*42.3*
2 Socialist Left (SV)	**6**	**4**	**2**
	5.4	*4.9*	*4.2*
1 Communist (NKP)			
	0.2	*0.3*	*0.4*
11 Miscellaneous			
	1.3	*1.3*	*2.0*

Key: **Seats** in bold, *Percentages* in italics.

References
Mini-acts about Norway 1987, Royal Norwegian Embassy, London.

Election Results: Portugal

	NATIONAL (Assembleia da República)					EURO-PEAN
	1987 Jul	1985 Oct	1983 Apr	1980 Dec	1979 Dec	1987 Jul
5 Centre Democrats (CDS)	**4** *4.3*	**22** *10.0*	**29** *12.4*	Democratic Alliance (AD)[1]		**4** *15.4*
3 Social-Democrats (PSD)	**14 5** *50.2*	**88** *30.0*	**73** *27.0*	**123** *44.4*	**118** *42.2*	**10** *37.4*
3 Monarchist Party (PPM)[2]	*0.4*					*2.8*
3 Democratic Renewal (PRD)	**7** *4.9*	**4 5** *17.9*				**1** *4.4*
2 Socialist Party (PS)	**59** *22.3*	**57** *20.8*	**100** *36.4*	**71** *27.1*	**73** *27.4*	**6** *22.5*
2 Democratic Movement (MDP)[3]	*0.6*					*0.5*
1 Communist Party (APU)[3]		**38** *15.5*	**44** *18.2*	**41** *16.9*	**47** *19.0*	
(CDU)[4]	**31** *12.2*					**3** *11.5*

PRESIDENTIAL

1986: Soares	1981: Eanes	1976: Eanes
51.3%	*56.4%*	*61%*
Support: PS and CDU	PS and APU	CDS,PSD and PS

Key: **Seats** in bold, *Percentages* in italics.

References
Portuguese Embassy, London.
Economist.

Notes
1 Governing alliance.
2 In 1979 the PPM had 5 parliamentary seats in the AD, in 1980 6 seats. They had no seats in 1983 and in 1985 stood two candidates as Independents on the Socialist Party list.
3 APU — Aliança Povo Unido – an alliance of the Portuguese Communist Party in which the MDP participated. The MDP had 3 seats in 1979, 2 in 1980, 3 in 1983 and 3 in 1985. Os Verdes first appeared on the APU list in 1983 when Antonio Gonzales sat as an Independent. He was followed by Maria Santoz who took the Independent seat for Os Verdes in 1985.
4 CDÚ — Coligação Democrática Unitária – new alliance formed by Portuguese Communist Party for 1987 elections. Two seats went to Intervention Democrática (ID) who broke away from MDP. Two seats also went to Os Verdes – Maria Santoz and Herculano Pombo.

Election Results: Spain

	NATIONAL (Cortes)			EURO-PEAN
	1986 Jun	1982 Oct	1979 Mar	1987 Jun
7 Popular Alliance (AP)		**106** *26.0*	**9** *6.0*	**17** *14.7*
	105 *26.0*			
6 Democratic Centre Union (UCD)		**12** *6.8*	**168** *35.0*	
3 Socialist Party (PSOE)	**184** *44.1*	**202** *48.2*	**121** *30.5*	**28** *39.1*
2 Social & Democratic Centre (CDS)	**19** *9.2*	**2** *2.8*		**7** *10.3*
1 Communist Party (PCE)	**7** *4.6*	**4** *4.1*	**23** *10.8*	**3** *5.2*
9 Catalan Conservatives (CIU)	**18** *5.0*	**12** *3.9*	**8** *2.7*	
9 Catalan Republicans (ERC)	**1** *0.4*	**1** *0.7*	**1** *0.7*	
9 Basque Nationalists (PNV)	**6** *1.5*	**8** *1.9*	**7** *1.5*	
9 Herri Batasuna (HB)	**5** *1.1*	**2** *1.0*	**3** *1.0*	**1** *1.9*
9 Euskadido Eskerra (EE)	**2** *0.5*	**1** *0.5*	**1** *0.5*	
9/11 Other regionalists/Miscell.	**4** *6.6*	*4.1*	**17** *12.7*	
10 Greens: Los Verdes	*0.2*[1]			*0.55*[2]
Alternative Verde	*0.1*			*0.34*
V.E.R.D.E.	*0.1*			

NATO Referendum March 1986: Yes *52.5%* 9,003,000 votes

No *39.8%* 6,829,000 votes

7.6% spoilt/blank ballot papers

(11,558,000 abstentions)

Key: **Seats** in bold, *Percentages* in italics.

References
Ministerio del Interior, Spain.
The Times Guide to the European Parliament, Times Books, 1984.
Oficina de Informacion Diplomatica 277, Spanish Foreign Ministry.

Notes
1 Los Verdes polled 31,560 votes in 5 out of 52 constituencies, Alternative Verde 29,065 over 7 constituencies, V.E.R.D.E. 28,114 over 6 constituences.
2 Lists for European elections are national. Los Verdes polled 107,001 votes, and Alternative Verde 64,847.

15: The European Greens

The European Greens arose out of the Coordination of European and Radical Parties, set up after the 1979 elections to the European Parliament by Die Grünen from West Germany, Agalev and Ecolo from Belgium, Mouvement d'Ecologie Politique from France, the Ecology party (subsequently renamed Green party) from the United Kingdom, Politieke Partij Radikalen from the Netherlands and the Partito Radicale from Italy. These parties came together with considerable enthusiasm, reassured to find that there were like-minded parties in other countries. Some were basking in impressive results in these elections. The French party had obtained the largest national score with 4.7% of the vote but, under the French electoral system, no seats. The German party too had failed to win seats with 3.2% of the vote but the Italian Radical party had won three seats with their 3.7%. Everyone felt very hopeful about the future.

Five main aims of the Coordination were identified:

1) to exchange information between member parties, including policy ideas;
2) to support each other's campaigns;
3) to make joint actions and press statements on European issues;
4) to hold seminars and develop policies on European and other international issues;
5) to develop a common statement or manifesto.

Roland Vogt of Die Grünen was the first coordinator, the declaration of Ecoropa was used as a basis for membership and the parties agreed early in 1980 to work on a joint platform for the 1984 elections to the European Parliament.[1] Inspired by the campaigning style of the Partito Radicale and the considerable charisma of its leader Marco Panella, the parties held a press conference in Stuttgart to announce the launch of the Green Fundraising Appeal in Rome on 5 April 1980.

The result of the appeal was very poor. Individual parties struggling to keep their heads above water at home found it difficult to raise interest in the empty coffers of the European Coordination. Despite shortage of cash and problems with the secretariat – which was transferred to the Dutch Radical party in 1981 – a start was made on the common programme. But by autumn 1982 everything ground to a halt, with a clear split in aims and style evident between the Radical parties (who also differ a lot among themselves) and the Green parties. Exasperation with the individualistic and anarchic Italian Radical party even extended to Die Grünen, who to this day refuse to work with them.

By December 1982 the Coordination had been joined by Miljöpartiet from Sweden, the Ecology party (now Comhaontas Glas) from Eire and Alternative Liste Österreich from Austria. Another French grouping, Les Verts – Confédération Ecologiste, joined in March 1983 and on the 31st of that month the Green parties formed a new Coordination without the two Radical parties. (The two French groups formed one party in February 1984.) The new Coordination kept the same aims as the old one, and at its October 1983 meeting it adopted the name 'The European Greens' and agreed a Joint Declaration of Aims (see Appendix I).

The Declaration was presented to a press conference in January 1984, which also announced that the parties would go into the forthcoming European elections with a common programme. Furthermore, successful candidates would formally represent those parties effectively disenfranchised by unfair electoral systems, for example in the United Kingdom. The First Congress of the European Greens was announced, to be hosted by Ecolo in Liège on 31 March/1 April 1984.

Everything seemed set fair for the elections, and hopes were high that there would be enough Greens elected to form an independent parliamentary group. This requires a minimum of 10 parliamentarians from at least three countries, 15 from two countries or 21 from a single country. The advantages of forming a parliamentary group are considerable, ranging from extra research assistance and office staff to the right to appoint a speaker and obtain seats on the various parliamentary commissions. (After the 1979 elections a technical group of 12 unattached parliamentarians had been formed in order to obtain these facilities. It included MPs from the Italian Radical, Belgian regionalist, Danish anti-EEC and Scottish Nationalist parties.)

However a sour note had been introduced at the January 1984 meeting of the European Greens. Up to then the coordination had been developing their common programme, to be launched at the Liège congress. Working with them was a new small Dutch Green party called De Groenen which had applied to join. Present and participating in these meetings had been two members of Die Grünen's European working group. But at the January meeting Günter Hopfenmüller, from the German party's executive, and Lukas Beckmann, the party's general secretary at that time, announced that Die Grünen wanted the European Greens to include the cartel of Dutch parties known as the Green Progressive Accord (see Chapter 10), to cancel the press conference and give them, Die Grünen, a week to produce an alternative common programme. As the programme under discussion had started as a draft from Die Grünen and had already been around the parties several times for amendment and ratification, the meeting was not enthusiastic about this idea. It also decided to go ahead with the press conference, even in the absence of Die Grünen, and to welcome De Groenen into the coordination. Many of the parties, who did not share Die Grünen's political history, were unenthusiastic about forming close links with the Green Progressive Accord. Not only was it an electoral cartel of existing (not specifically Green) parties but one of them was the Communist Party of the Netherlands. No one relished the prospect of having to spend the election campaign explaining their relationship to this party instead of explaining their Green policies for Europe.

This meeting marked the beginning of a long and frequently unpleasant low in the relationship between Die Grünen and the rest of the European Greens. While the constant pressure on the German Greens since they entered the Bundestag may understandably manifest itself in prickly behaviour, there is no real excuse for the arrogant and often contemptuous behaviour of some members of the German party who turned up at the meetings of the European Greens and who also meddled officiously in the domestic politics of the Netherlands, France, Spain, Denmark, Portugal and goodness knows where else. It may well be that these people are frequently acting on their own behalf for goals that do not always coincide with the Greens, but that does not remove responsibility for its ambassadors from the party at large. One of the co-founders of the 1979 Coordination, Petra Kelly, probably the best known Green in the world and someone who has done more than anyone to spread Green ideas in an honest and inspiring way, bitterly regrets the destructive behaviour of some members of her party towards the European Greens.

The Liège congress was effectively dominated by the 'non-participation' of Die Grünen in the coordination, with more than one session disintegrating into a debate between factions of the German party. However the European Greens were obliged to struggle on with Die Grünen because of the need to form a technical agreement to obtain reimbursement of expenses during the elections to the European Parliament due in June 1984. Part of the complicated rules concerning these funds meant that parties had to be part of a technical alliance of three or more countries and obtain at least 1% of the vote in their own country. The European Greens were prepared to include the Dutch cartel on a *technical* basis, but Die Grünen's representatives made a lot of fuss about attaching a *political* statement to the technical agreement. This they said was obligatory for their party back home. Pledges were made all round not to intervene in the Dutch elections and not to publicise the statement, which most parties found very weak in comparison to the Joint Declaration of Aims. The technical agreement, with the attached political statement, was signed in Paris on 28 April 1984 (see Appendix II).

But Die Grünen not only gave support to the cartel in the Netherlands, they also published the Paris statement in their European election programme, under the title 'Common Declaration of the Green, Alternative, and Democratic Radical Parties' and listing the names of the signatory parties underneath. The Dutch cartel, listed as the Green Party of the Netherlands, was later discovered to have signed a *second* technical agreement with the PSU, a small left-wing party in France, and the Partito d'Unità Proletaria, a small Marxist party on the list of the Italian Communist party.

In the event, the Dutch Green Progressive Accord did win two seats, the German Greens seven and the Belgian Green parties one each. The French Greens, who had been expected to win four seats, failed to reach the 5% threshold. (See Chapter 6.) Also looking for a home in a technical group in the European Parliament were two members from small Italian Communist parties, four Danish anti-EEC members, three regionalists from Belgium and Italy and the Radical party of Italy.

The Green Alternative European Link (GRAEL)

The GRAEL must be viewed as one of the more spectacular own goals by the Greens, and unfortunately most of the blame lies at the door of Die Grünen. At their congress in Karlsruhe in March 1984, after correctly denouncing the European Parliament as a thoroughly non-Green institution, Die Grünen decided to open up to all-comers their list for the forthcoming European elections. This resulted in only three of the first rotation of their 7 MEPs actually being members of the party. No wonder then that the subsequent attempts of the German party executive to subject these representatives to party discipline (i.e. rotation) failed dismally. In the event only two rotated at mid-term, another six months later, and all exhibited stronger commitments to their individual causes and interests than to any collective ones.

Although the European Green parties were unaware of it at the time (or if aware, unable to do much about it), the manoeuvrings of the representatives of Die Grünen over the signing of the technical agreement in Paris, and the subsequent duplicity of the Dutch cartel, were part and parcel of the preparations for the political shape of the new group in the European Parliament after the elections.

Pre-empting discussions with the other parties seeking to form a parliamentary group, Die Grünen issued a press statement declaring their political alliance with the Dutch cartel and the two Italian Marxists based on the political statement they had insisted be signed by the European Greens. The Belgian Green parties were put into an impossible position but by the summer had accepted the inevitability of having to work with the group as envisaged by the Germans in their press release. Paul Staes of Agalev made a last-ditch stand for a Green group by suggesting that the political grouping be formed on the basis of the Die Grünen programme rather than the political statement attached to the Paris technical agreement, but the Germans rejected this. A broader technical group, called the Rainbow Group, was established so that all the small parties could have access to the Parliament's special facilities. Inside this group, the German Greens, the two members of the Dutch cartel and the two Italian Communists formed the Green Alternative European Link (GRAEL). Ecolo and Agalev remained separate initially but eventually joined the GRAEL in an attempt to influence its work and its political direction. Only the Italian Radical party was excluded. Their disruptive behaviour in the previous technical group had rendered them universally unpopular.

Among those central to the manoeuvrings associated with the forming of the GRAEL was John Lambert, secretary-general of the outgoing technical coordination and supporter of Agenor, a very small international grouping of small left-wing parties. Lambert had held at least one pre-election meeting in which members of Agenor and Die Grünen had participated but to which no other Green party had been invited. The team of support workers Lambert established in the GRAEL gradually gained more power and importance than the disparate and mostly inexperienced new MEPs. As the 1989 elections approach it is also interesting to note how the GRAEL team has taken on a life of its own, promoting its corporate identity in the same way as the other political formations in the European Parliament. Like the Conservatives, the Socialists and the Liberals, the GRAEL seems to have forgotten that elections should be about *future* ideas and not about fossilising *past* notions.

By almost any standard, the GRAEL has been a phenomenal waste of time and energy. No coherent political message has emerged and no sensible strategy for using the platform and the resources of the European Parliament has been identified, never mind pursued. If the objective of the considerable wheeling and dealing of 1984 was to demonstrate that Green politics and the politics of the 'alternative' left were compatible, then this has singularly failed too. The GRAEL MEPs act largely in pursuit of their individual aims, and group meetings have sometimes been so acrimonious that the simultaneous interpreters lodged a formal complaint. The collected documentation and press releases of the GRAEL make, on the whole, sorry reading, especially when one German member went to the Basque country and issued statements in support of ETA. However, the efforts of individual MEPs like Undine von Blottnitz and Jacob von Uexkull from Die Grünen, and Paul Staes of Agalev, deserve special notice.

Unsurprisingly, apart from contacts at an individual level, and the occasional use of the European Parliament's facilities for meetings, the GRAEL and the European Greens mostly went their separate ways. The activities of the

European Greens continued modestly, lack of resources meaning that the meetings could do little more than increase the understanding of member parties about each other and facilitate a limited circulation of information. A more successful Second Congress, with the theme 'Getting Together', was hosted by the UK Green party in Dover, England on 22-24 March 1985 and attended by over 700 people from about 18 countries. Under continual pressure from Die Grünen to transform the European Greens into a 'broader' coalition of 'alternative' parties and groups, a working group made up of Paul Staes (Agalev), Ali Schmeissner (Die Grünen), and Michel Delore (Les Verts) was set up to examine how acceptable such an international grouping would be. It finally proposed *two* international organisations, one a Green Coordination and the other a Green Progressive Alternative Network. Only Die Grünen (not members) voted against this and the newcomers Luxembourg and Sweden abstained. The European Greens continued as before but the second network never got off the ground.

In 1986 the European Greens launched their first big campaign: Beyond the Blocs – for International Peace Year. Delegations were received by the US and USSR embassies in Brussels, and letters deploring the lack of steps being taken towards disarmament, let alone peace, were delivered to embassies in other countries. Various longer-term campaigning was planned but was understandably overshadowed by the nuclear accident at Chernobyl.

A change of heart by the federal committee of Die Grünen eventually brought the German Greens into the coordination early in 1987, and relationships began to improve. With their own growing success, member parties of the European Greens held the Germans in less awe than they did in 1984, and the Germans started to understand that the European Greens, despite the low-key profile forced on them by lack of cash, represented an international gathering of Green parties that merited attention, if not respect.

Since then, two more successful congresses have been organised, in Stockholm by Miljöpartiet in August 1987 on the theme 'Green Thinking for Global Linking', and by Agalev in Antwerp in April 1988 on the theme of local Green politics.

During 1988, the European Greens were joined by the Swiss Greens and Vihreä Liitto from Finland. The loosely coordi-

nated Federazione delle Liste Verdi in Italy are considering
how they might join. But requests for membership also came
from Spain and Portugal and the way the applications from
the last two countries were handled illustrates how the
European Greens themselves have not yet faced up to the
responsibility that goes with their existence. Perhaps remembering the experiences of the Netherlands, the European
Greens prevaricated over the problem posed by more than
one party from both Spain and Portugal applying to join (see
Chapter 14).

Future Prospects

The European Greens came together in the first place in
order to reinforce the confidence and efficiency of the member
parties, who were working in a political twilight at home.
Many positive things have emerged from the coordination,
including four well-attended international conferences. The
good working relationship developed by representatives at
the quarterly meetings has also been augmented by a
growing number of local party contacts, particularly
through twinning schemes. But since the end of the 1970s the
context has changed, and the European Greens have to
consider themselves as part of a world, not just a European
movement.

Discussion at the Stockholm conference revealed a strong
distaste for any sort of Green international organisation that
bore the remotest resemblance to any other political International. However, as demands on and expectations from the
European Greens mount, they have started to take a serious
look at how to develop their organisation and their activities,
helped by contributions from as far away as Australia.
Recent meetings of the 'Nordic Greens' and the 'South
European' Greens suggest a sensible way for the European
Greens to evolve and expand without running into problems
of scale.

In Eastern Europe, too, many groups are springing up that
want constructive but sensitively managed links with Greens
in the West. From further afield come requests for *sustained*
information about established Green parties and their policies, as people and groups struggle to put Green issues on the
agenda of public, if not political, debate in their own
countries. The time seems ripe, therefore, for the European

Greens to come out from behind their favourite slogan – Act Locally, Think Globally – and start thinking locally about how best to act globally.

Notes

1. Ecoropa is a non-political, non-profit-making European organisation with branches in about 10 countries. It is mostly concerned with the safety of ecological and natural systems and produces some excellent leaflets and pamphlets. For more information write to Ecoropa, Crickhowell, Powys, Wales NP8 1TA, UK.

Main Publications

Joint Declaration of Aims.
Think Globally – Act Locally (1984 European election programme).
From Two Blocs Towards One World, Campaign for International Peace Year, 1986 (booklet of essays).
Papers from the International Green Congress, Stockholm, August 1987 (may be ordered from Miljöpartiet).
Newsletter of the European Greens (quarterly by subscription).

A full list of publications, press releases and articles by and about the GRAEL is available directly from: Green Alternative European Link (GRAEL), European Parliament, 97-113 rue Belliard, 1040 Brussels, Belgium.

Studies of the European Greens

RUDIG W., 'The Greens in Europe, Ecological Parties and the European Elections of 1984', *Parliamentary Affairs* 38.
MÜLLER-ROMMEL Ferdinand, 'Ecology Parties in Western Europe', *Western European Politics* 5/1, January 1982.
RUDIG W. & LOWE P., *The Green Wave: a Comparative Analysis of Ecology Parties*, Polity Press, Cambridge, forthcoming.

Addresses

The European Greens
c/o Agalev
Tweekerkenstr 78
1050 Brussels
Belgium

tel: (32) 2 230666

Co-secretaries:
Bruno Boissière, Les Verts
Leo Cox, Agalev
Per Gahrton, Miljöpartiet
Sara Parkin, Green Party

16: NEW ZEALAND *Values Party*

*(name changed to Values, Green
Party of Aotearoa in 1986)*

Area: 268,704 sq. km.   *founded: 20 May 1972*
Population: 3.3 million (1986)   *members: not known*
Density: 12 per sq. km.

*Member: UN, The Commonwealth, OECD, Association
of South-East Asian Nations, Colombo Plan*
Official Languages: English and Maori
GNP per capita: US $5,276 (1985)

Background and Electoral System

The New Zealand Parliament consists of the 95-seat House of
Representatives which includes 4 seats for the Maori electorate. Maoris make up 9% of the population of New Zealand.

For the purposes of local government, which is at present
undergoing reorganisation, New Zealand is divided into 22
regions. Only 2 of them (Auckland and Wellington) have
directly elected regional councils. The rest are under the
newly constituted United Councils who are appointed by the
authorities under them. The regional sub-divisions are 88
counties, 10 districts, 128 boroughs and cities and 3 town
districts, as well as numerous other local authorities which
are either amalgamations of counties, districts, boroughs etc.
or which were created for specific purposes. For example:
river protection districts, electric power districts, pest
destruction districts.

For elections to the national parliament which take place
every three years the country is divided into 91 'European'
constituencies, each returning one member. It is also divided
into 4 'Maori' constituencies each returning one member.
Europeans may not be on a 'Maori' electoral roll, while
people of Maori descent may choose to be on either a

'European' or a 'Maori' roll, but not both.

National and local elections are conducted by the simple majority system. Candidates do not have to belong to a party but do have to be on an electoral roll and provide two nominees and a NZ $100 deposit. This is refunded to any candidate obtaining 30% or more of the vote.

Factors Influencing the Development of Green Politics

Outside influences, like opposition to the Vietnam war and the Limits to Growth debate, combined with internal changes and events to create the climate which led to the founding of the world's first national Green political party. Like Australia, New Zealand developed a new sense of national maturity and cultural confidence during the 1960s and 1970s. This included interest in and respect for the Maori culture, and brought a general questioning of the values which had dominated the rapid urbanisation of New Zealand over past decades.

The nationwide campaign in 1969 to save Manapouri Lake on South Island from a hydroelectric project did much to bring the issue of environmental protection to the notice of most New Zealanders. In the same year the Environmental Defence Society was founded and soon most university campuses had Ecology Action Groups. It was estimated that by 1973, one year after the publication of the Club of Rome report[1] and the UN Conference on the Environment in Stockholm, about 60 groups were concerned with environmental protection.[2]

There was also widespread concern about the French nuclear weapon testing programme in the Pacific and a growing interest in sustainable energy as well as mounting opposition to major urban development projects. Both major political parties adopted some policies concerning environmental protection but neither the National or the Labour party viewed the problems as being part of a 'general threat to human survival'.[3]

Values

As the name of the party implies, the impetus that led to its
founding was essentially one of values. In the words of its
founder Tony Brunt, many people were 'lying under the tap
marked Labour, waiting for a drop of moral leadership'.[4]
Brunt, a one-time journalist, canvassed his network of
contacts and friends about the possibility of a new political
party and was encouraged by the interest. The Values party
was founded at a meeting in Victoria University, Wellington,
on 30 May 1972 and received considerable publicity in the
months leading up to the November national elections. Its
election manifesto, *Blueprint for New Zealand*, with its call
for a new industrial democracy, struck a chord with many
people who were concerned about environmental degradation and who rejected the materialism which dominated
society. Although the party only stood in 42 of the then 87
constituencies it polled 2% of the national vote. And despite
the fact that Labour was returned to government with the
popular Norman Kirk as prime minister, Values was 'seen as
the party of the future with all the clever leaders of
tomorrow', and the one which made the environment, women
and peace *political* issues for the first time.[5]

The party spent a troubled year establishing an organisation able to cope with success. Conflicts arose over how to
structure a party devoted to decentralisation. At Values'
1973 conference a paper arguing that the party should have
no national organisation between elections was presented by
Guy Salmon. It was passed, leading to the collapse of local
branches and the party being unable to respond to growing
interest from individuals and the media. It is worth noting
that within a few months Salmon was serving on a National
party ginger group.[6]

However the 1974 Palmerston North conference managed
to restore some coherence to the party and, as the oil crisis
began to bite, it gained new credibility for its environmental,
no-growth economic and sustainable energy policies. For the
1975 national elections the party was able to contest all the
constituencies and polled an average of 5.2%, just short of
the percentage that gave Die Grünen 28 seats in the West
German parliament eight years later.

When Values went into the 1978 election with a carefully
prepared campaign and a detailed radical manifesto (which

brought admiration from fledgling Green parties around the world) they were convinced that they would increase their percentage and overtake the centre-right Social Credit party as the third force in New Zealand politics. The result, an average of 2.4% nationwide despite a candidate in every constituency, came as a tremendous blow, from which the party has never really recovered.

If only because it rose and fell before any other Green party had made any national impact at all, the reasons for Values' disintegration are worth examining.

When the National party, led by Robert Muldoon, won the election of 1975, Labour immediately set about polishing up its image and policies in time for the 1978 election. It also quite openly wooed the constituency that had been attracted to Values – young professionals, women and environmentalists. But in the end it never really mattered if voters thought the changes made by Labour were genuine or merely cosmetic, because by 1978 many potential Values voters were voting Labour for strictly tactical reasons. They wanted most of all to get rid of the controversial prime minister Robert Muldoon. Even if Values had not dissolved in major internal disputes after 1978 it is unlikely that the party's results would have been much different in 1981 when Muldoon won again, or in 1984 when the revamped Labour party, now led by David Lange, eventually regained power. Values contested 17 seats in 1981 and 30 seats in 1984, gaining a national average of 0.2% each time.

All the internal conflicts that had been previously soothed by success erupted in full force at Values' 1979 conference. In the battle for professionalism versus 'organic' organisation the latter won. But although the conflict seemed to be one of style it ran deeper than that. The Christchurch branch of the party had not only been mainly responsible for the 1978 election campaign but it had also dominated the party organisationally and intellectually for many years, frequently employing tactics and ideas that many party members felt belonged more to a traditional left-wing cadre party than to a Green party. So when party leader Tony Kunowski of Christchurch put his membership on the line by asking the conference to accept his model for professionalising the party, more was at stake than a benign plan for reorganisation. After he had lost the vote Kunowski and his supporters left the conference and the party. Some subsequently formed a Socialist Network.[7]

There is something to be said for the argument that Values was ahead of the times, and there is no doubt that enthusiasm for the party and its radical policies went beyond its actual electoral impact and apparently endures. Certainly, if the 1978 electoral setback had taken place in the context of a visibly growing Green political movement world-wide, the party might have survived the destructiveness that followed disappointment. They were pioneers but they were very alone. However, although many internal tensions over organisation and policy inconsistencies can be blamed for the decline of Values, the main reason for their poor results in 1978 lay ouside their control.

Future Prospects

Now the party membership is in hundreds rather than thousands, organisation is regionally based, and more a network of like-minded people than anything else. Electoral participation is not given a high priority (only 10 seats were contested in the 1987 national elections) and although Values members sit on local councils the election campaigns are no longer fought as a party political event. Most former members put their efforts into single-issue groups, many present members into local politics.[8]

However, as the economic vortex of the world moves to south-east Asia, the international pressure on the New Zealand Labour government can only increase. Although prime minister Lange has taken a strong anti-nuclear position, his principles have steadily become shipwrecked on the rocks of international trade, given New Zealand's heavy dependence on the export of its primary products. Lange's attempt to take a strong moral position over the sinking of the Rainbow Warrior, for example, was quickly compromised by his need to keep already glutted international lamb and butter markets sweet.

Internal pressures mount in New Zealand too. Enviromental and social problems have not disappeared after six years of Labour party rule. Recently a Royal Commission reported on a reform of the electoral system to provide fairer representation for the country's Maori population. The proportional system that they recommend will benefit other minority groups apart from the Maoris. Maybe the time of Values, the Green Party of Aotearoa, has yet to come after all.

Notes

1 Meadows et al, *The Limits to Growth*, Earth Island, London, 1972.

2 John Morton et al, *Seacoast in the Seventies*, Hodder and Stoughton, 1973.

3 Stephen Rainbow, 'New Zealand's Values Party – The Rise and Fall of the First Green party', paper prepared for the APSA Conference, Auckland, August 1987.

4 Tony Brunt, 'In Search of Values', in Brian Edwards (ed.), *Right Out*, Reed, NZ, 1973.

5 Janine McVeagh, Values International Liaison Secretary, personal communication, July 1987.

6 Stephen Rainbow, op. cit.

7 ibid.

8 Janine McVeagh, personal communication, July 1987.

Main Party Publications

Blueprint for New Zealand, 1972.
Beyond Tomorrow, 1975.
The Values Party Manifesto, 1978.

Linkletter, monthly newsletter, from Ruth Gardner & Stephen Symons, The Cottage on the Corner, 374 Barbadoes Street, Christchurch 1; tel: (64) 656 943

Study of Values

RAINBOW Stephen, 'New Zealand's Values Party – The Rise and Fall of the First Green Party', paper prepared for the 1987 APSA Conference, August 1987, Auckland, New Zealand.

Address

Janine McVeagh, international secretary
Wekaweka Valley,
Waimamaku
South Hokianga

tel: (64) South Hokianga 529

Organogram: Values
– Green Party of Aotearoa

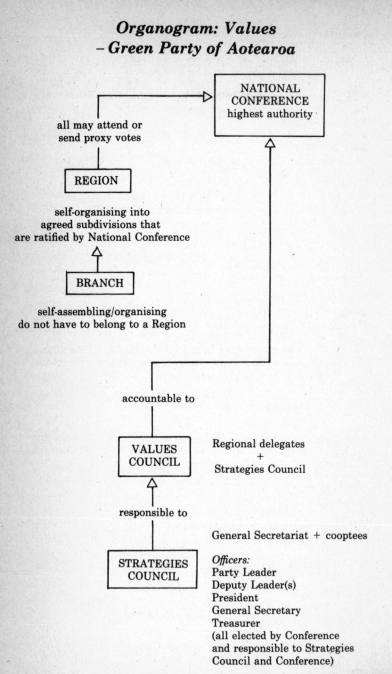

NATIONAL
CONFERENCE
highest authority

all may attend or
send proxy votes

REGION

self-organising into
agreed subdivisions that
are ratified by National Conference

BRANCH

self-assembling/organising
do not have to belong to a Region

accountable to

VALUES
COUNCIL

Regional delegates
+
Strategies Council

responsible to

STRATEGIES
COUNCIL

General Secretariat + cooptees

Officers:
Party Leader
Deputy Leader(s)
President
General Secretary
Treasurer
(all elected by Conference
and responsible to Strategies
Council and Conference)

17: AUSTRALIA

United Tasmania Group
founded: 23 March 1972 (dissolved 1976)

Nuclear Disarmament Party
founded: June 1984

Rainbow Alliance
founded: March 1988

Area: 7,682,300 sq. km.
Population 16.1 million (1987)
Density: 2 per sq. km.

Member: UN, The Commonwealth, OECD, Colombo Plan
Language: English
GNP per capita: US $11,172 (1984)

Background and Electoral System

Aboriginal cosmology revolves around the period known as the Dreamtime, when the formations of the landscapes – the trees, hills, mountains, rivers, rock, waterholes – were created by Ancestral Beings who were both men and animals at the same time, or who had the ability to transform themselves from one to another. When the creation of the physical environment was finished, the Ancestors left, leaving human children who, in turn, turned into animals, features of the environment or simply disappeared into the air, the earth or the sea. Thus the countryside is their testimonial to living humans: and it is also evidence of their existence.[1]

Few indigenous peoples have suffered more from coloni-
sation than the Aboriginal tribes of Australia. The arrival of
expatriated convicts (the last consignment was in 1867) and
adventurous British emigrants shattered their hunting and
gathering communities. Entire tribes were killed in bloody
confrontations with the newcomers, and many more succumbed to newly introduced diseases.

When Britain decided that its Australian colonies were
more trouble than they were worth, it started what was to be
a stormy process of uniting them into a self-governing federal
structure. The Commonwealth of Australia came into being
in 1901 and included the states of New South Wales, Victoria,
Queensland, South Australia, Western Australia and
Tasmania. In 1911, Northern Territory was transferred from
South Australia to the Commonwealth as was the site for
Canberra where building of the capital city started in 1923.

The Australian Parliament consists of a 76-seat Senate and
a 148-seat House of Representatives. Senators are elected
from the states for a six-year term, and the House of
Representatives has approximately twice the number of seats
as the Senate. This federal Parliament has limited and
explicit powers. Considerable powers are retained by the
state parliaments, including mining, forestry and Aboriginal
affairs. Certain local government functions are dealt with by
municipal, city, town, shire or district councils (total about
900). If a state law is inconsistent with a federal law, it is the
latter which prevails. However high court challenges are
quite common, for example by the Queensland state government over the listing of the Daintree rainforest as a World
Heritage Area.

Members of the House of Representatives are selected from
single-member constituencies by a preferential voting
system. Voters list candidates in order of preference, and if no
candidate has an overall majority the votes are distributed
according to preference until a majority is obtained. It is
difficult to win a seat under this system without holding
about 28% of first-preference votes. Senators are elected by
Single Transferable Vote from multi-member constituencies
and consequently require a much lower 'quota' to obtain a
seat – sometimes less than 5%. Most states have two houses
of parliament and operate electoral systems similar to the
national one.

Factors Influencing the Development of Green Politics

Cultural Confidence

Most Australians pin-point the success of the Australian Labor Party (ALP) led by Gough Whitlam in the 1972 federal elections as the turning point for their country. Although influenced by outside events like the Vietnam war and the development of the European Community, it was his robust and nationalistic approach to politics and life that gave Australians the kick they needed to wake up from the apathy of 26 years of Liberal rule and learn to say with pride and satisfaction: 'Yes, I'm Australian.' Their high standard of living was soon paired with a new confidence in home-grown intellectuals and a culture which is now met with respect around the world.

Some classic myths were debunked during this period too. The Great Australian Mateship was revealed for the smoke-screen of crude male clannishness it really was, which went some way towards making it easier for women to become more active in public life. And the habit, indulged in the name of egalitarianism, of attacking anyone in authority or anyone who 'did better' than their neighbours – known as 'knocking down the tall poppies' – was also unmasked as a dangerous recipe for chronic mediocrity. Perhaps inevitably, Australians went through strong reactions at this time of change, even over-reactions like the social cachet that became attached to having a convict ancestor!

Aboriginal Land Rights

There was also a straightforward guilt over the decimation of the Aboriginal population and their subsequent unjust treatment to be dealt with. On behalf of white Australians Whitlam tried to make up for 200 years of mistakes overnight, assuaging collective guilt by doling out lots of money and giving Aboriginals 'inalienable' rights to land in Northern Territory, north Queensland and New South Wales. (Although Whitlam was ousted by the governor-general in 1975, the new prime minister, Malcolm Fraser, nevertheless enacted this legislation.) 'Inalienable' rights means that the land cannot be bought and sold, but it rarely included land designated as a national park or the rights to exploit any mineral resources. These inadequate and, it must be said, unsubtle attempts at reparation did little to reduce the high rates of alcoholism and unemployment among the Aboriginal people. However, the 1988 celebrations of 200 years of white settlement in Australia and the Labor party's dithering over election promises they made to the Aboriginals has fired a new radicalism amongst Aboriginal leaders and rekindled a widespread and more thoughtful kind of guilt amongst everyone else.

Peace Movement

The brief whirlwind Gough Whitlam brought into Australian politics ended in 1975 when the conservative Malcolm Fraser came to power. The anti-nuclear lobby, however, continued to find hope in the promise of the Labor party's firm opposition to the whole nuclear cycle:

> ...the provision of Australian uranium to the world nuclear fuel cycle creates problems relevant to Australian sovereignty, the environment, the economic welfare of our people, and the rights and well-being of the Aboriginal people.
>
> The lack of adequate permanent disposal of uranium is the major obstacle in the path of the nuclear industry but other important problems are present as well, such as health hazards to miners in underground mines, safety and security of fuel from theft and terrorisationists (sic), proliferation of nuclear weapons, safety of nuclear reactors, security and contamination of long-term wastes. AN AUSTRALIAN LABOR GOVERNMENT WILL MAINTAIN ITS PRESENT POLICY OF OPPOSITION TO URANIUM MINING AND NUCLEAR POWER.[2]

But in the same way as the Aboriginals were to be disappointed by Labor's return to power in 1983, so was the anti-nuclear movement. Jo Vallentine, a Western Australian teacher, was inspired 'to take the struggle for nuclear disarmament into the political mainstream' in 1983 after mentioning to Mr Hawke her concern that the Labor party would renege on its anti-uranium mining postion. 'I told Mr Hawke that it would make a lot of people very upset with the party and may prompt them to show their displeasure in the ballot box. To which he replied with that famous sneer: "Who else are they going to vote for?" '[3] The 1984 ALP conference voted to open the Roxby Downs uranium mine and six months later Jo Vallentine won a seat in the Senate.

But despite Jo Vallentine's election (and subsequent re-election in 1987), the Australian peace movement is in as much disarray as its counterparts in other countries. Years of campaigning have resulted in little tangible success. US bases remain, uranium mining and exporting goes on and nuclear warships and submarines regularly visit Australian ports.

The Green Bans

The Australian Green Bans are one of the best-known examples of a successful labour-environment movement coalition. They started in the early 1970s in Hunters Hill, a select suburb of Sydney. During the biggest uncontrolled building boom in Sydney's history a group of women, frustrated in their attempts to conserve the last bit of bushland (Kelly's Bush) left in their area, went to the New South Wales Builder's Laborers Federation (BLF) for help. They were prompted to do this by remarks made in a local paper by Jack Mundey, the union's then secretary: 'In a modern society, trade unions must broaden their vision and horizons and become involved in wide-range social, political and environmental activities... Not only has the trade union movement the right to intervene, it has the responsibility to do so.'[4]

As a result of this meeting the BLF developed a policy of work-bans on environmentally unsound projects. Jack Mundey eventually coined the term Green Ban, feeling it more in keeping with the far-reaching and moral action the union was taking than the traditional 'black' bans – strikes over workers' pay and conditions. For each Green Ban, starting with the 'battle for Kelly's Bush', the union insisted that a public meeting be held by the people or groups requesting the ban. By demonstrating that there was a strong local sympathy for the ban they were able to avoid accusations of indulging in covert political activities. The bans (42 in all) covered different schemes and met with varying successes, but they saved over 100 historic buildings and many open spaces.

But the story of the Green Bans doesn't have a happy ending. When the New South Wales government failed to break up its troublesome building workers union it got the federal union to do it for them. As was later revealed, the federal union secretary Norm Gallagher received 'commissions' from two of Australia's biggest developers; though he was gaoled, this happened too late to save the Green Bans movement. Jack Mundey went on to become an alderman on Sydney city council, which was now 'dominated for the first time by independents who were largely of a "Green" flavour and who were opposed to the worst excesses of inappropriate urban development. They were so successful that the NSW state Labor government sacked the council in April 1987.'[5]

Conservation Movement

> We cannot speak for other things. But we know that we, at least, need natural beauty and that our human beings resonate with nature, its forests, seashores and mountain grandeur. We may not say it well – or at all – except by the pictures we hang on our walls, the books on our shelves, the gardens we eke out of suburban confines or grow upon window sills and bathroom ledges.

> Our bodies and minds are made for wildness. Through millions of years, every human cell has been created and made ready for the Earth's terrain. The spread of our toes, the grip of our hands, the curl of our ears to catch the faintest movement of air molecules by fur, feather or fin: billions of wilderness cells making us up.[6]

In densely populated Europe few of us have been lucky enough to have contact with the powerful vastness and beauty of natural wilderness. Our physical environment, even when walking in the countryside, is full of other people and human artefacts. Fortunately the vastness of Australia's wildernesses and the low density of its population have made it easier for a growing number of people to understand that these wild areas must be protected. In the words of Bob Brown again, they are conscious of 'the value of wilderness; the need for large areas of wild Earth to be kept intact; the very concept of wilderness as a place with no roads, fences, factories or kiosks; the wisdom that we have no right to send other species to extinction; nor to fell a forest without asking whether people, ten generations from now, would give that act their warrant.'[7]

This consciousness was only just developing in April 1971 when the Lake Pedder Action Committee (LPAC) was formed in Tasmania to oppose the planned flooding of Lake Pedder by the Hydro-Electric Commission (HEC). Although this protest was ultimately to fail (Lake Pedder was flooded in 1974) the experience gained from this campaign ensured that the next battle, for the Franklin river, would succeed. Not only did the Franklin blockade become a world-wide campaign, but it and the subsequent strategies of the Australian conservation groups offer the environmental movement everywhere a powerful lesson in new ways, or to be exact new *combinations* of ways, of putting their demands at the top of political agendas.

Green Politics

United Tasmania Group

The Liberal government in Tasmania collaped in March 1972 when the Centre party member who held the balance of power resigned. In view of this the Lake Pedder Action Committee called a meeting in Hobart on the 23rd of the month. Their campaign against the flooding of Lake Pedder had so far revealed extensive complicity between the HEC and success-ive governing parties in Tasmania, including the previous Labor government that had approved the scheme in the first place. The campaigners therefore saw little hope for their cause in the impending election. However, frustration and anger at their inability to influence the decision-makers led the meeting to agree that:

> ...in order that there is a maximum usage of a
> unique political opportunity to save Lake Pedder,
> now an issue of national and global concern, and
> to implement a national, well-researched conser-
> vation plan for the state of Tasmania, there be
> formed a Single Independent Coalition of primarily
> conservation-oriented candidates and their
> supporters.[8]

There are several definitions as to what constitutes a
political party, but a basic requirement is that a candidate is
nominated for public office. So, whether you count the day
when the decision was made to contest the election or the
election day itself (21 April 1972) as the magic date, it seems
certain that the United Tasmania Group formed at the
Hobart public meeting was the world's first Green party.[9]

The month-long campaign, co-directed by Dr Richard
Jones, stood 12 candidates in 4 of the 5 Tasmanian multi-
member constituencies, concentrating on Denison and
Franklin, where the LPAC was strongest. The result state-
wide was 3.9% with pockets of around 7% in Denison and
Franklin. The United Tasmania Group came within 200 votes
of winning a seat in Hobart.

Although it never managed to win any seats in 10 elections
up to its dissolution in 1976, the UTG did push environmentalism and its values into the political arena. The party
developed a comprehensive platform based on a New Ethic
(published in 1972) which prompted the *Examiner* of 26
August 1976 to comment: 'Dr Jones' little party has produced
more teasing relevant ideas for Tasmanians than all the
other party policy writers put together.' Some of them were
even taken up by subsequent governments.

The Tasmanian Wilderness Society

In the same way that the United Tasmania Group grew out of
the Lake Pedder Action Group, so activists of the UTG were
involved in founding, out of some small action groups, the
Tasmanian Wilderness Society (TWS). In fact, 19 of the 23
people present at the inaugural meeting of the TWS held in
August 1976 were active members of the UTG. The formation
of this new pressure group annoyed the established, but

rather conservative, Tasmanian Conservation Trust, because this was not the first time that members of the UTG had deliberately set out to radicalise the conservation movement.

> The party {UTG} was also instrumental in the 'carefully orchestrated coup' which replaced the established Australian Conservation Foundation {ACF} executive through democratic elections. The ACF had been established in 1965 as the first national conservation body concerned with the whole range of conservation issues. Due to the 'palace revolution' of 1973 the ACF was transferred from a conservative club to a lobby group more critical of the government. As a result the ACF today is no longer seen as lagging behind or as reluctant to fight the establishment and in recent years has developed quite radical policies on such controversial issues as woodchipping.[10]

The Tasmanian Wilderness Society was founded in August 1976, one year after the short-lived Whitlam Labor government was replaced by a Liberal/National party coalition in the House of Representatives and shortly before the Australian Democrats party was born. This new party did develop a reputation for taking on board the demands of pressure groups and was for some time seen as the natural political vehicle for minority issues. Its policies on nuclear and environmental matters were broadly acceptable to the developing Green movement, but weak economic and conventional defence policies and a hierarchical organisation dominated by parliamentarians made it appear like any another party committed to 'politics as usual'. Currently the Democrats party has 7 seats in the Senate but no seats in the House of Representatives.

However, the Democrats party was of little use to the TWS in 1976. The society came into existence specifically to save Tasmania's south-west wilderness (one of the last three temperate rainforests on Earth) from destruction by yet another hydro-electric scheme, this time on the Franklin river. Lessons learnt from the failure at Lake Pedder proved very useful to the new campaign. As Bob Brown puts it:

We had a view from their shoulders. We began the

campaign years before the Hydro-Electric
Commission poured the first load of cement. With
such a headstart there was time to meet the
'experts' on their own ground – to argue economics and employment as well as environment... By
1982, when the heavy machines rolled south down
the Franklin valley and were barged up the
Gordon to Warner's Landing, the nation knew
what was at stake... Thanks to a warmhearted
group of wilderness workers: to the thousand
arrested or jailed, to the donors, the letter-writers,
the stall-holders, shop volunteers and voters.
Thanks most of all to the wild river's wilderness
and its articulate self-advocacy: through television, books and newspapers the river had found a
transformed Australian audience. The nation,
now aware of this heritage, demanded a stop to the
destruction.[11]

This time the campaign was successful. Not only was the
Australian public alerted to the need to save the Tasmanian
wilderness but people around the world also took up the
cause. Under substantial pressure the ALP led by Bob Hawke
pledged itself to save the Franklin river. When Labor won the
1983 national elections they kept their promise and, through
the high court, forced the Tasmanian state government to
stop the scheme in June 1983. In that same year, Bob Brown,
who had been director of the Wilderness Society during the
campaign, was elected to the Tasmanian House of Assembly
(lower house) from the Denison constituency. He and Gerry
Bates currently sit there as Green Independents. Another
veteran of the campaign, Norman Saunders, now sits in the
federal Senate as environment spokesman for the Democrats
party.

The Nuclear Disarmament Party

Disgust at the ALP's U-turn on its anti-nuclear policies and
distaste for some areas of the Democrats party platform
inspired a group of people attending the 1984 Palm Sunday
peace march in Canberra to form a new party, the Nuclear
Disarmament party.

The party rapidly grew to 10,000 members and in the

December 1984 elections to the federal Parliament was able
to stand candidates in all Australian states. The NDP polled
over half a million votes (6.8%) and its candidate for Western
Australia, Jo Vallentine, won a Senate seat. Apart from
disenchantment with the Labor party the NDP's rapid
success can be attributed to two factors. First, the publicity it
received through its New South Wales candidate Pete
Garrett (lead singer with the popular rock group Midnight
Oil who only just missed being elected), and secondly, its
simple three-point platform:

> (i) to prohibit the stationing in Australia or
> passage through Australian waters or airspace of
> any nuclear weapons;
> (ii) to close all foreign military bases in Australia;
> (iii) to terminate immediately all mining and
> export of uranium.[12]

But that simple platform was also to cause the ultimate
downfall of the party. 'It was probably the only political party
in Australia's history to announce, just before the election,
that most of its policies would be decided after the election'
(*Australian*, 29 April 1985). At its inaugural national conference in Melbourne at the end of April the most prominent
members, including Jo Vallentine and Pete Garrett, walked
out when the 300-member Socialist Workers Party (usually
described as Trotskyite) stacked the conference and defeated
a key motion for a ballot of the whole membership on the
principle that members of other parties would be ineligible to
join the NDP.

Although greatly diminished and only spasmodically
active since this take-over, the Nuclear Disarmament party
lives on. Even to its own surprise and despite a swing of 6.1%
against it, the party did win a Senate seat in July 1987
through its New South Wales candidate, Robert Wood. Wood
was a founder of Paddlers for Peace, a brave band who paddle
their kayaks in front of visiting US warships. Vallentine,
who sat as an Independent since leaving the Nuclear Disarmament party, also managed to keep her seat in 1987, if by a
whisker. Neverthless the rise and subsequent fall of the
Nuclear Disarmament party has left many people feeling
very disappointed that an important chance for the Australian anti-nuclear movement was wasted.

'Vote For The Forests' (VFTF) Campaign

During the 1983 federal election a coalition of environmental
groups involved in campaigning for the south-west
Tasmanian wilderness decided to mount a pressure campaign
on the major parties in some marginal seats, rather than
stand candidates themselves. They estimate they were
responsible for seven seats going to the 'better' (i.e. less
environmentally dangerous) candidate.[13]

For the July 1987 elections the TWS and the Australian
Conservation Foundation targeted 11 marginal constituencies with a well-prepared and sophisticated 'Vote For The
Forests' campaign. The campaign ('{we've} not a lot of
money, but we've got a lot of people')[14] leafletted voters and
sponsored what was acknowledged to be a brilliant tv and
radio advertising campaign under the slogan 'The forests
can't vote...but you can'.[15] In the 11 marginals voters were
urged to vote for the ALP for the House of Representatives
and Democrats for the Senate. To maximise the benefits of
preference votes under the Australian electoral system,
voters were shown how to distribute their votes between the
other candidates and parties on 'How to Vote' cards that
were handed out at the polling stations.

The final results showed a national swing of 1.31% *away*
from the ALP, but in the 11 targetted seats the swing became
0.89% *towards* the ALP. Vote scrutineering at some of the
polling stations showed an average of 12.5% of ALP voters
following the VFTF 'How to Vote' ticket rather than the
ALP's own suggested ticket. The VFTF campaign claimed it
had contributed an average of 2.2% of the ALP vote and
reckoned that seven of the targetted seats went to the ALP as
a direct result of the VFTF campaign. [16]

Despite some scepticism about the statistics, prime minister Bob Hawke formally acknowledged that the 'Greenies'
had brought in about 2% of his votes.[17] He also gave them
their reward in the shape of nominating the Queensland
Daintree rainforest as a World Heritage Area and appointing
Senator Graham Richardson as minister for the environment
with increased powers.

Future Prospects

It is difficult to assess the future prospects for Green politics in Australia. The ingredients seem to be in place – direct political involvement (e.g. the Nuclear Disarmament party and the Independents in the federal Senate and in some of the State parliaments); carefully targetted and sophisticated pressure from the movements (e.g. environmental and Aboriginal rights, the Green Bans) – but somehow they have not yet achieved the right mix.

An attempt to do so (inspired by the Second Congress of the European Greens in Dover, UK) was made in Sydney at easter 1986 when a Getting Together Conference was organised by the Liffey group working out of the Hobart offices of the Tasmanian Wilderness Society. Perhaps over-anxious to be inclusive, the conference was sidetracked by a Future Congress that was quickly organised on the same day by people describing themselves as coming 'from the non-conventional culture'.[18] Now the debate about Green politics in Australia has turned inwards and, at the moment, the 'non-conventional culture' faction is calling the tune. Based mainly in Brisbane and Melbourne, they have developed a New Political Movement which includes an 'elite' who came together after the take-over of the Nuclear Disarmament party by the extreme left. The movement has been augmented by other local groups and people attracted via the Getting Together and Future congresses.

Internal arguments over a name for a new party were resolved by a 'plebiscite' of the members, who chose 'Australian Greens'. However the Melbourne group objected that this was 'too environmental'. A new poll somehow managed to produce 76% in favour of the name 'Rainbow Alliance'.[19]

The first conference of the Rainbow Alliance, grimly entitled 'Remaking Australia, People in Control of Politics, the Economy and the Environment', was held on Labor weekend, March 1988. About 500 people attended the conference to debate the key question 'What kind of economy do we need if we are to achieve economic justice, political democracy, ecological balance and genuine security?', but almost all the various factions of the alternative movements seem to have come away dissatisfied. Watching the conference carefully was the Socialist Workers Party, already branded as the villian of the piece for shattering the Nuclear

Disarmament party. The SWP's attempts with the Australian
Communist party to bring the left together under a Charter
Group had fallen apart in November 1987, which made the
Rainbow Alliance the only remaining scene of political
action outside the major parties. However, without a trace of
irony, their paper *Direct Action* bemoaned the fact that the
plenary sessions were dominated by a small number of the
Melbourne organisers (23 March 1988).

Not surprisingly, people like Jo Vallentine and Bob Brown
are not entirely enthusiastic about this turn of events. Brown
would prefer a coalition of Independents and Vallentine is
openly concerned about the dubious decision-making
processes that the new group favour. They are both keeping
their options open and are joined in this by groups like the
Green Electoral Movement which is based mainly in South
Australia. Meanwhile, further forward on the political stage,
the Democrats party is waxing ever greener, Senator
Norman Sanders has been making headlines with his rev-
elations that Australian uranium goes into the international
enriched atomic soup and therefore into nuclear weapons
(*Canberra Times*, 22 April 1988) and the new environment
minister is being attacked by members of his own party for
protecting the environment too assiduously (*Australian*, 25
March 1988).

Notes

1 Burnam Burnam, in Drew Hutton (ed.), *Green Politics in Australia*,
Angus & Robertson, Australia, 1987, p. 94.
2 'Australian Labor Party Policy on the Environment', 1980, p. 64.
3 Jo Vallentine, in Drew Hutton (ed.), p. 55.
4 Jack Mundey, in ibid, p. 107.
5 Personal communication from Bob Brown, 1 September 1987.
6 Bob Brown, in Drew Hutton (ed.), p. 38.
7 ibid, p. 44.
8 K. McKenry, 'A History and Critical Analysis of the Controversy
Concerning the Gordon River Scheme', *Pedder Papers: Anatomy of a
Decision*, University of Queensland Press, St Lucia, 1976, p. 23.
9 Pamela Walker, 'The United Tasmania Group, an Analysis of the
World's First Green Party'. A paper presented to Eco Politics II
Conference, University of Tasmania, May 1987,
10 ibid.
11 Bob Brown, in Drew Hutton (ed.), p. 44
12 David Turbayne, 'The Nuclear Disarmament Party', paper for the
Second Congress of the European Greens, Dover, 1985.

13 Bob Brown, personal communication, October 1984. David Barnett ('Green Power', *The Bulletin*, 4 August 1987) says 5 seats is a more reasonable number but adds: 'that was still a factor of enormous significance'.
14 Jonathan West, director of TWS, quoted in *Time*, 22 June 1987.
15 The Australian National Opinion Polls (ANOP) said it had been the most effective of all the election tv advertisements.
16 Report on 'Vote For The Forest' campaign, Tasmanian Wilderness Society and Australian Conservation Foundation, 19 July 1987.
17 *Sydney Morning Herald*, 17 July 1987.
18 Eric Mack, *New Leaves* 14/15, October/November 1987.
19 Drew Hutton, ibid.

Green Movement Publications

New Leaves, PO Box 294, Stones Corner 4120, Queensland.
Edgeways, PO Box 1330N, Hobart 7001, Tasmania.

Studies of the Green Movement

HUTTON Drew (ed.), *Green Politics in Australia*, Angus & Robertson, Australia, 1987.
WALKER Pamela, 'The United Tasmania Group, an Analysis of the World's First Green Party', paper presented to Eco Politics II Conference, May 1987, University of Tasmania.

Addresses

Senators Jo Vallentine
and Robert Wood
Parliament House
Canberra 2600 ACT

tel: (61) 62 721211

Rainbow Alliance
PO Box 494
South Brisbane 4101
Queensland

Green Electoral Movement
c/o Andrew Allison
22 West Street
Torrensville 5031
South Australia

Tasmanian Wilderness Society
130 Davey Street,
Hobart 7000
Tasmania

tel: (61) 2 349366

Nuclear Disarmament Party
Box 414
Canberra City 2601 ACT

tel: (61) 62 866686

18: UNITED STATES
Green Committees of Correspondence

founded: 10-12 August 1984
Members: about 100 groups

Area: 9,116,758 sq. km.
Population: 238.7 million (1985)
Density: 26 per sq. km.

Member: UN, Organisation of American States, NATO,
OECD, Colombo Plan
Language: English
GNP per capita: US$ 11,338 (1984)

Background and Electoral System

A great deal of inspiration for the European Green movement
has emanated from the United States of America. It came
from activists such as Martin Luther King Jr and Ralph
Nader; from campaigns like the one which stopped American
intervention in Vietnam; and from lobbies that gave teeth to
the Environmental Protection Agency and kept nuclear
power at the bottom of the list of means of energy production.
Important too has been the influence of writers such as
Rachel Carson, who warned of the planet's limits in absorbing the consequences of human activity;[1] Lynn White, who
gave the seminal lecture 'The Historical Roots of Our
Ecologic Crisis' in December 1966;[2] Lester Brown, who, as
director of the Worldwatch Institute, provides brilliant
analyses of the complicated global problems we face;[3] and
Theodore Roszak who described so powerfully the whole
'counter-culture' which has influenced more than one
generation:[4]

It seemed that what was falling apart – or at least

being roughly shaken – was an ominous, world-wide technocratic system which the governing elites of the advanced industrial societies had been assiduously rigging up since the end of World War II. I may have pressed the analysis further than others by observing that the rising forces of dissent, in their search for the root causes of our public ills, were probing well beyond the immediate issues of war and social justice; they seemed intent upon subjecting many of our most closely guarded psychological commitments and subliminal cultural orthodoxies to critical examination.[5]

American writers have also contributed greatly to the theoretical underpinnings of Green thinking; Fritjof Capra in *The Turning Point*,[6] Murray Bookchin in *Towards an Ecological Society*,[7] Kirkpatrick Sale in *Human Scale*,[8] and Jonathan Schell in *The Fate of the Earth*[9] are only a few of the better known examples.

Why then does the 'cultural revolution' seem to have been more successful in Europe than it has in the USA? One explanation is that many countries in densely populated Europe have provided Greens with an accessible political system, enabling them to spread their ideas and channel their protests via political programmes. The huge, diverse and more thinly populated USA has not. In America the Green revolution appears to have taken more a private than a public form, as people come to terms with the implications of their analysis of society's ills. As Roszak puts it, people are realising that 'the needs of the person are the needs of the planet...the rights of the person are the rights of the planet.' This means, he suggests, that 'we live in a time when the very private experience of having a personal identity to discover, a personal destiny to fulfil, has become a subversive political force of major proportions.'[10]

The latest wave of books on deep ecology seem to bear this out,[11] as do the writing of feminists like Charlene Spretnak[12]. What is not yet entirely clear, however, is what form Roszak's subversive political force will take, if and when it goes public.

Based on the Constitution of 1787, American national government has three branches – executive, legislative and judicial.

The president is elected for four years by an electoral college equal in number to the total of Senate and House of Representative seats. These are in turn elected by popular vote after the celebrated primaries and caucuses which take place before the big party conventions where the candidates are finally chosen. Traditionally the president carries out his duties via executive departments, the heads of which form the president's cabinet. The heads of these departments and the judges of all the federal courts of law are appointed by the president and require confirmation by the Senate.

The legislative branch, Congress, is made up of two houses, the Senate and the House of Representatives. Regardless of its population each state elects by simple majority vote two Senators who serve six years. The Senate has power to initiate bills (not revenue ones), to amend or reject bills initiated by the House of Representatives and to ratify international treaties (but not agreements) entered into by the president. The House of Representatives has 435 members elected from the states in proportion to their population for two years, and is more important for budgetary policies. Most US elections are conducted under a simple majority system.

Candidate registration (ballot qualification) rules also vary from state to state, and some states have introduced complex laws to discourage the growth of third parties. Most states require a party to collect a number of signatures from registered electors in order to obtain 'ballot access'. California, for example, requires 713,000 signatures. Although Illinois requires fewer signatures (25,000), they must include at least 200 each from 50 of the 102 counties. It is estimated that, in order to to get onto the ballot in all 50 states, a party must collect around 2.2 million signatures.

Public funding in advance of the biggest event on the electoral calendar of the United States, the election of the president, is restricted to the two major parties and is of course matched by massive private funding. It is estimated that Ronald Reagan received nearly $40 million in public money for his 1980 campaign. Smaller parties may receive funding *after* the election but only if they obtain at least 5% of the vote. The best commentary on the rules for media coverage of candidates comes from Jim McClellan. He notes that in the 1980 Citizens Party presidential campaign Barry Commoner, the candidate, received less than three minutes on network evening news. This was roughly the same amount of coverage that was given to Ronald Reagan's old co-star, Bonzo the chimpanzee, during the campaign.[13]

Factors Influencing the Development of Green Politics

As well as the environmental warnings catalogued in Carson's *Silent Spring*, the 1960s saw the growth of the black civil rights movement, triggered by the refusal of Rosa Parks to give up her 'whites only' seat on a bus in Montgomery, Alabama. Echoing the American revolution, students and activists from the north bussed down to the south to help the black communities with their protest, fired by the charismatic Martin Luther King Jr and his evocation of the power of non-violent resistance.

Although the 1960s saw the counter-culture manifest itself in ways that ranged from hippies to health freaks, it was above all preoccupied by the involvement of the USA in the war in Vietnam. When seven members of Students for a Democratic Society were charged with conspiracy in 1968 for their anti-Vietnam war activities in Chicago, they became heros in the eyes of many young people. The rapid growth of the women's liberation movement in America owes much to the connections women made at this time between the public politics that led to war and the personal politics that led to women's subservient role in society. However, the collective frustration of an entire generation that had been told it had everything, but realised it wanted something different, seemed to peak on Earth Day, 22 April 1970.

By comparison to the 1960s, the 1970s were an anti-climax. The traditional American way of seeking change is through formal lobbying organisations, inevitably concentrated in Washington DC. During the 1970s the peace and environmental groups came in off the street and joined in the lobbying process with a will. They were greatly helped by the fact that 'ecology' had become fashionable. Being into cycling, recycling, solar energy and alternative lifestyles was definitively 'in'. The supposedly non-political nature of the lobbies also permitted experts and scientists to take part without compromising their professional positions. The lobbying organisations vied with each other over the number of prestigious names they could squeeze onto their letterheads, and jealously guarded their relationships with politicians, civil servants, church leaders, business and other influential people and institutions. President Nixon set up the Environmental Protection Agency in 1969 to fight 'our war on pollution' and from 1972, seven years before the accident at Three Mile Island, orders for nuclear reactors were being cancelled.[14] In 1975 America withdrew from Vietnam.

However, three groups in particular were not impressed either by the speed or the extent of change.

Early Days

Campaign for Economic Democracy

In 1976 Tom Hayden, one of the 'Chicago seven' who had been tried for conspiracy as a result of their anti-Vietnam war activities, polled over 1.2 million votes (36.7%) in California when he stood as candidate for the Democratic party nomination to the US Senate.[15] Although failing to secure the nomination, his result inspired him to form the Campaign for Economic Democracy (CED), based on the ideas and the style of the now defunct Students for a Democratic Society.

After three hard years spent building the Campaign into a state-wide political movement through meetings, actions, organisation of local chapters and some small and occasionally successful forays into local elections, Hayden published his 'Vision for the 80s' in *CED News* of September 1979. This vision was less a prescription for the future than a catalogue of the problems in hand, such as centralised power, uneven wealth distribution, unemployment, inflation, sexual and racial discrimination, pollution, health hazards and product safety. However, Hayden also quoted some research done by Professor Archie Carroll of the University of Georgia, which revealed that three-fifths of the executives he interviewed admitted they would commit unethical acts to prove loyalty to their superiors.

Starting in Harrisburg, Pennsylvania on 23 September 1979, Hayden and his wife Jane Fonda (another veteran of the anti-Vietnam war campaign) set out on a tour of almost 50 cities in 15 of the key 'primary' states for the 1980 presidential elections. The tour was described by its supporters as an effort to 'rally progressives across America behind a program of renewable energy, public control of giant corporations and control over inflation in life's basic necessities: energy, housing, food and health care'. Its detractors saw it more as the next logical step in the Tom Hayden self-promotion campaign. Whatever its objective, it failed. The Campaign for Economic Democracy did not become a nationwide organisation, Tom Hayden returned to Californian politics and dissolved the CED in 1987.

The Citizens Party

A few weeks before the Hayden-Fonda tour, on 1 August 1979, the National Citizens Organising Committee sent representatives of its 100 founding members to a press conference in Washington DC to announce the founding of a new national political party, the Citizens party. The founding convention eventually took place in Cleveland, Ohio in April 1980, confirming a member of the founding committee, Barry Commoner, as the party's presidential candidate. Commoner, a biologist, author of *The Closing Circle*[16] and long-time activist for improved conditions in the workplace, gave the party its intellectual personality, and Stanley Weiss, a businessman, gave it its budget. LaDonna Harris, a Comanche Indian with long experience in Indian affairs, women's, health and social issues was Commoner's running mate. A programme not dissimilar to the Campaign for Economic Democracy was adopted, but explained in more positive and friendly terms on a leaflet decorated with the party's logo, a fir tree.

The party managed, sometimes after taking legal action, to get onto the ballot in 37 states, but even so scored a disappointing total of only 234,294 votes in the 4 November 1980 election that saw Reagan replace Carter in the White House.[17] This was a long way short of the announced objective of 5% of the total national vote.[18]

It was also the beginning of the end for the party, although its newspaper *Citizen's Voice* was able to announce in March 1982 that chapters had been formed in 48 states and that to date the party had seen candidates win four local elections (the biggest win being to King County, Seattle school board with 69%) and come second in ten others. The chapters became more independent in style and programme from the

financially broken national party and the idiosyncratic
behaviour of Barry Commoner. Some continued to be locally
active and supported the candidature of Sonia Johnson in the
1984 presidential elections. Author of *From Housewife to
Heretic*[19] and nationally famous for her hunger strike in
support of the Equal Rights Amendment during which she
chained herself to the White House railings, Johnson encir-
cled the Citizens party fir-tree logo with the feminist symbol
and polled 72,200 votes (0.07% of the total).[20] By this time,
however, Commoner had declared his support for Jesse
Jackson's Rainbow Coalition.

The New World Alliance

While the Campaign for Economic Democracy and the
Citizens party were seeking to break into American national
politics via the presidential race, the New World Alliance
was one of several groups which sought a breakthrough for
its ideas via a networking process. Its political vision
included healing, rediscovery, human growth, ecology, participation, appropriate scale, globalism, technological creati-
vity and spirituality.

The Alliance originated from a 21-page questionnaire sent
by Mark Satin, author of *New Age Politics*,[21] 'to 350 people
involved in a variety of personal-growth and social-change
activities'. A governing council was formed from respondents
and the New World Alliance founded in December 1979. The
purpose of the Alliance was to 'articulate new decentralist/
planetary politics, launch practical and realisable projects
and to serve as one of the organisational vehicles for
transformation'.[22] After heady initial ambitions for multiple
activities ranging from an 'on-going traveling political
consciousness-raising seminar' to a 'planetary outreach
project', Mark Satin himself has eventually settled down
to producing an interesting monthly newsletter called *New
Options*, which in March 1988 reported a circulation of over
10,000. If its letterhead sporting a list of 100 'advisors' is
anything to go by, this monthly may have succeeded in
upending the lobbying process. Now the illustrious seem to
be lobbying the citizens!

Recent Developments

These three examples of attempts to bring 'new' politics to
the American electorate were probably doomed before they
started. The vastness of the United States makes organising
anything nationally extremely expensive and time-
consuming, and the electoral system presents a virtually
unassailable barrier to new political parties. In fact, no third
party has been nationally successful since the creation of the
Republican party over the slavery issue in 1860, and although
it is possible for third parties to win in local elections it is also
expensive and difficult.

But another reason why the domination of American
politics by the Democratic and Republican parties has never
been broken is put forward by Kirkpatrick Sale. He believes
that any attempt to put forward a coalition of ideas, policies
and parties is futile in the US (and, he suspects, elsewhere).
The several attempts to present the American electorate with
a hodgepodge of left-liberal-radical parties and ideas over the
last few decades have all failed, including the Rainbow
Coalition of Jesse Jackson which deployed considerable
publicity and money in the 1984 presidential election campaign. Sale believes the best ideas tend to be picked off by the
Democratic party, leaving the unpopular ones behind.[23]

Since Jesse Jackson's 1988 attempt to win nomination as
Democratic candidate for the White House, the same might
be said of the candidates. However, the points of Jackson's
1988 programme which were highlighted in his fundraising
leaflet did not even nod in the direction of Green politics and
he was very ambiguous even about nuclear arms. In a review
of the presidential candidates, the magazine of American
Friends of the Earth, *Not Man Apart*, pointed out (Jan-Feb
1988) that Jackson did give sound speeches on environmental
matters, but had no track record to prove that his actions
might follow his rhetoric.

So, two decades after the passion of the Sixties fizzled
away, what hope is there for Green politics in the 1990s? Has
Roszak's subversive political force sunk back into its
armchair and put its carpet slippers on for good? If the age
group of many of the prime movers in the new culture and
politics described in a recent book by Brian Tokar is
anything to go by, then the answer is definitely no:

In the emerging Green movement, we can see the
beginning of a different way. We find people
openly embracing a need for community and an
ethic of cooperation. We meet a reactivated citi-
zenry standing against war and injustice, and
rebuilding a peaceful society from the ground up.
We discover social change work that is integrated
into the daily life of communities all across our
continent, spreading its message by example. We
feel the birth pangs of a new culture of empower-
ment and a new politics of celebration.[24]

Four main strands stand out in the United States Green
movement at the moment: the 'monkey-wrenchers', the
bioregional movement, the social ecologists, and the
Committees of Correspondence.

The Monkeywrenchers

Inspired by *The Monkey Wrench Gang*,[25] an amusing novel by
Edward Abbey, Dave Foreman resigned from his job as a
Washington-based lobbyist for the Wilderness Society and
founded the group Earth First!. Earth First!'ers specialise in
using direct action to defend the environment. This includes
putting their own bodies in front of bulldozers and spiking
trees with nails to render them useless as lumber. Accused of
terrorist activity, Foreman shrugs it off. 'Going round
pulling up survey stakes is not terrorism. It's simple self-
defense.' The founder of Friends of the Earth, David Brower,
defends the monkeywrenchers: 'They're spiking trees that
shouldn't be cut, by an industry that's only concerned about
the short run. The environment movement has gotten very
drowsy, and I think Earth First! is giving it CPR {cardiac
resuscitation}. I admire people who put their bodies where
their mouth is.' Although concentrated on the West Coast,
Earth First! is a rapidly expanding movement with a growing
number of international connections. They produce a journal
which claims 10,000 subscribers. An admirer of the deep
ecologists, Foreman sums up his philosophy like this:

The more we got involved in Earth First!, the more
we began to question the assumptions of technological civilisation and to realise that it isn't reform-

able. I think of us as being on the Titanic. There
are icebergs ahead and nobody's in the pilot cabin;
everybody's arguing about rearranging the deck
chairs. I just want to make sure there are some
lifeboats outfitted, you see?[26]

The Bioregionalist Movement

A bioregion is a part of the Earth's surface whose
rough boundaries are determined by natural
rather than human dictates, distinguishable from
other areas by attributes of flora, fauna, water,
climate, soils and land-forms, and the human
settlements and cultures those attributes have
given rise to.[27]

The bioregion is the domestic setting of the community just as the home is the domestic setting of
the family.[28]

Kirkpatrick Sale, a leading figure in the bioregion
movement, is convinced that the only way forward for Green
politics in the USA is to learn the lessons of deep ecology,
basing a new political movement on the single principle of
ecology and concentrating all political activity at the level of
the bioregion. 'Ecological consciousness,' says Sale, 'is not
just another good thing, one more pillar; it is, rather, the only
sane and rational way to embed the human project in these
historic times.'[29]

Bioregionalists believe that if people can relocate themselves into sustainable 'bioregions' then there is a chance for
human survival. They extrapolate the logic of restoring the
balance between everyday human existence and the
immediate environment into every area of human activity:
political, spiritual, social. Consequently the bioregionalists
are drawn to the developing 'deep ecological' philosophy
which regards human beings as 'just one constituency in the
biotic community' instead of as separate from and in control
of the nonhuman world.

Social Ecologists

Although his writing enjoys more recognition in Europe
than in the US, another key figure in American Green
politics is Murray Bookchin, director of the Institute for
Social Ecology in Vermont. Bookchin is a self-confessed
anarchist who has produced some thought-provoking work
on social ecology that is useful reading for Greens around the
world. Sadly, Bookchin seems to have fallen into the habit
that he condemns in so many others – narrow dog-
matism – and the logical trap that lies in wait for anar-
chists – obsession with the self. This is a shame, as he is quite
correct that the terrain for Green politics should be 'neigh-
borhood assemblies {and} town meetings' and he does apply
ecological thinking to social organisation in an interesting
way.[30]

Bookchin vehemently attacked the deep ecologists at a
conference sponsored by the Committees of Correspondence
at Amherst, Massachusetts in July 1987.[31] He was worried
about what he saw as a flight into religion and possibly
fascism threatened by the deep ecologists and the more
spiritually oriented Greens. This he felt might cause people
to lose sight of their social responsibility to overcome the
domination of human over human in an over-preoccupation
with the domination of human over nature. Much of this
conference was overshadowed by his clash with Charlene
Spretnak, principal spokesperson for the spiritual point of
view.[32] A brisk article in *Earth First!* magazine suggests that
Bookchin is demonstrating sour grapes at being eclipsed by
the interest in the philosophical and spiritual dimension of
Green politics. The article also sees Bookchin's 'tirade' at
Amherst as being part of the, not unexpected, pre-emptive
strike on the 'green Greens' by the 'red Greens'. 'What is
worth noticing in the fusillades by Bookchin and other leftist
critics...is not the words but the mood. Is this the approach of
nice people, of true humanitarians, or of people interested in
exercising power over others?'[33] The scene appears to be set
for a long and somewhat ferocious exchange of views.[34]

The Committees of Correspondence

In 1984 Charlene Spretnak and Fritjof Capra co-authored a
book called *Green Politics*.[35] It looked in detail at the German

Green party, its programme and its activities, and more generally at Green parties in other countries. The book then devoted 33 pages to suggesting that the Green alternative could also happen in the USA. After examining different organisational options they clearly favoured the organic, networking one, and cited the journal *New Options* which had offered to provide a temporary clearing-house for the new American Green movement. Within months of the book being published, *New Options* reported enquiries from over 500 people.[36]

In May of the same year, the First North American Bioregional Congress was held at Excelsior Springs, Missouri. Kirkpatrick Sale reported in the *Nation* (16 June 1984) that Green politics as a way of promoting the bioregional message was exhaustively (and exhaustingly!) discussed. An organising committee was formed at this congress to prepare the founding meeting of what became the Committees of Correspondence. This took place in St Paul, Minnesota on 10-12 August 1984.

The meeting was called by Charlene Spretnak, Harry Boyte (co-author of *Backyard Revolution*),[37] Catherine Burton (co-founder of Earth Bank), Gloria Goldberg (coordinator Institute of Social Ecology) and David Haenke (convenor of the North American Bioregional Congress). It was attended by 62 activists from Green-oriented movements. The name for the organisation was taken from the grassroots political networks that had existed during the American revolution, an interregional committee was established to encourage 'multi-levelled movement building' and ten key values were adopted around which local groups were expected to rally: ecological wisdom, decentralisation, grassroots democracy, community-based economics, global responsibility, inclusiveness, feminist values, personal and social reponsibility, non-violence and future focus.

The organisation has grown steadily and now has over 100 local groups 'confederated' into regional committees.[38] The size of the groups and their activities varies greatly. Some quickly became involved in elections and members have been elected to local office in five states – Connecticut, Michigan, North Carolina, Texas and Wisconsin. Groups in Maine, New Hampshire and Vermont have contested elections unsuccessfully but been rewarded with local publicity. Other groups have concentrated on different issues: protecting a coastline, protesting against mass burning of waste household refuse, anti-nuclear campaigns, often in alliance with other protest groups like Clamshell and Earth First!.[39]

By most standards in the United States, the Committees of Correspondence remain a very small organisation. But already they are attracting the attention of troublemakers. In March 1986 a meeting of Mid-Atlantic Greens from Philadelphia, Washington, New York and New Haven got together to consider candidates for the 1988 presidential elections. The *Philadelphia Inquirer* of 22 March 1986 described the meeting as being like a flashback to the 1960s. One speaker was Abbie Hoffman, founder of the Youth International Party (Yippies), best known for its street theatre and for nominating a pig for president in 1968. Another leading figure, Dana Beal, said the conference called for unity amongst Greens, but *Synthesis* (August 1986) argued that the Mid-Atlantic Greens had actually managed to strain the 'inclusiveness' principle of the interregional committee to its limits. Beal likes to call the ten key values the 'ten commandments', and at another conference in May 1987 in Chicago these values were diminished by Beal and his colleagues to a simple appeal to 'the four big alternative constituencies' – peace, environmental, human rights and social justice' (*Synthesis*, July 1987).

When the Committees held their first big conference in Amherst, New England at the beginning of July 1987, over 1,500 participants rallied to the theme of the conference – Building a Green Movement. Reporting in *Green Letter*, Jerry Gwathney remarked: 'As it should be, the conference meant something different to everyone. The long-term outcome of the gathering will not become known for some time. But what is clear at this point, is that the conference sparked ideas and motivated many of the participants to go home and pursue tasks of green organizing.'[40] Since the Amherst conference, pens have been very busy arguing about whether there should be a national organisation or whether this would spoil the network already established.

From the outside, however, the Green Interregional Committee of the (now formally Green) Committees of Correspondence looks indistinguishable from a national organisation. Their meeting at the end of August 1987 adopted a prospectus for events over the next three years. First a mini-conference to discuss Green strategy and political issues in 1988, then a Green Continental Programme

Conference in 1989 and a Green Continental Congress in 1990 which would serve as a founding convention, presumably of the US Green party. The only downbeat note in their otherwise very courageous and ambitious plans came with the first step they proposed for preparing the mini-conference. Local groups were asked to send in 'one-sentence descriptions of what they believe the key areas should be. Persons should limit themselves to no more than 5 key areas.' It is hard to feel anything but sad that American Greens, with their rich heritage of such inspiring holistic writers, should be reduced to such a reductionist exercise.

Future Prospects

In the American edition of *Seeing Green*, Jonathon Porritt sees the many different parts of the American Green movement as pieces of a patchwork quilt waiting to be stitched together.[41] Unfortunately he doesn't extend his metaphor to speculate how and when the needle(s) will be wielded, nor does he reflect on the way in which the completed quilt might overcome the immensely powerful American state.

Brian Tokar, like a lot of American Greens, talks in evolutionary time-scales and sees the process of affecting change as important as the changes themselves:

> A major hope for Greens everywhere lies in the development of new community-based institutions and experiments in local democracy...{so that} as the system increasingly fails to satisfy many people's most basic needs, the search for alternatives can evolve to an entirely new level.[42]

Jim McClellan, on the other hand, suggests that the time for change in America may be nearer:

> Once before in American history, the major parties lost both their sense of direction and their constituencies. They offered a string of presidents – Taylor, Fillmore, Pierce, Buchanan – who were only a little less memorable that Nixon, Ford, Carter and Reagan.'[43]

If history does repeat itself as McClellan suggests, it might then look as if the most important thing Roszak's subversive political force could be doing right now is some pretty nifty needlework. Their moment for taking their alternatives to an entirely new level could be nearer than they think.

Notes

1 Rachel Carson, *Silent Spring*, Houghton Mifflin, New York, 1962.
2 *Science* 155/3767, 10 March 1967.
3 See *Building a Sustainable Society*, Norton, New York, 1981, and the subsequent *State of the World* reports for 1984, 1985, 1986, 1987, 1988 (Norton).
4 Theodore Roszak, *The Making of a Counter Culture*, Anchor/ Doubleday, 1961.
5 Theodore Roszak, *Person/Planet*, Granada, 1981.
6 Wildwood House, 1982.
7 Black Rose Books, Québec, 1980.
8 Secker & Warburg, 1980.
9 Pan Books, 1982.
10 Theodore Roszak, *Person/Planet*, loc. cit., p. 23.
11 See for example Bill Devall and George Sessions, *Deep Ecology* , Gibbs M. Smith, Salt Lake City, 1985.
12 See for example Charlene Spretnak, *The Spiritual Dimension of Green Politics*, Bear & Co, New Mexico, 1986.
13 Jim McClellan, 'Two-Party Monopoly', *Progressive*, 28 January 1981.
14 John Valentine, *Atomic Crossroads*, Merlin Press, 1985.
15 *America Votes*, 1976, p. 65.
16 Alfred A. Knopf, New York, 1975.
17 This was 0.3% of the total vote, and 3.3% of votes cast for 'others', i.e. neither Republican nor Democrat. *America Votes*, 1980, pp. 19-20.
18 'Historical Background', paper issued by Citizens Party in 1980.
19 Doubleday, New York,1981.
20 *America Votes*, 1984, p. 40.
21 Delta Books, New York, 1979.
22 New World Alliance leaflet.
23 Kirkpatrick Sale, 'Green Politics in the USA', personal communication, October 1985.
24 Brian Tokar, *The Green Alternative*, R. & E. Miles, San Pedro, 1987, p. 150.
25 Avon, Philadelphia, 1975.
26 Quoted in Dick Russell, 'The Monkeywrenchers', *Amicus Journal*, fall 1987.
27 Kirkpatrick Sale, "Bioregionalism – A New Way to Treat the Land', *Ecologist*, 14/4, 1984.
28 Thomas Berry, 'Bioregions: The Context for Reinhabiting the Earth', Committees of Correspondence working papers, available from Berry at

Center for Religious Research, 5801 Palisade Avenue, Bronx, NY 10471.
29 Kirkpatrick Sale, 'Green Politics in the USA', loc. cit.
30 Murray Bookchin, *Towards an Ecological Society*, Black Rose Books, Québec, 1980.
31 Copies of the speech from Bookchin at Green Perspective, PO Box 111, Burlington, VT 05402.
32 John Rensenbrink, 'The Great Green Gathering of 1987', in *Peacework*, Cambridge, Mass., September 1987.
33 *Earth First!*, 1 November 1987.
34 *Synthesis* 26, December 1987.
35 Paladin, 1985.
36 *New Options*, 27 August 1984.
37 Temple University Press, Philadelphia, 1980.
38 List of local/regional Green groups, Committees of Correspondence Clearinghouse, January 1988.
39 See various issues of *Green Letter*.
40 *Green Letter*, 3/6, no date.
41 Jonathon Porritt, *Seeing Green*, Basil Blackwell, New York, 1984, p. 224.
42 Brian Tokar, *The Green Alternative*, R & E. Miles, San Pedro, p. 147.
43 Jim McLellan, op. cit.

Main Publications

Green Letter, PO Box 9242, Berkeley, California 94709, USA is the 'official' newsletter of the Committees.

Earth First! PO Box 5871, Tuscon, Arizona 85703.
New Options, PO Box 19324, Washington DC 20036.
Synthesis, PO Box 1858, San Pedro, California 90733, USA.
Utne Reader, PO Box 1974, Marion, Ohio 43306.

Main Studies of Green Politics

CAPRA Fritjof & SPRETNAK Charlene, *Green Politics*, E. P. Dutton, New York, 1984. Although mostly devoted to a study of the West German Green party, this book ends with a consideration of the possibilities for Green political activity in the United States.

TOKAR Brian, *The Green Alternative*, R. & E. Miles, San Pedro, Ca., 1987.

WOLFE Alan, 'Why Is There No Green Party In The United States?', in *World Policy Journal* 1/1, 1983.

Addresses

Green Committees of Correspondence Clearinghouse
PO Box 30208
Kansas City
Missouri 64112

tel: (1) 816 9319366

Earth First! (address as above)

Institute for Social Ecology
PO Box 384
Rochester
Vermont 05767

North American Bioregional Project
HCR3 Box 3
Brixey
Missouri 65618

tel: (1) 417 6794773

Organogram: Green Committees of Correspondence

'A grassroots movement capable of national campaigning and comitted to a value-centred, principled approach to working' (*Synthesis* 25, July 1987).

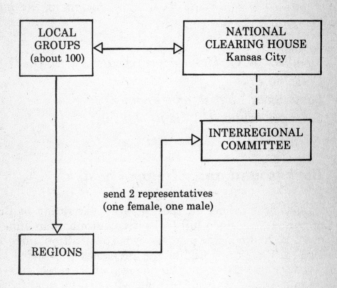

National Clearing House: acts as central mailing address and information exchange.
Regions: are a federation of local groups. Membership is automatically granted unless another group raises questions. Then the matter is discussed in the Interregional Committee.
Interregional Committee: is an ongoing meeting ground and forum for regional representatives. 'Our purpose is to identify and facilitate exchanges of information, ideas, resources, money and proposals to encourage local, regional and interregional organising' (*Committees of Correspondence newsletter*, summer 1985, preview issue).

19: CANADA

The Canadian Green Party

Area: 9.2 sq. km.
Population: 25.6 million
Density: 3 per sq. km.

founded: August 1983
members: not known

Member: UN, The Commonwealth, OECD, NATO, Colombo Plan
Languages: English and French
GNP per capita: US $12,940 (1985)

Background and Electoral System

Canada was formed in 1867, as a confederation of British provinces. It gained full legislative autonomy in June 1931 and has had control over its own constitution since April 1982. A Charter of Rights and Freedoms was added to the Canadian constitution in the same year. This recognised the nation's multi-cultural heritage, affirmed the existing rights of native peoples, confirmed the principle of equalisation of benefits among the ten provinces and strengthened their rights over natural resources.

Though Canada remains a member of the Commonwealth, the governor-general acts as non-executive president. He appoints members of the 104-seat Senate, but the 282-seat House of Commons is directly elected in proportion to the population of each province.

The provinces have full power over their own affairs, provided they do not interfere with the action and policy of the federal administration. They each have a lieutenant-general appointed by the governor-general and their own legislative assembly. Local government, its organisation and its powers, comes under the jurisdiction of each province.

For elections to the federal Parliament, Canada is divided into 282 single-member constituencies (ridings) and uses the simple majority voting system. Provincial elections use the same system with some slight variations. Only candidates obtaining 15% of the vote in any riding are eligible for public funding and all candidates require a deposit of Can $200 which is refundable if 10% or more of the vote is polled. Rules for gaining ballot access in provincial elections vary. The Ontario Greens, for example, had to collect 10,000 signatures to register their party while the British Columbia Greens only needed 50 signatures to do so.

For a party to gain national status, it must have candidates in 50 ridings. This gets the party's name on the ballot paper and makes it possible for donors to claim tax rebates on their contribution to the party between elections.

Factors Influencing the Development of Green Politics

Despite the huge size and low population density of Canada, awareness of the problems of environmental degradation is fairly well developed. It is estimated that more than half of the 12 million tonnes of acid deposited annually on eastern Canada comes from the United States, which gives Canadians ambivalent feelings towards their powerful southern neighbours.[1] The summer 1987 issue of *New Catalyst* lists over 70 'environmental hotspots' for British Columbia alone. Heading the list are six 'outstanding issues' – a dam on Peace river; off-shore oil exploration; raw sewage, industrial waste and air pollution in Greater Vancouver; uranium mining; watershed damage through extensive logging; and native land claims.

Early Days

The first attempt to establish a Green party in Canada was made by Jim Bohlen, co-founder of both the Sierra Club of West Canada and of Greenpeace. (Bohlen was on a Greenpeace ship next to the *Rainbow Warrior* when it was sunk in

Auckland, New Zealand). In 1980 he brought a collection of people from the 'alternative movement' together at a meeting in Saskatchewan. However, as the group were not even able to agree on whether the press should be allowed to attend the meeting, they decided there was little chance of them cooperating in the forming of a new political party. Bohlen eventually became active in the British Columbia Greens.

Later, in 1982, a group of people decided to press a resolution at a congress of the British Columbia New Democratic party (a social-democratic party founded in the 1930s) demanding that the Valhalla area in Kootenays be made into a wilderness park. When the resolution never even made the floor there was great disappointment among the environmental lobbyists. Once again the possibility of a new party was discussed. This time the discussion was serious enough for one man, Paul George, to go to Victoria and register a provincial Green party. Thus in February 1983, amid much publicity, the registration of the British Columbia Green party was confirmed and Adriane Carr installed in the obligatory post of president.

Without any delay the BC Greens entered the electoral field. They stood candidates in four ridings for the November elections to the 69-seat provincial parliament, scoring about 1.5% of the vote.[2] Their electoral debut prompted some criticism about the new party 'splitting' the vote. But as British Columbia has been ruled for most of the past 35 years by a conservative Social Credit party, with the New Democrats as the only opposition holding a mere 22 of the 69 seats, the Greens were not too worried by this. They reckoned the New Democratic party needed to feel its monopoly of opposition under threat to make it give serious attention to environmental issues. So instead the Greens concentrated on attracting as wide a variety of members as possible and on developing the party's basic principles:

> a) to carry on the functions of a political party;
> b) to work towards achieving the goal of nuclear and general disarmament, and world peace through the non-violent resolution of conflict;
> c) to work towards achieving the goal of a conserver society;
> d) to work towards an economic system based upon sound environmental and ecological principles;
> e) to work towards developing a society that

accepts responsibility for and upholds the inalienable rights of all life forms and natural processes that share the earth;

f) to develop a community-based democracy with local decision-making and control; and

g) to undertake all such other activities consistent with these purposes which the society's elected representatives consider appropriate.[3]

A National Party?

The publicity given to the founding of the BC Green party gave the necessary nudge to people in other Canadian provinces who were considering taking a similar step. The Ontario Green party was founded in June 1983 and groups got together in Québec, Manitoba, Alberta and Saskatchewan.

With remarkable speed a national party was registered in August 1983 by the Ontario Greens, and the Canadian Green party held its founding conference 'The Gathering of the Greens' at Carleton university, Ottawa on 4-6 November 1983. According to the attenders list 174 people were present: 129 from Ontario, 22 from British Columbia, 9 from Québec, 5 from Alberta, 4 from Saskatchewan, 3 from Manitoba, 2 each from New Brunswick and Nova Scotia and one from Northwest Territories. Observers and guests came from West Germany, the USA and UK, and a Toronto organiser, Jutta Keylwerth, announced that nationwide the new party already had a membership of between three and four thousand.[4]

But beneath the optimism reported in the papers the meeting hit serious snags. 'It became pretty clear over the convention weekend that most of those in attendance wanted a party which did not look or act like one; an organisation that would not organise; and leaders who would not lead. That is pretty much what they got.'[5]

Despite the ambivalence towards any formal national organisation, never mind the sheer logistics of building a national party from scratch in a country the size of Canada, the Greens managed to put up 60 candidates in the federal elections of September 1984. Twenty-six Greens stood in Ontario (11 in Toronto Metropolitian area); 19 in British

Columbia; 7 in Alberta; 4 in Québec; 2 in Saskatchewan and 1 in Prince Edward Island. The total vote polled was 26,957, 0.2% of the total vote and 0.9% in the constituencies where they stood.[6]

By the time their provincial elections of May 1985 came around, however, the Ontario Greens had run out of steam (and perhaps money). They only managed to present 11 candidates.

Future Prospects

Because of the difficulties posed by the electoral system and the size of the country (Ontario alone is three and a half times the size of West Germany), Green politics in Canada remains very much a local affair. The national party is more or less in limbo and no further attempts have been made to hold national meetings. Communication between activists takes place on a local networking basis.

Back in British Columbia, however, Green politics has become increasingly influenced by the concepts of deep ecology, bioregionalism and feminism, and has focussed round an excellent quarterly regional paper called *The New Catalyst*.[7] Local groups grew stronger and in 1985 Seymour Treigner of Naniamo took over from Ontario's Trevor Hancock as president of the national party.

When 9 Green candidates stood in the provincial elections of November 1986 they scored an average 1.3% of the vote. But Paul Watson, director of the Vancouver-based Sea Shepherd Conservation Society, managed to poll 15,000 votes when he and six other Greens contested the Vancouver civic elections on 15 November 1986. The overall average for these elections was around 8%. There is little doubt that the Greens were helped by the news six days before the election that two members of the Sea Shepherd Conservation Society had sunk a couple of Icelandic whaling ships in Reyjakvik harbour.

> To look into a whale's eyes, and know it is regarding you intelligently, changes your life. To me, whales are like the canary in the mine: if they go, that's it for all of us, the whole human race.[8]

The swashbuckling exploits of Paul Watson's organisation and his open participation in the democratic political process in British Columbia are interesting. Watson is very clear about the guidelines under which his crew works. No explosives, no weapons and no action to be taken if there is the slightest possibility of injury to human life. He is also quite clear that he is merely policing the regulations of the International Whaling Commission which Iceland was blatantly contravening. America had reneged on its pledge to impose fishing and trade sanctions on any country doing this so Watson imposed his own justice, reckoned to amount to just under US $10 million worth of damage. Since 1979 the society has sunk five illegal whalers without causing a single injury or attracting a single legal action. The society's most vehement supporters are evidently women over 65 and include British schoolchildren who raised $25,000 for an anti-whaling campaign near the Faroe islands.

The society's other campaigns include preventing the killing of wolves, mostly done to protect the trophy hunting of caribou and moose which is increasingly big business, and the spiking of trees with nails to render them worthless for timber. 'Property damage is always justified in defence of any living thing. The right of something to live takes precedence over somebody's right to own,' affirms Watson. He is also quite clear about the importance of a political party 'that is neither right nor left' taking an ecological standpoint on issues. To him the New Democratic party is positively *anti*-environmentalist because it refuses to come out against nuclear power. The party leader Ed Broadbent has two reactors in his home constituency and it supports uranium mining in Saskatchewan.[9]

The potent combination of radical non-violent action, feminism, electoral participation and a high quality journal make British Columbia's Green movement one to watch.

Notes

1 Norman Myers (ed.), *The Gaia Atlas of Planet Management*, Pan Books, 1985.
2 *Toronto Star*, 10 November 1983.
3 Constitution of the Green Party Political Association of British Columbia, revised version, 1985.
4 *Toronto Star*, 10 November 1983.

5 Vaughan Lyon, 'The Reluctant Party: Ideology Versus Organisation in Canada's Green Movement', *Alternatives* 13/1, December 1985.
6 Canadian Federal Elections, Appendix D, *Canada Statistics*, 1984, p. 69.
7 First issue, November 1985. P O Box 99, Lillooet, British Columbia.
8 Benjamin White, quoted in Dick Russell, 'The Monkeywrenchers', *Amicus Journal*, fall 1987.
9 *New Catalyst* 8, summer 1987.

Main Party Publications

Ontario, British Columbia, Quebec and Saskatchewan parties all produce newsletters.

The New Catalyst, quarterly newspaper, PO Box 99, Lillooet, British Columbia V0K 1V0.

Main Studies of the Canadian Greens

McROBERT David, 'Green Politics in Canada', *Probe Post: Canada's Environmental Magazine*, October 1985.
LYON Vaughan, 'The Reluctant Party: Ideology Versus Organization in Canada's Green Movement', *Alternative* 3, University of Waterloo, December 1985.
HARDING Jim, 'The Founding of the Canadian Greens – a Report and Analysis of the Politics', undated paper available from Green Party of Canada, address below.

Addresses

Green Party of Canada/Parti Vert du Canada
c/o 831 Commercial Drive
Vancouver
British Columbia V5L 3W6
tel: (1) 604 2548165

Green Party Political Association
of British Columbia address as above

Green Party of Quebec/Parti Vert du Québec
c/o Yves Blanchette
1206 du Mont-Royal Avenue East
Montréal
Québec H2G 1Y1

tel: (1) 514 5261700

The Ontario Greens
PO Box 1912
Brantford
Ontario N3T 5W5

tel: (1) 416 6988207

Contact addresses for other provincial parties and local chapters may be obtained from the British Columbia address.

20: WORLDWIDE

Introduction

'The environment knows neither borders nor parties. It is
essential to develop joint efforts for environmental conservation at the regional level.' This message was sent to the
meeting of Central American presidents in summer 1987 from
another meeting held in May the same year. The earlier
meeting had brought together every major non-governmen-
tal conservationist organisation in Central America plus
delegates from similar organisations in South America,
North America and Europe. As one of the delegates, Gerardo
Budowski from Costa Rica, pointed out: 'The search for
ecologically sustainable development is the same as working
for peace.'[1]

The rapid growth of environmental groups in Central and
South America is matched by similar developments in Asia
and Africa. Also interesting is the burgeoning of ecological
groups in East European countries where governments are
faced with some of the worst environmental pollution in the
world. In all countries where the democratic rights of citizens
are either absent or miserably reduced, the distinction
between political party and pressure group which applies
elsewhere becomes, of course, irrelevant.

Unfortunately it is not possible to chronicle all of the
initiatives here. Not only are they springing up so fast that it
is difficult to keep track of them, but quite a lot of the news
that comes to Europe from different sources is hard to check
out without engaging in long and costly research. From a
position of such ignorance, it would therefore be entirely
wrong and probably counterproductive to issue what might
be misinterpreted as 'benedictions from Europe' to newly
announced Green parties or groups. Some parties do appear
quite genuine. The Brazilian Green party, for example, say
they are well on the way to fulfilling the conditions for
legalising their party, which entails establishing their

presence in nine of Brazil's 22 states and being active in 20% of the municipalities of those states.

In Japan, matters are less clear-cut. A small group of anti-vivisectionists have established the ambitiously named Earth Green Federation which grew out of the Japan Green Federation they founded in November 1984, but their relationship to the Midori No Yo (Green party) is unclear. Also active in Japan is the Seikatsu Club, a consumer cooperative founded by a Tokyo housewife which has remarkable ecological and social standards. Aware of the political nature of their club's work and frustrated by the lack of interest from local politicians, some of the predominantly female membership contested elections under the slogan 'Reform from the kitchen'. After their first success in 1979, there are now 31 elected members – all women.[2]

In some countries, on the other hand, there are groups or parties employing the word Green in their title which smack more of front organisations for not-so-democratic governments or sinister cults, and there may well be other courageous and genuine groups hard at work who have not seen fit (or been able) to make their existence known to the rest of the world. For example, a Humanist party (alternatively called Futuro Verde or Green Future) is becoming increasingly active in South and North America and in Europe. Its origins are said to be in an Argentina-based organisation called The Movement or The Community, and its manner of recruiting and influencing members seems to owe more to pseudo-religious sects such as the Moonies or that of Jim Jones than to anything else.

This chapter, therefore, concentrates on four non-party political initiatives which have already received a considerable amount of publicity. They offer particularly inspiring and different examples of how the basic need of all people to secure a healthy and life-sustaining everyday environment for themselves is being used as a potent political tool, as human beings try to resolve some of the dreadful conflicts in which they have become entangled. In Poland and Hungary, for example, demands for environmental protection are closely linked with demands for the basic human rights of free association and expression, while in India and Kenya ensuring the survival of the forests is closely linked to the condition of women and the development of sustainable local economies.

Poland

> Being downwind of the Chernobyl explosion was
> only the latest in a string of misfortunes in a
> country in which environmental devastation has
> become a feature of everyday life. According to
> government reports (many of which are not
> intended for public distribution), air, water and
> soil pollution are so hazardous in Poland that the
> health of at least one-third of the country's popu-
> lation is at risk; that is, roughly thirteen million
> people now living there are likely to acquire
> environmentally induced cancers, respiratory
> diseases, or a host of other illnesses. In most major
> cities, air pollution is fifty times higher than the
> established limits allow. Water quality is declin-
> ing so rapidly that within the next few years the
> nation's entire supply – rivers, lakes, and
> wells – may be unfit for any use, including
> industrial. And as much as one-quarter of the
> country's soil is too contaminated for safe
> farming.[3]

Even if only some of the statistics are true, the title of the
dirtiest country in the world does seem to belong to Poland,
where economic growth from rapid industrialisation has
taken priority over all considerations for the health and
safety of either people or the environment.

In September 1980, in Cracow (perhaps the most polluted
city in Poland), a group of shop stewards, journalists, doctors
and academics formed Poland's first independent environmental pressure group, the Polski Klub Ekologiczny
(PKE — Polish Ecology Club). The group organised discussions and collected evidence 'so that it could intervene
effectively...in the most dramatic and serious cases of environmental danger and destruction'.[4] The organisation grew
quickly, established branches in the 17 historical regions of
Poland – in 1976 these were replaced by 49 vovoidships
(administrative provinces) – and was perfectly aware of the
political nature of its existence. Lack of formal central
organisation makes total membership of PKE difficult to
estimate, but it is certainly now measured in thousands.

PKE's successes have included the closure of the aluminium smelter in Skawina after a massive local campaign, involving people claiming compensation through the courts for damage to their health, but the organisation also had to come to grips with the broader implications of its campaigns – loss of jobs, regeneration of polluted land and so on. Relationships with the trade union Solidarity were established, shortly before it was banned under martial law.

In July 1981, Solidarity set up a commission for 'Man and the Environment' to 'speed up union activity working for environmental protection and the rational use of natural resources...through social pressure and control...and cooperation with interest groups and institutions concerned with environmental issues, planning and control.'[5] Some of the groups with whom Solidarity envisaged working were the Naczelna Organizacja Techniczna (NOT — Association of Scientists and Technicians), the Liga Ochrony Przyrody (LOP — Nature Conservation League) and the Polish Ecology Club.[6]

The declaration of martial law and the banning of Solidarity at the end of 1981 concentrated protest in Poland on the issues of human rights and civil liberties. PKE reaffirmed its status as an 'independent, apolitical and areligious social movement of those people who are aware of dangers connected with the unsettlement of biological balance caused by the epoch of technical development, industry and the consumptive (sic) way of living'.[7]

Then in 1985 a new organisation appeared on the scene. In March, twelve people fasted for a week in Podkowa Lesna (near Warsaw) to protest at the imprisonment of Marek Adamkiewicz, who had been given a 2½-year prison sentence for refusing to take the military oath pledging fraternal allegiance to the Soviet Union. At a seminar on peace and human rights held during the hunger strike the idea of establishing Wolnosc i Pokój (WiP — Freedom and Peace) was born. By November the movement had published its declaration of principles, identifying the main themes of human rights, national liberation, the threat of war and the international peace movement, environmental protection, world hunger and humanitarian assistance, human development and tolerance.[8]

Membership of WiP requires only a will to take part in its activities which, because the group insists on openly publicising these activities and does not hide names or addresses of participants or petition signers, can mean considerable harassment by the authorities, including arrest leading to fines and/or imprisonment. At present a loose federation of groups in 11 Polish cities, WiP has roughly 100-200 activists, but considerably more supporters; petitions have been signed by up to 10,000 people. The group knows that its strategy will keep its membership small, but it feels it has an important role to play in influencing change in Poland. 'Freedom and Peace is very close to Solidarity as far as its principles are concerned, but its sphere of activities differs,' is how one activist who was arrested for his involvment with WiP put it.[9]

After the nuclear accident at Chernobyl in April 1986, it was WiP who organised some of the first demonstrations in Eastern Europe and they have also mounted protests against the construction of nuclear plants in Poland. The WiP campaign against the Siechnice steelworks led to the local council deciding to close it down, which represents the group's most significant environmental success to date. During one of the demonstrations which was considered illegal, several participants were arrested. As WiP point out in a letter sent to the UK Green party shortly afterwards, these arrests show how fine the line between environmental protection and human rights can be – Article 71 of the Polish constitution states that it is every citizen's duty to protect the natural environment.

The broad platform of WiP, the youth of its activists, and the support they inspire by their open, courageous demonstrations and their commitment to non-violence and personal responsibility, pose major problems for the Polish authorities. When WiP held a seminar in May 1987 in a Warsaw church that attracted over 200 supporters and activists from 17 countries, the government did subject several organisers and participants to considerable harassment but they did not prevent the seminar from taking place.

> The fact that 20 conscientious objectors are not in prison, the closing of the Siechnice steel mill, and the holding of the seminar demonstrate that WiP is having an effect. Schooled in the experience of Solidarity and fueled by its own energy and determination, WiP is enlarging the space for independent initiative and, thereby, for the establishment of a pluralistic society.[10]

WiP's newsletter *Co Bylo?* (*What's Been Happening?*)
details the trials, harassments, demonstrations and so on
connected with the conscientious objector movement and
prints reports on environmental issues gleaned from the
Polish and foreign press. In December 1987 and January 1988
Co Bylo? noted the authorities' (relatively) more flexible
stance on alternatives to military service – i.e. less heavy
fines, shorter prison sentences, at least one person allowed to
work in the health service instead. It also noted an article
which appeared in the Wrocklaw evening newspaper (7
January 1988) about a report by the Polish academy of
sciences in Zabruz on the Siechnice steelworks. The article
said the report exonerated the plant from significantly
polluting ground water with its waste dumps and reported
that the management of the plant and the workers as well as
local politicians were in favour of modernising and reopen-
ing the works.[11]

Hungary

Not very far north of Budapest, the Danube gives up its job as
border marker between Hungary and Czechoslovakia,
indulges in a few beautiful bends and then dips down towards
the Hungarian capital. The bends with their marshy islands
are framed by some of the few hills in Hungary and are
already listed by UNESCO as land of special value that
merits protection. Further upstream the river-bank forms a
major source of shore-filtered water. Due to lack of sewage
and waste treatment, the river itself is bacteriologically and
chemically filthy, but the special combination of bank pebble
size and fall of the river means that the water is literally
sieved into what is recognised as Europe's biggest drinking
water supply (10 cubic kilometres of pure water).[12] As 1,500
out of Hungary's 3,500 communities are without safe
drinking water and it is estimated that around 2½ million
people have to collect their water in plastic containers or
from tankers, it might be imagined that these huge natural
reservoirs would be subject to strict conservation measures.[13] But no, work is going ahead to build a series of dams,
canals and concrete river-bank reinforcements that even
official figures show will be an uneconomic investment. The

dams will also change the river so drastically that the water filtering power of the river bank will be destroyed and the drinking water irredeemably polluted. It will also turn one of the most beautiful spots in Hungary into an industrial landscape.

The history of the Gabcikovo-Nagymaros dams goes back a long way and Hungary has waxed hot and cold over the project for decades, albeit mostly because of the cost. Slovakia has been keen on the project all along, because the canal will help to overcome the fickle seasonal behaviour of the natural river and make Bratislava's long-held dream of becoming a major river port come true. However, Czechoslovakia has no money at all. The final push to the project came when the Austrian government had to abandon its own project to dam the Danube at Hainburg after vigorous opposition from the Austrian Green movement in December 1984 (see Chapter 1). It solved its problem of having a lot of investment, plant and contractors all dressed up and ready to build a dam by simply shifting the whole project downstream in 1986 to countries where public protest is proscribed. Austrian environmentalists and Green parliamentarians described this as no less than 'ecological imperialism'. To repay Austria for the 'loan', Hungary signed an agreement to provide 1,200 gigawatt-hours of high-peak electricity between 1996 and 2015. Seasonal variations in the flow of the river mean that Hungary will have to build another power plant in order to assure a continual supply of this electricity.

Hungarian protest against the project started in 1981 when biologist Jànos Vargha wrote an article critising it in *Tudomàny*, a popular science magazine. Opposition mounted amongst professionals and ordinary citizens. Even the presidium of the Hungarian Academy of Science publicly suggested that the work should stop and some politicians did too, only more privately. But political pressure to stifle establishment protest grew and in 1984 Duna Kör (Danube Circle, sometimes known as the 'Blues') was formed. Petitions were collected, marches were organised, leaflets were distributed, MPs were lobbied, international press conferences were held – all in the face of government bans on such activity. In 1985 Duna Kör became the first East European organisation to receive the Alternative Nobel Prize, and Vargha travelled to Sweden to receive it. But all to no avail. The attachment of the then Communist party secretary János Kádár to such 'prestige' projects, and the desire of the party to balance its economic links with the Soviet Union by similar links to non-Communist countries prevailed. The intervention of Austria swept aside any remaining official doubts, the project went ahead and the Blues retreated for a rethink.

Then in January 1988, Hungary became the first East European country to appoint an environment minister. Significantly he has a special remit for water management. The replacement of the elderly Kádár by glasnost-friendly Károlyi Grosz in May brought further freedom of action to the growing number of dissident groups in Hungary and demands for reform came out of the back rooms onto the street and into public debate. However, like its counterparts, Hungary's Communist party has considerable structural inertia and resistance to change, and at the end of August a proposal to parliament calling for a ban on associations warned groups not to go too far too fast.

Nevertheless, in September, Duna Kör – in collaboration with the World Wide Fund for Nature, the International Rivers Network and local groups such as the Association of Young Democrats – organised the first meeting since 1956 to be both openly critical of the current policy of the Hungarian government and to receive that government's official blessing. Contributors from several countries joined Hungarian experts to explain that no big dam project anywhere in the world had been anything but a disaster and that the dams on the Danube would be no different. Despite claims from Water Board engineers that they had heard nothing to convince them the project should be abandoned, the meeting and subsequent street demonstrations were widely reported in the Hungarian press.

Lifting the lid off the opposition to the Danube dams can only have been done under orders from the higher echelons of the Commuist party. It seems likely that they did not properly understand the costs of the whole Nagymaros project to Hungary until quite recently. However, no government, whatever its political hue, likes to admit it has made a grave economic misjudgement, especially in a country with a large external debt and anxious to inspire confidence in foreign investors. As member of parlimanet Szabó Kálmán put it at the meeting: 'The problem is not that we do not know what is in the budget, but that there is no hope of coming up with a counter suggestion.'

Karolyi Grosz needs face-saving excuses to get Hungary out of its contracts with Austria and Czechoslovakia. The evidence offered at the meeting and the large number of citizens who are actively protesting the project should be enough for him to argue this case with Austria, which was forced to abandon the Hainburg dam for similar reasons. A petition now running to about 2,000 signatures is being courageously collected in Czechoslovakia which, combined with outside pressure ranging from the influential World Wide Fund for Nature to the vice-president of the Austrian parliament and the European Parliament, may help persuade that country to review its side of the contract.

However, one thing was sorely missing from the meeting and its final communiqué – the 'counter suggestion' that the perestroika-inclined veneer of the Communist party will also need if it is to shift the stubbornly conservative bulk of the party. Alternative energy sources and energy efficiency and conservation techniques, plus the evidence that they are not only environmentally desirable but also cost-effective and job-creating, must be the subject of another official conference in Hungary very soon. Convincing the legions of Water Board engineers and bureaucrats that they are more likely to be redeployed than fired will be essential if the world-famous Danube river is to be saved from a cladding of cast iron and concrete. The work of Duna Kör is not yet finished.

India

The slogan of the Chipko Andolan (Movement to Hug) is 'ecology is permanent economy'. It was coined by Sunderlal Bahuguna, a Gandhian activist and philosopher who spread the Chipko message by his 5,000-kilometre walk through the Himalayas in 1981-83. The movement was born in April 1973 when villagers in Gopeshwar in the north of India embraced trees to prevent loggers from a company in distant Allahabad from cutting them down. Over the next few years the Chipko protests spread through the Indian state of Uttar Pradesh and in 1980 the then prime minister Indira Gandhi ordered a 15-year ban on 'green felling' in the Himalayan forests.

Since then the movement has spread to other states of India, to Himachal Pradesh in the north, Karnataka in the south, Rajasthan in the west and Bihar in the east, as well as to the Vindhyas in central India where further bans on felling have been obtained.[14]

Crucial to the success of the movement has been the support and involvement of women, who know best of all the importance of the forest for the provision of firewood, food, animal fodder and herbal cures and treatments. Many villagers who depended on the forest for their everyday livelihood also discovered the longer-term effects of deforestation when the monsoon rains washed the soil off the denuded hills and sometimes buried their villages under mud slides. The links between protecting the trees and their own survival were often tragically reinforced.

Reporting on the movement in 1981, the United Nations Environment Programme remarked: 'In effect the Chipko people are working a socio-economic revolution by winning control of their forest resources from the hands of a distant bureaucracy which is concerned with selling the forest for making urban-oriented products.' However, Chandi Prasad Bhatt, one Chipko activist who has worked long and hard to encourage local industries based on the conservation and sustainable use of forest wealth for local benefit, puts it like this: 'These trees provide a voice for our problems. The women of this area, one can say, have got a voice because of the trees. And today it is possible that many matters have been understood by the men in the villages; that because of the trees the women's voices have got strength.'[15]

Kenya

As Kenya has one of the highest rates of population growth in the world, and 90% of that population lives in rural areas and depends on firewood for its energy needs,[16] it is not surprising that the last decade has seen tree planting become a national pastime for both the government and for many voluntary groups in Kenya.

However, one voluntary organisation, the Green Belt Movement, stands out not only for being among the first but also for the way it has concentrated on women. It is the women of Kenya who have to walk further and further to find sources of fuelwood and, as it is they who also do most of the work and child care, this means family income and diet suffers too. Sometimes it is so difficult to find wood that women can be obliged to change their families' diet to foodstuffs that require little cooking. This all too often leads to kwashiokor and other diseases associated with malnutrition.

Founded by Professor Wangari Maathai, chairperson of the National Council of Women of Kenya who went on to develop the idea, the Green Belt Movement planted its first trees on World Environment Day, 5 June 1977. There are now more than 1,000 'public' green belts of over 1,000 trees each in communities and schools and about 20,000 'private' green belts in farmers' fields. Women's groups now run about 65 community tree nurseries.[17]

Wangari Maathai was very aware that women did most of the work involved in any development programme, although they were rarely consulted as to its appropriateness and usually poorly rewarded by it:

> The period for talking and complaining about the status of women was coming to an end and it appeared appropriate for women to talk around development issues and cause positive change in themselves, environment and country. Development issues provide a good forum for women to be creative, assertive and effective leaders and the Green Belt Movement, being a development issue, provided the forum to promote women's positive image.[18]

The movement taught women how to collect seeds from indigenous species of trees and grow them in nurseries before setting them out in bigger plantations. Employment was created for the previously unemployable – the physically handicapped, school leavers, the old and the desperately poor. As well as the skills necessary to establish the plantations and ensure the survival of the trees, the movement provided formal and informal education on diet, family planning, health, prevention of soil erosion and flooding, sustainable agriculture and forestry techniques. As the number of plantations grew, so the information and skills were transferred to more and more communities.

The Green Belt Movement is a very good example of how a development programme should work. It is designed for local people by local people, run and controlled by local people to whom the benefit accrues, yet it also has a strong educational emphasis which includes the broader issues affecting those people. In the words of Wangari Maathai these are: 'the inter-relationships between environment, energy, food production, population, political stability and peace'.

Notes

1 *Earth Island Journal* (USA), summer 1987.
2 Paul Ekins, 'Japan and the Living Economy', *Resurgence* 128, May/June 1988.
3 Jean Pierre Lasota, *The Sciences*, July-August 1987, quoted in *From Below*, p. 90 (see note 8).
4 Katarzyna Wojtkowska, 'The Polish Ecology Club', *Tygodnik Solidarność* (*Solidarity Weekly*) 14, 3 July 1981.
5 'Proposals for Protection of the Natural Environment', in *Social Politics of the Union*, a booklet for delegates at the First National Congress of Solidarity, Osrodek Prac Spoleczno-Zawadowych (OPS-Z — Solidarity's research and advisory body), 1981.
6 Rafael Serafin, 'The Greening of Poland', *Across Frontiers*, Berkeley, California, summer 1984.
7 Letter from PKE to UK Green party, 1984.
8 'Chronology of Freedom and Peace', in *Ruch Wolność i Pokój*, series of articles from *WiP Bulletin* translated into English, Warsaw, 1987. For the full text of the Principles see Appendix III in *From Below: Independent Peace and Environmental Movements in Eastern Europe and the USSR*, a Helsinki Watch report, October 1987.
9 *From Below*, loc. cit., p. 80.
10 ibid, p. 95.
11 *Co Bylo?*, 12-18 December 1987, 16-22 January 1988, translated by Toni Berrison, UK Green party.
12 Làszlo Sòlyom, 'Hungary: Citizens' Participation in the Environmental Movement', *IFDA Dossier* 64, March/April 1988.
13 Judit Vasarheli, 'The Danube Project and the Danube Circle', *END Journal* 30, October/November 1987.
14 Jayanta Bandyopadhyay and Vandana Shiva, 'Chipko: Rekindling India's Forest Culture', *Ecologist* 17/1, 1987.
15 André Singer, *Battle for the Planet*, Pan, 1987, p. 80.
16 *World Development Report*, Oxford University Press, New York, 1985.
17 Paul Harrison, *The Greening of Africa*, Paladin, 1987.
18 Wangari Maathai, 'The Green Belt Movement: Building Blocks for Sustainable Development', paper given at The Other Economic Summit, London, 1985.

Poland

Polski Klub Ekologiczny
(Polish Ecological Club)
Palac 'Pod Baranami'
Rynek Gl 27
31010 Kraków

tel: (48) 12 221884

Wolnosc i Pokój
(Freedom and Peace)
c/o Tomasz Wacko
ul. Gersona 7/10
Wroclaw 51-664

Hungary

Duna Kör (Danube Circle)
Bosckai út 31
1113 Budapest

tel: (36) 1 661583

India

Chipko Information Centre
PO Silyara via Ghansali
Tehri-Garhwal
U.P. 249155

Kenya

The Green Belt Movement
c/o National Council of
Women of Kenya
Moi Avenue
P O Box 67545
Nairobi

Brazil

Partido Verde
Rua Dr Francisco Muratori 45
Lapa-Rio de Janeiro

Japan

Midori no tò (Green Party)
6-42-12 Asakusa
Daitò-ku
Tokyo

Seikatsu Club
2-26-17 Miyasaka
Setagaya-ku
Tokyo 112

tel: (81) 3 7060031

Appendix I:
Joint Declaration of the European Green Parties

As the twentieth century approaches its end, the Green movement is offering real hope for the future. This it does by aiming to return power to the citizen, to make it clear that a better way of life need not depend on a higher standard of living, to restore the balance between the human race and the rest of nature, radically to rethink relations between the rich and poor peoples of the world and to defend the cause of peace.

Green politics are a fact of life in more and more European countries. In order better to fulfil the aspirations of an increasing number of their citizens, the Green parties have decided to work together closely, at an international level, for the ecological aims they already pursue at the local, regional and national levels. We intend to extend this cooperation to Green movements in both Eastern Europe and on other continents.

The elections to the European Parliament in June 1984 will offer an opportunity to stop those who, in pursuit of continued economic and industrial growth, are undermining the basis of life itself, either by supporting pollution and other damage, or by encouraging war. These tendencies are to be found in all traditional parties, whether they claim to be of the left, the centre or the right. The millions of citizens who already share an ecological viewpoint know that such tendencies will be removed only if there is a fundamental change of mind by everyone concerned.

We in the Green movement believe that Europe should no longer be governed, or misgoverned, by central authorities. The diversity of its cultures, of its peoples and regions is one of Europe's greatest assets, to be conserved and developed for the benefit of every European; true sovereignty can only come from a federal structure which takes that diversity into account. Such a structure, which should ultimately consist of regions rather than nation states, must also be established in a way that respects the dignity and responsibility of all citizens: political, social and economic decisions must be taken by those who have to bear the consequences of them. A truly democratic Europe will be made possible only through decentralisation of institutions, constant dialogue between citizens and those making decisions at various levels, open discussion of problems, free access to all official documents and files, referenda at the will of the people, and the granting of the vote to immigrants, which is a matter of particular importance in elections to the European Parliament.

We in the Green movement do not want a Europe whose governments are heavily involved in the accumulation of weapons while every year millions of people are dying of hunger and poverty. Indeed, the terrifying gap between those who have too little and those who have more than they know what to do with is one of the most likely causes of a future war, and the evening up of living standards must be a priority in the struggle for peace.

In the light of this we must radically transform and diversify our agricultural policies which are currently heavily subsidised and based on industrial methods which exploit animal and plant life, and instead promote nutritional self-sufficiency both for our own regions and for those of the Third World.

Therefore continuing research into ecological and nutritional adaptation on our planet constitutes a main aim of the Green movement's peace strategy.

In conjunction with this, the Green movement advocates civilian-based, non-violent defence, rather than the traditional concept of armed defence. We also call for a stop to the arms trade, for an independent European defence strategy and for a unilateral first step towards multilateral disarmament.

The Green movement is opposed to any growth based on soaring energy production in industrialised countries since this brings intolerable pressure to bear on the environment. Moreover, excessive consumption leads to a depletion of the energy resources of the planet at the expense of Third World countries. We oppose the use of nuclear energy, as an expensive, out-dated, inhuman and extremely dangerous technology that creates environmental problems persisting for thousands of years. Instead, we wish to see an energy policy which is based on real needs, promotes energy conservation, rational use of energy and the use of locally produced renewable resources.

The Green movement rejects an economy based primarily on productivity, on the concentrated means of production, on irreversible environmental damage (partly due to uncontrolled waste disposal), on the creation of artificial needs, on the prevention of self-fulfilling activities, and on the accentuation of inequalities between continents, regions and social groups thereby leading to widespread unemployment. We wish to break totally from the liberal capitalism of the West and the state capitalism of the East, and want a third path which is compatible with an ecological society. We favour regenerating the economy from the bottom up, making it human and sustainable, creating a system of community-based self-reliance, giving priority to respect of the ecosystems. We want positive discrimination in favour of human-scale economic activity producing socially useful, lasting and environmentally compatible products which meet the real needs of society. We favour human-scale organised businesses, involving the participation of workers, consumers and those living in the immediate vicinity. We are in favour of a signficant reduction in working hours, work-sharing, and a general redistribution of income and resources.

This declaration marks the creation of a European Green Coordination, the members of which hereby underline their commitment to cooperate closely within this framework and to pool aims and means thus creating a genuine Green international.

23 January 1984, Brussels, Belgium

Appendix II:
The 'Paris Declaration'

Our common commitment for a new Europe, neutral and decentralised, with autonomous regions, each conserving their own cultural independence, is based on the following points:

* We are opposed to the stationing of nuclear weapons in East and West Europe, we are for total disarmament and for the dissolution of the power blocs and the military blocs.

* We are for environmental policies that uncompromisingly respect the ecological balance; we are against pollution of the air, water and earth, and we are against the concreting of nature and the countryside.

* We are for the equality of women in all sectors of social life.

* We demand measures against unemployment and the reduction of social welfare, which, whether in the interest of the workers or the consumers, must be not only at an economic level but also at a social and work level.

* Policies with regards to the Third World must be based on equal relations with the people of the Third World. We are for a reorganisation of economic relations between Europe and the Third World, and for a closer cooperation between solidarity movements and Third World movements in Europe.

* We are for the free expression of the fundamental rights of the people, one of the conditions most important to bring us to an emancipated, ecological society.

* We recommend an ecological form of agriculture and we wish to preserve jobs in the smaller and middle-sized agricultural businesses.

The Technical Alliance

The following political groups:

Ecolo and Agalev (Belgium)
Die Grünen (West Germany)
Les Verts Europe – Ecologie (France)
Comhaontas Glas (Eire)
Déi Gréng Alternativ (Luxembourg)
CPN, Groene Partij Nederland, PSP, PPR, (Netherlands)
De Europese Groenen (Netherlands)
Ecology Party (United Kingdom)

sign a declaration for a technical alliance for the European elections of June 1984, so conforming with the regulations of the European Parliament for the purpose of the funds destined for reimbursement of the expenses of political groups who have taken part in the European elections of 1984 as published in the Official Journal of the European Community of 29 October 1983, no. C 293/1.

Dated 28 April, 1984

Table 1

Green Parties in the 1984 Elections to the European Parliament

Country/ Party	Green Party Votes	as % of Poll	Total Votes	Total Electorate
Belgium	.		5,725,837	6,975,677
Ecolo	220,704	3.9[1]		
Agalev	246,879	4.4[1]		
Denmark	-	-	2,002,622	3,804,660
France	680,080	3.4	20,180,944	36,880,688
West Germany	2,025,972	8.2	24,851,371	44,451,981
Greece	-	-	5,956,060	7,790,309
Eire	5,242	0.5[2]	1,120,416	2,413,404
Italy	-	-	35,098,046	44,438,303
Luxembourg	60,152	6.1[3]	162,898	214,434
Netherlands	67,423	1.3[4]	5,297,621	10,476,161
United Kingdom (excluding NI)	74,176	0.2[5]	13,312,898	41,917,313
Northern Ireland	2,172	0.3[6]	685 317	1,064,035
TOTAL	3,382,800	3.1	114,394,030	200,426,965

References

The Times Guide to the European Parliament, 1984.
Official sources from several countries.

Notes

1 Ecolo and Agalev gained 9.9% and 7.1% respectively in their different language regions and one seat each. The percentages given in the table are for Belgium as a whole.

2 This result represents one candidate for Comhaontas Glas who stood in one of Eire's four European constituencies.

3 The figure for valid votes cast is an approximation as the electoral system in Luxembourg gives each elector 6 votes.

4 This is the result for De Groenen. The votes cast for the Green Progressive Accord (GPA) were 296,516, 5.6% of the total valid vote for the Netherlands which gave them 2 seats.

5 The nationwide percentage represents 17 Green Party candidates in 17 of 81 single member constituencies under a simple majority voting system.

6 Northern Ireland is a single multi-member European constituency. The figures given here are for the first preference votes in a Single Transferable voting system.

NB: Apart from Great Britain, all countries use some system of proportional representation for elections to the European Parliament and are subject to different rules concerning reimbursement of election expenses. More details may be obtained in document PE 112.905 (April 1987) available free from the European Parliament Information Services, Plateau de Kirchberg, 1601 Luxembourg. After the European Court upheld a case brought by a member of Les Verts (concerning the use of funds intended for general information purposes in the election campaigns of parties already represented in the parliament) there will be no finance available from the European Parliament in 1989 to parties not already represented. Stricter rules will apply to the use of information funds by sitting members of the European Parliament.

Table 2 *Election Results Summary*

Country & Name of Party	Year founded	Number of members[1]	Elect System	local seats	No of MPs/year first elected		No of MEPs/year first elected	
AUSTRIA			E					
Die Grüne Alternative	1986	?		+	8	1986	n.a.	
BELGIUM			G					
Agalev	1982	1,300		+	11	1981[8]	1	1984
Ecolo	1980	1,000		+	6	1981[8]	1	1984
DENMARK			G					
De Grønne	1983	800		+	-		-	
EIRE			C					
Comhaontas Glas	1981	c.300		+	-		-	
FINLAND			H					
Vihreä Liitto[2]	1987	?		+	4	1983	n.a.	
FRANCE			B					
Les Verts	1984	1,200		+	-		-	
GERMANY			D					
Die Grünen	1980	40,000		+	44	1983	7	1984
GREECE			I					
no party	-	-		-	-		-	-
ICELAND			G					
Kvennalistinn[3]	1983	?		+	6	1983	n.a.	
ITALY			G					
Liste Verdi	1987	?		+	14	1987[8]	-	
LUXEMBOURG			H					
Déi Gréng Alternativ	1984	125		+	2	1984	-	
NETHERLANDS			F					
De Groenen	1983	?		+	-		-	
NORWAY			H					
De Grønne[4]	-	?		+	-	n.a.		
PORTUGAL[5]			E					
[5]	-	-		+	2	1983	-	
SPAIN			H					
Los Verdes[6]	1985	700		+	-		-	
SWEDEN			G					
Miljöpartiet de Gröna	1981	6,500		+	20	1988	n.a.	
SWITZERLAND			H					
Die Grüne Partei / Le Parti Ecologiste	1983	4,000		+	9	1979	n.a.	
UNITED KINGDOM			A					
Green Party	1973	8,000		+	-		-	
NEW ZEALAND			A					
Values Party	1972	?		+	-	n.a.		
AUSTRALIA			J					
Green Independents[7]	-	?		+	2	1984[8]	n.a.	
USA			K					
Ctees of Correspondence	1984	?		+	-	n.a.		
CANADA			A					
Green Party of Canada	1983	?		-	-	n,a.		

Electoral Systems

A Simple majority in single member constituencies.

B Double ballots in single member constituencies.

C Proportional representation by Single Transferable Vote in multi-member constituencies.

D Effectively proportional: combination of simple majority in single member constituencies and straight party list.

E Proportional representation with straight party list.

F Proportional representation with one national constituency.

G Proportional representation with sub-national constituencies, allocation of remainders assures overall proportionality.

H Proportional representaion with sub-national constituences but with no overall proportionality assured.

I Effectively non-proportional as second distribution of seats goes to leading parties.

J Alternative (preferential) voting in single member constituencies – not proportional. Senate: proportional representation with multi-member constituences and preferential voting.

K Presidential elections: simple majority to elect 'electoral college'. States use wide range of systems for other elections, mostly simple majority.

Notes

1 Some parties are organised as federations or networks. Not all know how many members they have.

2 Although not officially registered as a party at the time, the first Green councillor in Finland was elected in 1980 (see Chapter 5)

3 The Kvennalistinn (Women's Alliance) do not formally associate themselves with the Green parties but do have a very Green programme (see Chapter 14).

4 No Green party has been formally registered in Norway, but some candidates were elected to local councils in 1987 using the title Green (see Chapter 14).

5 Three parties lay claim to the Green title. One of them, Os Verdes, has two members of parliament elected through an alliance with the Communist party. All of them have locally elected councillors (see Chapter 14).

6 Los Verdes is the only nationally registered Green party. Also active are Confederacion de Los Verdes and a number of local groups. Only Los Verdes has elected councillors.

7 Two senators sit in the national parliament, one as an Independent Green, the other as a member of the Nuclear Disarmament party. Two Green Independents sit in the lower house of the Tasmanian parliament.

8 These numbers include members of lower and upper houses of parliament. Agalev has 5 senators and Ecolo 3. Liste Verdi has two senators, and both Australian seats are in the Senate.

Bibliography

This bibliography does not pretend to be a comprehensive list of the influences on Green thinking, nor does it cover all the books referenced in *Green Parties*. It may, however, be taken as a starting point for people coming to Green politics for the first time. My selection has been influenced by the response to a question I asked of some Green party activists in different countries: which books do you think best represent the *ideas* that have influenced your party's founding and development? To find out more about the *issues* that concern Greens I recommend *A Green Manifesto* by Sandy Irvine and Alec Ponton, Optima, 1988. It has an extensive bibliography. The books below are listed in order of publication, and those with a particularly useful bibliography or set of references are marked with an asterisk. As with references elsewhere in this book, place of publication is London unless otherwise indicated.

SCHUMACHER, E. F. *Small Is Beautiful*, Abacus, 1974. Translated into several languages, this is the book that led many people into Green politics.

* FROMM Eric, *To Have or To Be*, Jonathan Cape, 1978. Despite his fondness for Marx and Freud and his somewhat pessimistic outlook, Fromm manages to explain how we might transform ouselves from the 'having mode' to the 'being mode' of human existence.

BOOKCHIN Murray, *Towards an Ecological Society*, Black Rose, Montreal, 1980. Mincing no words, Bookchin defends the relationship between ecology and anarchism against the intrusion of Marx.

* ROSZAK Theodore, *Person/Planet*, Granada, St Albans, 1981. The most stirring explanation of what the politics of the person really are and how they can lead to planet-saving politics.

SKOLIMOWSKI, Henryk, *Eco-philosophy*, Marion Boyars, 1981. A description of a new philosophy that sticks to examining the meaning of life rather than the 'meaning of meaning'.

* *CAPRA Fritjof, The Turning Point*, Wildwood House, 1982. A theoretical physicist, Capra describes how the change from a scientific to a holistic view of the world is taking place, its implications for a new vision of reality and its consequences to our social and political structures.

* BROWN Lester et al, *State of the World 1984/1985/1986/ 1987/1988* (annual volumes), W. W. Norton, New York. By highlighting different aspects each year and by prefacing their extensively referenced books with a brief but consistently brilliant overview, the Worldwatch Institute team produce the most useful and readable of all the reference books which deal with the human predicament.

* PORRITT Jonathon, *Seeing Green*, Basil Blackwell, Oxford, 1984. Still by far the best and most readable 'primer' of Green politics.

BAHRO Rudolf, *From Red to Green*, Verso, 1984. The story of Bahro's personal journey from a member of the East German Communist party to an inspirational member of the West German Green party.

* EKINS Paul (ed.), *The Living Economy*, Routledge & Kegan Paul, 1986. With contributions from or references to everyone who is anyone in the world of Green economics, this book is the best starting point for anyone interested in this crucial area of Green thinking.

Heretic Books

The Heretic imprint was relaunched in spring 1988 as an independent publishing company serving the Green movement. Other recent publications include:

William Johnson
THE MONK SEAL CONSPIRACY

A thrilling personal story of the campaign to save the Mediterranean monk seal in the politically sensitive waters of the eastern Aegean, leading to a confrontation with the Greek secret service which international conservation organisations failed sadly to handle.
224pp, £4.95.

Marjorie Spiegel
THE DREADED COMPARISON: race and animal slavery

A pungent essay on the parallels between black slavery in America and the treatment of animals today, with graphic illustrations. Topics covered include 'slaves and masters', 'the destruction of security', 'transportation', 'hunting', 'secrecy', 'power', 'oppression in language and literature' and 'profits over all'. With a Preface by Alice Walker.
112pp, £3.95*

John Seed, Joanna Macy, Pat Fleming and Arne Naess
THINKING LIKE A MOUNTAIN: towards a council of all beings

A practical introduction to 'deep ecology' by its most prominent exponents, focusing on collective workshops and rituals. Includes 'beyond anthropocentrism', 'evolutionary remembering', 'our life as Gaia', readings and meditations.
96pp, £3.95*

The full Heretic catalogue is available from:
Heretic Books Ltd, P O Box 247, London N17 9QR.
To order by mail, please add £1 per book.

* Available in North America from New Society Publishers.